Actors Talk About Shakespeare

Actors
Talk About
Shakespeare

Mary Z. Maher

An Imprint of Hal Leonard Corporation
New York

Published in 2009 by Limelight Editions
An Imprint of Hal Leonard Corporation
7777 West Bluemound Road
Milwaukee, WI 53213

Trade Book Division Editorial Offices
19 West 21st Street, New York, NY 10010

Printed in the United States of America

Book design by Mark Lerner

Library of Congress Cataloging-in-Publication Data

Maher, Mary Z.
  Actors talk about Shakespeare / Mary Z. Maher.
    p. cm.
  ISBN 978-0-87910-364-4 (pbk.)
  1. Shakespeare, William, 1564-1616—Dramatic production. 2. Shakespeare, William, 1564-1616—Stage history. 3. Actors—Interviews. I. Title.
  PR3112.M34 2009
  792.9'5—dc22

                              2009019124

  ISBN 978-0-87910-364-4

www.limelighteditions.com

In memory of Janie Edmonds, the best archivist that ever was

Contents

Acknowledgments

There are so many people to thank. First of all, the actors themselves. All of them gave time and took the risk of having their ideas featured, narrated, and encapsulated. They were straightforward and direct, and they wanted their work documented (which fed right into my willing hands). Often, a welcome helper liaisoned between myself and the actor, settling matters of detail, correcting information, supplying addresses and solutions. These include the remarkable Amy Bradley, Tracy Motley, Richard Clifford, Roy Brown, Paul Parlee, the faithful Mary Gladstone, and the exceptional Tamar Thomas, who handles details so masterfully. Dana Werdmuller and Marcus Cato fielded my special requests of Shakespeare Santa Cruz. Kudos to these people, who were ready to go the extra mile and make my life easier.

Thank you to a colleague and special friend, John Andrews—he and I have worked together for years, since one or the other of us would have the right contact in the theater world. I treasure his unending support.

Next, the archivists, most often women, some of whom became dear friends. First and always on the list is Janie Edmonds at the Stratford Shakespeare Festival. Janie knew everything and everybody and how to reach the most distant fact. Alas, we lost her to cancer in 2009. The capable and efficient Ellen Charendoff follows in her footsteps. Next come the workers at the now defunct Theatre Museum, which used to be in London. I remember swanning into the study smelling of the cosmetics I had bagged in Covent Garden gift shops while the staff tried to not notice the perfumed air as they filled my requests for newspaper clippings. There were gentle helpers and polite nudges at the Royal Shakespeare Company Archives, where all details theatrical can be obtained, and I was allowed to digress and pore over the promptbook of Peter Brook's *A Midsummer Night's Dream* while bees buzzed at the window—Marian Pringle, Sylvia Morris, and the efficient Helen Hargest were superb. Finally, the sharp rough-and-tumble of the Billy Rose Performing Arts Library, set in fashionable Lincoln Center with its surrounding New York traffic and vitality. The video chap was especially patient and did not ask me to leave when I laughed too raucously over Kevin Kline's Benedick.

Deeply valuable were people who edited for me. Chief among these was my trusty friend Judy Maher, who can spot a bad verb tense from a running horse and fix all manner of uncomfortable wordings and other errors. A compliment from her is hard-won but enormously truthful. Best of all, she slashes and chops with fearless precision, heedless of my feelings.

Readers who helped along the way were townies around Ashland, who have accumulated many years of theatergoing—Jeani and Jon Kimball; Lue Douthit, the dramaturge at the Oregon Shakespeare Festival; and Alan Armstrong, the knowing audience member and my favorite sounding board, who worked for years offering National Endowment for the Humanities workshops on Shakespeare in performance. Thanks also to John A. Wilson, my codirector on many Shakespeare projects, who gave advice. A mentor who helped with aspects of publishing was the author of a wonderful book on writing nonfiction, Elizabeth Lyon, knowledgeable and endlessly giving. I appreciate my dear friend and chief adviser, Mary Sybil Marx. Photographers Michal Daniel and Rich Hein were particularly creative and amenable artists.

I am especially grateful to the Mechanicals—Brenda Richards and Christi Schulz, who talked me down from the ledge many a time. Not to forget my trusty Knight of the Computer Glitch, Chris Zwemke. Without him, I would be dead in the forest.

Agent and diplomat June Clark, as well as Limelight Publisher Michael Messina gave me the final boost to complete a book long in the creation chambers. And thanks to editors Carol Flannery, Marybeth Keating and Angela Buckley.

Although I haven't mentioned them elsewhere, who could omit the reassuring, unconditional love of calico Thisbe and the dark king of shadows, Oberon.

Mary Z. Maher
April 2009
Ashland, Oregon

Introduction

In writing about Shakespeare over the span of a college teaching career, there are a few facts—and lack of them—that have piqued my interest. One is that we know virtually nothing about how Shakespeare's company of actors really performed—what they looked like onstage, how or if they rehearsed, how they thought about "the work," and what their relationships were to their colleagues, on- and offstage. Shakespeare's lead actor Richard Burbage is mostly documented in an epitaph, even though all the major roles—including Hamlet, Lear, Macbeth, and Othello—were written for him. We are not even sure if actors blocked the scene or followed the same patterns of movement each night. The records are sparse, and there is not a rack left behind.

In 1982 I made a trip to the flagship Oregon Shakespeare Festival in Ashland, where I now live. That summer, an actor named Mark Murphey played the first Hamlet I'd ever seen onstage. After the intermission, I followed a father and his young son back into the theater. Hanging on to his parent's hand, the son looked up anxiously and said, "He isn't really crazy, is he, Daddy?"

We are all attracted to these gilded creatures that strut and fret their hour upon the stage. We marvel at their effortless reality, their glorious voices, their flexible bodies. They fascinate us, draw us into death and tragedy and pity and fear. Though the spell is broken in the end, we remain in awe of their ability to make a magic we really cannot deconstruct. "How did you do that?" is the question constantly asked of actors.

Shakespeare performed onstage is different from Shakespeare on film, from the community theater production of *Kiss Me, Kate*, from the historical pageant done in Ohio. How is it different, and how is it the same? What skills might one need to become a classical actor? What background and training are important? What kinds of study and process does a classical actor achieve? My goal here is to explore actors' perceptions and comments as they release issues and expectations about performing Shakespeare.

Although the actors interviewed transition easily from film to television to stage work, each has faithfully returned to Shakespeare throughout his or her career. Each understands profoundly that classical acting demands a heightened level of commitment to language so challenging that it places pressure on the performers to use consummate technique. Kevin Kline claims that acting Shakespeare requires a different set of muscles altogether. Stacy Keach asserts that a Shakespeare role trains performance instincts afresh each time. Breath support, as well as a honed voice and clear diction, merges with many other demands—an acute analysis of all the detailed artifice in these texts, studying the character from image-saturated language clues, understanding the difference between poetry and prose, understanding each phrase, each paragraph, each response. "Now," as Peter Brook says, "keep it loud and at the same time, keep it *natural*." Z'ounds!

Why would an actor sit down with an interviewer to talk about the acting process *after* the show has closed, the set is struck, and the traces of performance have vanished into thin air? Because each one has something to say and wants to leave a legacy. Somewhere inside is the deep knowledge that Shakespeare immortalized: actors "are the abstract and brief chronicles of their time," and they do reflect "the very age and body of the time"—its "form and pressure."

These actors' observations, insights, and opinions about their craft provide a treasury of talents, tactics, and tales for other actors and for audiences who also return to Shakespeare.

About the Actors

The meat of the interviews is in those very qualities that grace those who do the job well: resilience, savvy, relationship skills, intellectual curiosity, stamina, a thirst for work, a fat dollop of imagination, and a gallon of sheer guts. Consider, as well, that acting onstage involves a measure of financial sacrifice; one takes a sizable salary cut compared to the paycheck for work on film or television.

Kevin Kline has elements of the mystic about him, certainly a settled and confident man. He plays piano beautifully and thinks nothing of crossing the ocean to see a really good actor at work. He says that if you watch and listen to an artist really closely, you will see *something else* coming off of the performance, a glimpse into the performer's soul. Now I always watch for that.

Nicholas Pennell taught me about the sanctity of "the work," a term actors use quite often. When I requested an interview he asked me, "Are you one of Claribel's kids?" Claribel Baird was an iconic, god-like professor who taught Shakespeare at the University of Michigan. Nicky knew her well, and I had been one of her students. She wore Dior to class and drummed text into us and sometimes out of us. Once I answered yes, Pennell gave me all the interview time I wanted. Six months later, he was dead of lymphoma.

Derek Jacobi is precisely articulate about "the work" and talks about it in phrases that shimmer. He exemplifies how much intelligence is needed to perform Shakespeare, how much focus and energy and sheer brilliance have to be surging in the mind, under and behind the lines.

Kenneth Branagh embodies the importance of entrepreneurship and learning to sell one's own projects. He formed his own theater company in his twenties, continues to direct many stage productions of Shakespeare, manages to get his Shakespeares on film financed by major companies, and has even directed an opera. He's always having ideas, building on prior work to stimulate his creativity, and supporting and networking with other actors. No wonder young fans call him "the Kenergizer"!

These are just samples. There is so much to admire in hallmark actors and a very great deal to *learn*. That is my first hope, that when you read about their acting process, you do it comparatively. Indeed, I was a willing student.

About the Interviews

Actors are initially edgy about being trapped in a room with an interviewer. Once they warm to the subject, they encounter who they are and want to communicate their work. I am inspired by their concentration and focus, their need for precision. Something takes over—they find their groove.

I've established some uniformity in the chapters by asking each actor the same general questions during the interview. These were designed to get at what she or he actually does, as opposed to what ought to be done according to the how-to books. The questions addressed the actor's training, background, and early mentors. They explored how each prepares for the role, including both personal and study-oriented research, as well as the special challenges of Shakespeare's language and matters of using the voice when speaking the verse.

I asked about working with directors, so the actors' comments address the collaborative process of theater when artists come together and negotiate, relinquishing vested interests in order to turn out a polished product. Some actors have had long-term or short-term affiliations with a theater company, and special insights develop in those cases—for example, Geoff Hutchings's experiences as a clown with the Royal Shakespeare Company during its 1960s renaissance, Tony Church's teaching duties at the Guildhall School in London and the Denver Theater Center, and William Hutt's and Martha Henry's years with the Stratford Festival company in Canada.

When I am actually interviewing, I often follow an interesting conversational thread that the actor has begun. One gets rich results that way. Once I am writing, I organize the material into topics in a prose-essay format, and I also edit the information. Spoken discourse is highly redundant, filled with qualifiers, and often the pronouns and other referents are unclear. Descriptions about performance are abstract and have more than one meaning, and the meanings can be slippery, so I made a decision to be the guiding voice.

My final insurance is to run the essay by the actor so the story being told can be verified as belonging to the actor and not to me. I am after a composite here, not a journalistic report of what happened at the scene of the crime. More important, an actor's creative process should be set within the context of that career and its trajectory. Plucked out of its own setting, the information loses specificity and weight.

My approach offers a sense of what Shakespeare actors mean by "the work." Inevitably there will be differences. For example, about the details of text analysis, each actor treats the punctuation in Shakespeare's dialogue in his or her own particularized way. Zoe Caldwell assigns a certain weight to each comma, semicolon, and period in Shakespeare's texts as she decides how long an actor should pause. She finds this practice especially useful when teaching. Nicholas Pennell used Wite-Out on all punctuation when he studied the verse, because part of his creative process in "new-minting" the language was creating his singular way of delivering the speech. He'd listened to scholars talk about the printing of Shakespeare's folios and quartos and decided that we will never know for certain which punctuation marks are authentic.

Is one of these methods *absolutely correct* and another *dead wrong*? Of course not. There are a number of effective ways of using punctuation in performance—for example, as a pause or to vocally lift a parenthetical expression—and a number of approaches that audience members may not notice the results of at all. Acting is a performance art, an art that is ephemeral and mostly phenomenon, and its effects influence audience members in a variety of ways. Each actor has evolved his or her methods of analysis, dissection, and comparison inside the research and rehearsal process. Each finds an *individual* journey to the end result, one that has worked well and produced an enduring career as substantial proof. Now readers have the luxury of choosing, weighing, discerning, perhaps even self-validating as they read about artists who have earned their spurs in Shakespeare.

The actors in this book believe that acting Shakespeare is tantamount to earning a black belt in performance art. I have focused on stage performances because text is fuller there (film versions regularly cut 50 to 70 percent of the language), so stage versions offer a fuller rendition of the characters in the play. The two art forms differ significantly in terms of size and scope of acting. Stage acting shifts and grows each night. A screen performance provides us one taste, one sequence of filming, at one point in the life of the screenplay. Most actors claim that if you acted the same way onscreen that you act onstage, you'd look ridiculous. The reverse is true, as well—if you were to act onstage in the same way you act onscreen, your performance would never project to an audience, because it would be too small. So, I've worked in the mode that Shakespeare's actors chose, where the actor (rather than a cameraman or an editor) controls more of the performance.

About Finding the Actor's Process

When I first interviewed Derek Jacobi, I impulsively bought a gorgeous bouquet of apricot-colored roses on the street en route to his house. We wrapped up the interview early because he had a voice-over job scheduled. He said, "But you must come back so we can finish." A week later he showed me the roses on his coffee table, fresh as the day I'd brought them. I reminded Kenneth Branagh, on our second interview, that our agreed time was up, and he said, "I'll just go have a pee and then you can take all the time you want." Nicholas Pennell gave me several hours of interview, over a span of a week. At the end, I told him a funny story and he laughed so hard he pounded his fist upon the table and the tape recorder jumped all about. Stacy Keach gave me a poster of his *King Lear* in profile—he wrote on it, "Look—no teeth! Thanks for the great interview!" I was touched because all were helping *me* by talking about close-to-the-bone topics.

Choosing the performers to include in the book was key—one must remain open to letting the actors actually choose *you*. The selection process involves personal taste, but for me, these are actors who consistently present a real person in a Shakespeare role, who deliver the lines understandably, and *especially* who carry me into the performance— take me out of the workaday world and sweep me into the play.

Since acting styles do change over time, I asked each performer (and often did not have to ask), "What do you know about acting Shakespeare that you did not know at the beginning of your career?" The answers revealed a surprising amount of historical shift in decorum and manners over time and also showed that the inner and outer substance of the actor's process got "more *real*," which is one of the fidgety words one has to deal with in writing about acting.

One thing became enormously clear as I focused on the actor's process: there is no single correct way to perform Shakespeare. Let me repeat that: *there is no single correct way to perform Shakespeare.* Furthermore, all of these artists are highly intuitive and certainly creative. If you are looking for a codified way, an orderly sequence of rules—abandon hope now. The best actors of this generation differ in methods and in means. All would agree that "remaining open"—even to changes of mind as well as changes in method—is extremely important, and all are extraordinarily disciplined as they work.

A precise definition of *process* is elusive, and the word is certainly fluid. Process begins to develop from an actor's formal training and then from how he or she watches other actors at work. In both of these instances, technique starts shaping itself early—ways of using the voice for maximum clarity; training the body for general movement, dance, and stage combat; exploring vocal, facial, and bodily expression and how each can inform a role; and learning to listen and react to one's partners onstage. These skills remain foundational. All can be practiced and improved on, and they are also components of the acting process. Other details of study—unscrambling a long speech, searching out surface and deep meanings, memorizing lines—grow and become richer with experience, especially as an actor works within a *variety of performance spaces.* What is intriguing about the actors described here is how they layer technique into their own realities onstage, creating interest, complexity, and freshness in a character.

Usually an actor learns a very basic form of character analysis. That component draws carefully from the writing, what most actors call *text.* In play scripts and especially in Shakespeare, text is all a performer has to go on, because there are so few stage directions. Since the language is a mixture of poetry and prose, as well as certain Elizabethan performance conventions (soliloquies, prologues, epilogues, tirades), this text has a special place in training and in practice. There are many prescriptive "how-to books" and also books that focus on text in only one role. Here, hallmark actors articulate their own developed ideas as these have emanated from the context of a career.

There is variation in actor training: some actors went to drama school; others went from university straight into the profession; some skipped postsecondary-school education of any kind. I am recording not "how-to" but "how I do it" from a selection of proven classical actors who get cast again and again. The goal is to do more than become a character: process results in making Shakespearean dialogue sound real and natural and, above all, it leads to getting something more than the plot across to an audience. Character creation and verse speaking are not two separate entities—they are intertwined.

An important learning curve about process happens on the job. Derek Jacobi was a mentor to Kenneth Branagh (remembering that Gielgud said of Jacobi, "He's playing all my roles"), as was Richard Burton to Jacobi. Zoe Caldwell was always an avid learner and in-the-wings observer. Teachers also figure in as influences. The narratives here show that actors get encouragement and considerable help from a special person along the way, including other colleagues who are cast members. The directors one has are influential. All of the Canadian actors in this book—Martha Henry, William Hutt, and Nicky Pennell—mention the changes in their own process when they began working with director Robin Phillips in the Stratford Festival company in Canada. Without exception, these actors stayed alert, aware, observant, keyed-up during rehearsal, and watchful during performance.

I've always told my students that 50 percent of the character comes from the text and 50 percent of it from their own personality. Heaven knows what the real percentage is, but the actor's instrument (unlike the bassoonist's) is a composite of himself and his life experiences. Add to this what the opera singer refers to as "pipes," the physical and vocal gifts the performer got from family genes. The actor's *score* is in my opinion very different from a musical score, so all actors need heavy-duty work in reading scripts to discover a character's needs and drives—much more so in Shakespearean drama, because understanding has to precede performance, and dealing with the text is the hard part. It takes doing one's homework, tenacity, and practice.

Process also includes *actual performance*—how to "be in the moment," the current coinage of having truth and reality onstage. Note, as you read, how each actor describes this modern adage in his or her own words. The pressure to be "real" and to "really go there" onstage has intensified with the spate of new Shakespeares-on-film that happened around the release of *Shakespeare in Love*. The quality of being natural onstage—no matter what the actors say or what you read or what you think you understand—is something that will always be a bit inexplicable, somewhat shrouded in mystery.

Issues in Acting Shakespeare

My interviews turned up information on both old and new issues in acting Shakespeare. One that is perennial is the question of "naturalistic speech," taking a language that is over four hundred years old and making it sound not only real, but also *meaningful*. Some speeches have mellowed, like fine wine, and are imbibed with communal pleasure by the audience. Other bits remain obscure and tantalizing. One absolute standard that never changes is that the actor needs to understand a line before it can be successfully communicated to an audience. By the way, that phenomenon—the lightbulb of finally getting the meaning of a line—can happen to an actor halfway through the run! Furthermore, notions of how to speak the verse shift a bit from decade to decade, and this hue and cry for sounding natural is partly a reaction to an earlier historical period of handling the language in a more declamatory way. Today, if audience members can follow the talk emanating from the stage, they will probably describe it as *natural*.

An issue often overlooked is the intelligence of the actor. The sense of achievement from ferreting the character clues out of Elizabethan English is a process most good classical actors really, really *dig*. I do not measure this facility by the amount of training or place of schooling, yet we all agree that it takes a nimble mind to grasp and portray a character via dense, ornamented language.

An important influence generates from the number of "concept productions" that directors subject audiences (and especially actors) to. By now, we've all seen production designs with seven Ariels flown in on a helicopter and a Caliban playing the slots in Las Vegas. In the conversations here, opinions vary about what to do with a director who has an "idea" of the play. Actors usually negotiate this hot-button issue with a generous and politic response, en route to a persuasive appeal.

Finally, it is important to constantly rediscover that there are no iron-clad rules in playing Shakespeare. The consensus of these actors, however, is that they like to leave the actual performance open to possibility. Nowadays, actors do not rehearse a play in order to perform it the same static and immobile way each night, because that closes down creative options and shuts the valve of energy and discovery. Interestingly enough, this rather modern notion of edginess appears to *increase* the amount of preparation done beforehand.

Even today, a precious few stage performances are filmed, and those that exist are like viewing the shadow of a shadow. Video recording an outstanding production is something theater companies rarely include in the budget. Although biographies get written, they explain little of the daily endeavor of acting, what its forms and pressures were, how it worked. Sadly, the history of our greatest stage actors is fragmentary or lost. We remember their romances, their peccadilloes, their long gowns and tuxedos, their Tony speeches—but we do not properly record *over time* their art and their artistic process, the place where all the work gets done.

Documenting these performers, for the curious actors and the loyal audiences who venerate and are thrilled by Shakespeare's words, is my passion. I am sharply aware that these performers have taught me more than I could ever possibly have discovered on my own. Playwright August Wilson remarked that "The true critic does not sit in judgment. Rather, he seeks to inform his reader, instead of adopting a posture of self-conscious importance in which he sees himself a judge and final arbiter of a work's importance or value." Clearly, Wilson understood the actor's process.

Actors Talk About Shakespeare

KEVIN KLINE AS LEAR IN THE 2007 PRODUCTION OF *KING LEAR* AT THE JOE PAPP PUBLIC THEATER. (PHOTO BY MICHAL DANIEL)

1

Kevin Kline

I Can Add Colors to the Chameleon

Kevin Kline has the uncanny gift of doing comedy and tragedy equally well. During the first two decades of his career, *New York* magazine called him "at once dashing and daft"[1] and described his ability to move from "swash-bungler to tyrant to buffoon to prince—equally adept at slipping on banana peels and reciting soliloquies."[2] Indeed, this movie star has forged a career as a serious stage actor with a fortuitous comic strain, a "Shakespeherian rag" pervading his work like a leitmotif. Rather than living in Hollywood, Kline retains New York City as his home base, traveling out to make films in a variety of locations around the world.

Kline's screen credential began in the early 1980s and includes classics like *Sophie's Choice, Pirates of Penzance, The Big Chill, Silverado, Cry Freedom, Dave, Life as a House, In and Out, Trade,* and of course, the unforgettable *A Fish Called Wanda,* for which he won an Oscar for Best Supporting Actor. In 1990 he played Hamlet onstage and on public television. In 1999 he played Bottom the Weaver in a film version of *A Midsummer Night's Dream,* and he was Jacques in Kenneth Branagh's HBO production of *As You Like It* in 2007.

Onstage, Kline interspersed his film work by performing leading roles in *Richard III, Henry V, Hamlet* (1986, 1990), *Much Ado About*

Nothing (Benedick), and *Measure for Measure* (the Duke). He was a triumphant Falstaff at Lincoln Center in 2004 and a masterful *King Lear* in 2007. He has also performed in Brecht, Chekov, Shaw, and Restoration plays. He is associate artist with the New York Shakespeare Festival and has earned Tonys, Drama Desk, and Golden Globe awards, as well as the Golden Quill Award for acting Shakespeare. Frank Rich declared, "Next to Mr. Kline, most other American classical actors of his generation are mere pretenders to the throne."[3]

Kline was raised in a family that was deeply involved in the arts and had a respect for both imagination and divine inspiration. A flair for comic invention appeared as early as age ten on a family vacation, as he was intently reading beside a swimming pool:

> He . . . slowly stood up, strolled over to the diving board, walked
> to the end, and—still reading the magazine—dove into the wa-
> ter. When he surfaced, he swam to the side of the pool, got out,
> and went back to his chair—never once taking his eyes off the
> magazine.[4]

Kline's Jewish father ran a large toy and record store in St. Louis, and his Catholic mother insisted on a classically based literary education for him at the Benedictine-run Priory School. His father was a tenor who wanted to be an opera singer and loved to quote long passages of Shakespeare. With a heritage like that, Kline jokes that he should run for mayor of New York.

Kline starred in Plautus's *Mostellaria* in high school, but the search for his bliss began at Indiana University, where he majored in piano and music studies. He took an acting class, and while he watched auditions for *Macbeth*, the director called him onstage to read. He wound up cast as a bleeding sergeant. Although he appeared in university productions, his heart belonged to the Vest Pocket Players, a coffeehouse theater built, managed, and directed by fellow students. This hands-on experience gave him the confidence to declare that he wanted to be an actor.

Kline's sister Kate was one of his early mentors. An artist and writer who steered him toward art films and more aesthetic interests, Kate had read about Juilliard, a prestigious conservatory that was adding an acting school. There, Michel Saint-Denis and John Houseman had the idea of forging an understanding of style for the American actor in dealing with classical works. Kline was a founding member of The Acting Company—cofounded by Houseman—after completing his studies at Juilliard. The result was four years of bus touring, 110 cities and 34 states from 1972 to 1976. Members of The Acting Company received their Equity cards, as well as invaluable work experience in regional theater, as they energetically discovered a way to make period drama work: "In Arkansas, you could hear a pin drop when we did *School for Scandal*. They weren't blasé, they hadn't seen it all, and they weren't going because it was a hot ticket. They were starved and curious."[5] Kline was also getting exposure, which led to the part of Bruce Granit in the 1978 Broadway musical *On the Twentieth Century*, his first Tony Award and the signature role that introduced the mercurial range of his abilities.

At Juilliard, he had stage speech from Edith Skinner (her book *Speak with Distinction* is still revered) and studied voice with Elizabeth Smith. Classes in mask work disclosed his physical fearlessness and an uncanny skill for shtick and slapstick. This gift generated creative touches like the Pirate King dueling with the conductor's baton during the overture to *The Pirates of Penzance*. In film roles remarkable for their range, Kline became known as an actor's actor who defies type and establishes the guts of each role, refusing to repeat or stereotype himself. He plays characters varying as widely as Donald Woods (*Cry Freedom*) and Bottom the Weaver.

His function as an actor is not to fulfill expectations but to serve the play. The study of acting is a lifelong process. He loves to explore the craft, to talk about acting and all its allied skills: "I like variety,"[6] is how he explains it. "You always try not to repeat yourself, but at the same time you can't *not* do something just because you've done it before. Otherwise, you'll end up not walking or talking."[7]

The key to Kline's acting philosophy is the idea of the actor taking authorship: the actor creates his own role and the gestures and voices that flesh it out. In stage practice, the director is often a Svengali-like creature who has an "idea" of the character in his head; actors can be treated as meat on a meat hook that must do as the director says. Kline resists this notion and insists that the actor has a brain and uses his own resources in creating a character:

> The author of the play is Shakespeare, but the actor has to own the character he is playing. Olivier aptly said you marry yourself to the character.
>
> I can always tell when comic business has been imposed on actors as opposed to having been *found* in rehearsal. There's an aura, this kind of visible odor if they're not in tune with themselves when they are performing somebody else's idea. Now, if the idea resonates, then it's yours, you are now the author. If it doesn't, it will always look or feel alien.
>
> You can steal from other actors? Of course. We've been stealing from the generations that have preceded us, especially when you play a classic part. You've confiscated it, appropriated it. If a line reading or piece of business is merely borrowed, that's no good. You must make it *yours.* Occasionally you watch an actor and you think, there's something wrong here. He's imitating. He's not playing from his own engine—something has been grafted onto this "machine" as Hamlet calls it.
>
> I always get shivers when an actor comes in to audition and says, "Oh, I really want to play Macbeth. I have an idea about how to play him."
>
> Why bother? What's the adventure? Where's the discovery?[8]

Kline emphasizes that ownership is a concept that has boundaries and can be mastered over time, as an acting career matures:

> I think the best directors give an actor a note [a suggestion] with the implied proviso, "If this resonates for you." If it doesn't, then you must discard it. Otherwise, it will look like glop suddenly, which will take the actor and then the audience out of the flow.
>
> Every actor has a different threshold. You say to yourself, am I really happy doing this work or am I just making a director happy? That takes a lifetime to find out.

I'll give an idea a try. If it doesn't work after a while, then I'm going to campaign for "Please, can we find another way—I'm giving up too much here and I'm losing something vital." It's a very interesting juncture in any area of work. To know when you've compromised yourself is a useful kind of self-knowledge.

Occasionally directors do take on the role of a marriage counselor. I usually prefer to work out our differences on our own, keeping it private and personal.

From ownership evolves responsibility. If an actor has been responsible for the generation of his character, then he will enter the rehearsal process with a positive, collaborative energy. There will be an "instinctive commitment where the acting will come alive in a much richer way." Kline is not interested in the actor who comes into rehearsal and thinks, "I'll simply do what the director tells me, collect my paycheck, and be on my way once the show is over." A quality production depends on group effort, the process of discovery freely entered into: "I want to work with actors who have a personal connection to the production and to the role and to the theater—someone with a deeper purpose."[9]

Essential to ownership is a great deal of personal security. Kline had a college friend, Harold Guskin, who became a sounding board and discerning critical eye. He helped Kline mine his own talents: "Harold keyed me in to some things about myself." When Kline enrolled in acting courses at Indiana University, he was obsessed with finding the right way to perform. He was still forming his identity, and Guskin was a mentor:

Guskin opened the whole discussion about being an artist. He would ask me, "How do you feel about this line you are going to say?" I would retort by asking him what was the right way? How would Brando say it, how would Olivier say it? He would respond, "Who cares? How do you feel? What does it mean to you?"

How would I say it? It was this wonderfully thrilling, scary thing! It led me to suddenly think, "Who am I?" Yes, that is what acting is all about! This was a great revelation. They call it "personalization" in the acting books.

That's the first great gift he gave me. Followed by the notion of being in tune with yourself. That was far more important than the right way and the wrong way. Some of the best acting is not "the right way." The best kind is where you redefine what it is each time out.

Guskin was blissfully free of rules and theories.[10] He had nothing for sale—no books, no systems. Yet he'd gathered a huge and varied arsenal of ways and means to coax a good performance from the actor. Kline adds: "He believes that actors are athletes of the spirit, who have to be trained to show us those places in the heart where we . . . hide feeling away."[11]

Kline confesses to a certain healthy cynicism about theater school, listing all the paraphernalia that Guskin eschewed:

He didn't teach "substitution." If you have to substitute [to hearken back to an incident from your own memory bank of experience which will summon up an appropriate emotional response to the situation in the play's world], it's because you're getting nothing from the other actor in the scene, and nothing from the director, and nothing is working. Then, okay. Make this other actor into your mother, someone you're in love with or angry with or whatever's appropriate . . . but it should be the last desperate resort.

Guskin said wonderful things that got the actor free of the stuff that drama school taught, that you read in books, that you thought acting was. He made you get in touch with yourself.

Use what's there. It's all about what's happening now. Tonight. Not in rehearsal six weeks ago. Not in the book you read. Trusting that your instinct in the moment is not only valuable but that that's all you have. That's the only thing of interest.

These conversations were helpful to Kline because Guskin's approach was neither obscure nor enigmatic but very direct. Excuses and footnotes were not allowed:

Working on a role, I'd been looking at the speech where my character breaks down and cries. I told him—we're coming up to the scene tomorrow, and as I look at it, I don't think I do have to cry. I mean I don't have to take that as my choice.

He said, "Yeah you do. You have to cry. Just find out how."

You see, I had found a way to avoid the real work here. He would say, "I lost you there, on that line. Where are you now? You're intellectualizing, you're commenting on the character, you're entertaining us, but you're not facing the work."

Some directors and some acting teachers have a means of making you articulate the one thing that keys right in to what is going on in the play. Guskin never reduced it to the banal. It was talking about ideas in a way that made them instantly translatable into dramatic choices. He brought the work to its essence.

One thing Guskin urged on Kline was the final push, the ultimate gesture: "That's what he often said: 'I think you've got to go all the way with that.'" This prod toward perfection was probably the impetus for freeing Kline's natural gifts:

> Once when we were rehearsing a very serious play he was directing, I was clowning around during a tech rehearsal. He said to me, "If ever you had the kind of freedom to be absolutely foolish and to go to that extreme, if you can do in a part what you just did for the last fifteen minutes, it would be magic, it would be *heaven*."

One can see how important this element of risk, going for broke, laying one's inner self out there, is essential in an artist's process. Kline does just that—is true to himself—in a long list of sublime character moments: Otto making love to Jamie Lee Curtis in Italian phrases that sound suspiciously like menu items in *A Fish Called Wanda*, the Pirate King pinning his foot to the floor with his own sword, the long fall backward onstage after Hamlet's second soliloquy, Benedick falling from the tree where he was hiding in *Much Ado*, Howard Brackett dancing to "I Will Survive" in *In and Out*, Cyrano climbing into the performance from the side boxes. These are creative notches on the actor's belt, and they come from letting the imagination go and being relaxed enough to let the magic happen.

Such precepts as his basic philosophy of ownership evolve partly from the personality of Kevin Kline, who is not only intellectual and likeable, but also given to introspection, to perhaps thinking too precisely on a subject. He has a way of springing perceptive ideas out of experience. He believes something unusual and vital—that whenever a performer performs, there is "always something else coming off that actor." This applies to singers and pianists and other artists as well: there is always an air rising from the performer that allows you to see into his or her soul. Over time, that piece of information begins to be not only evident, but surprising. If one has intuition, these vibes or auras or whatever they are, truly exist and communicate—sometimes commenting about the play or the piece played, sometimes commenting on the state of the artist's life in that moment.

When Kline decided to direct and also to play the lead in his own *Hamlet* in 1990, his ideas expanded. I was invited into the rehearsals for that project and to the video recording of it for PBS later on. One thing that stood out was the sheer quality of the endeavor. Every artist working on it was the best New York had to offer, from costumer Marty Pakledinaz to lighting designer Jules Fisher to text coach Elizabeth Smith, his former teacher at Juilliard.

Kline believes that his concept for the play was in the casting: "I think the style of the production is what actors you choose." He was intrigued by something Wilfred Leach (who directed him in *Henry V*) announced to the cast on the first day of rehearsals: "My concept is to do the play." Beyond that and an invested trust in his actors, Kline set about encountering Shakespeare directly, without the intervention of an elaborate design concept or needing to set the play in an exotic locale: "No matter how much you surround them with scenery or costumes, it is the actors themselves that are really going to dictate the style."

Hamlet was clearly its own triumph,[12] filled with the challenges that Kline relishes and fraught with potential land mines. He had decided not only to direct the play this time around, but also to play the lead, a task achieved by only a handful of the greats: Gielgud, Olivier, Irving, and Tree. In retrospect, Kline felt that Gielgud was right—one should play Hamlet only in repertory, acting it two or three times a week as opposed to eight times a week:

> I have been asked, "Why is Hamlet the hardest role for actors?" Because it draws on everything. You need every bit of spiritual, psychic, emotional, and physical reserve to play it. It happens at such a pitch that you've got to be *full* when you go onstage. You need to cast an actor whose emotions are very accessible and communicable. In fact, you need an emotional wreck to play Hamlet, one of those actors that is so highly strung and neurotic that if you look at him funny, he'll burst into tears.
>
> Sometimes I find it very difficult, watching stage productions, to give a damn about Hamlet. He's a problem. I don't care about him when he dies—sometimes I'm sorrier for Horatio!
>
> It may be because I'm not made to empathize—because some actors play him as "a guy like me." The character has to be larger in scope than that. As big as life gets, that's what Hamlet has to be—any Shakespearean role, really.

Kline begins from a tutored and experienced lens:

> The complexity of the characterization is so much a part of Shakespeare's genius. I subscribe to the theory that the character plays you, when it comes to the great roles—that an interpretation cannot be circumscribed by an idea. When a director says he has an idea about Henry V, it must be a *large* idea that can embrace the scale of just about any of Shakespeare's characters, because they're full of paradox, of contradiction and ambiguity.
>
> Just when you think, "Henry is a hero," you understand that he's a *flawed* hero, capable of sainthood and great villainy. How do you deal with his saying "kill the prisoners?"—because the French killed our boys, so now the English kill the French prisoners. Or with Henry's hanging Bardolph—he "would have all such offenders cut off." Bardolph was one of Henry's old friends! Henry exemplifies that wonderful gray area in Shakespeare, not

just good guys and bad guys, or people to root for and people not to root for.

That's why Branagh's version of *Henry V* is so interesting. Olivier's film didn't really encounter the play—instead, he did selections from a play that served his propaganda purposes. Branagh made it a play *about* war. It's not a prowar play nor an antiwar play. Shakespeare's play is encompassing—it can ennoble and embolden, bring out the best and the absolute worst that humanity is capable of. So many of his characters are caught up in the war between their ambivalent moral polarities, their animal nature and divine nature.

Kline brought up this same point about King Lear, a certain doubleness found in Shakespeare's characters, being neither entirely good nor entirely evil. Perceiving this kind of detail in Shakespeare contributes to the reality of the character, makes him human rather than iconic, and it offers grist for the actor:

> We don't get the sense that Lear was always an ideal father. One of his daughters says "he hath ever but slenderly known himself." Peter Brook explored that in a production with Paul Scofield—who made Lear seem unruly and undisciplined. But Albany described him as "this saintly old man," madded by his daughters, a noble man wrongly used. Lear has both of these characteristics. He has imperfection, as well as the potential to be great. The actor and the director have to deal with that in performance.[13]

Once that character composite is in place in the actor's head and heart, Kline recommends giving over to it totally, offering a commonsense tagline:

> In performance, I think you just have to let the role take *you*. Let it play you. Rehearsals should be about letting the play go through you, experiencing it, you taking your cue from the text.
>
> I find with any of the great parts, the notion of "finding the character" is something that defies the usual kind of analysis. You

cannot have a pre-created idea, because the hallmark roles have everything—they are what they seem and they have the opposite of that as well. Submit to it, try to be truthful to the words, but jump in. Have fun, be naughty, be a pig—I did with Falstaff. He is not a man sitting around being depressed—that didn't interest me. Be as indulgent as the character can be. If I wasn't enjoying myself, I had failed.

I no longer think in beats and objectives. I gave that up years ago. It's more about being there.

Kline talks about the double consciousness that operates in an actor during performance. There is a kind of split in an actor's mind, where one part of him is monitoring and watching and even being a sort of director. The paradox is that the actor tries to use and yet subdue that consciousness:

I think it's the hardest thing for actors to articulate, even to one another. It is probably a book unto itself—the psychology of actors in performance. So much of the craft is creating ways in which you almost trick yourself into having something happen rather than manufacturing something into happening.

Yet each time onstage, you have to keep finding new ways to play the part.

There is that "third eye," as Derek Jacobi calls it, which is looking at the performance from inside the actor. It monitors events, comments on the performance, says, "Ouch, I did the wrong thing," or "*That* sucked." Ideally, you want to get rid of that voice, in a way. You don't want it so critical that it locks you up. However, it's always there to answer you when you ask, "What is my next line?" It always responds, "And now you say *these words*" and it gives them to you. The situation is such that you want to forget that you know those lines, and how to say those lines, that you have rehearsed them for eight weeks and performed them for six months—so that they can sound fresh. You have to keep finding new ways to do those lines, to make it look new each time over the length of a show's run, plus how do you reconcile that it's not going to be the same success level each time you do them! You must remain vigilant and yet carefree. You have to care and not care. You have to let the third eye observe and keep the third eye shut.

Same way with listening to yourself—you have to have the third ear there but not listen to it. The ear is always there saying, "Am I being clear? Am I making myself understood? Did I hit the final consonant of that word hard enough? Was I communicating at the same time?" So, you'd like to be able to turn the third eye and third ear off, but they never really go off. I am not sure it is a measurable, quantifiable entity; nonetheless, people ask me what percentage of the third eye is there.

I have read that researchers have hooked up electrodes and found that when actors were acting grief or joy or other major emotions, the electrical impulses registered the same as when a person was actually feeling them. That makes perfect sense to me, that the autonomic nervous system would send off identical signals. It's part of how we are human, why we are doomed to be who we are—we fool ourselves so often into patterns of behavior that are comfortable, or at least familiar, as opposed to having pure responses to things. You cannot have a pure response and still be who you are, in an odd sort of way. If you know what I am talking about. Or maybe I don't know what I am talking about. Finally, remember that we all have less than inspired nights. Part of the art of acting is doing it well on a bad night. We can't always have the muses within us.

It's like Geoffrey Rush says in *Shakespeare in Love*: "It's a mystery." And some of it should always remain a mystery.

Kline makes the point that there is a certain amount of day-to-day crafting and polishing, much of which should *not* be explained:

Acting is like sculpture. You have a big hunk of stone and you just keep chipping away until what's left is the elephant. You get rid of what doesn't work, and what's left is what works, hopefully. Find out how not to do it. In so doing, you find out how to do it.

I don't want to define Hamlet in inexplicable paradoxes. I want to just let it be.

Someone said to Picasso, "Can you explain the painting?" And he answered, "If I could explain it, I would be a writer." He's saying, "I painted it. *You* interpret it."

When Kline plays a role, all of his efforts focus on digging through the text, looking at words and meanings and structural entities rather than reading literary critics:

Obviously, I feel very strongly that an actor should do a very rigorous analysis of the text. *Analysis* is the wrong word. You take your *cue* from the text. You've got to know exactly, precisely, what you're saying. You can't generalize. That's one of the common fatal flaws in Shakespearean acting where things go wrong. An actor will say, "I know generally what he's saying here," and then begins emoting. No. You can't let an audience infer things from a general feeling—well, I suppose you can, but the audience is losing a lot if the actor can't hit all the notes. You have to know very specifically what Shakespeare is saying so that you can be the author of those performed words.

Before you do that, you have to know what they mean. Part of that is interpretation, but part of it is understanding Shake-speare's language. You may have to make a decision based on an appraisal of a scholarly footnote. Really go digging and find the one that there's some controversy over—what the word means or the phrase means precisely. I have used the dictionary, con-cordances, the Cambridge editions, finding the meaning that makes the most sense and resonates emotionally within me.

Paraphrasing is a good tool—if that helps you to understand what you are saying—but you have to be careful there, because you can paraphrase a line and alter it. The paradox is that you have to use Shakespeare's words, not yours.

I trust myself more than I did ten years ago, when I might have read Josephine Tey's book on Richard III [*Daughter of Time*], for example. Today I would say that's a very interesting but totally useless theory if I'm going to play Shakespeare's *Richard III*. The critics are not writing for actors nor looking at a text the way an actor does. Criticism may spark an idea that is dramatic and resonates in you, but you have to discern what's useful and what's un-useful.

Kline weighs and sifts when he looks at text and makes a very practical decision, based on that particular production's requirements:

> Scholars and dramaturges do not write for actors. As they discuss the plays, you think—that's all very interesting but it has nothing to do with *how to make a scene work onstage*. The idea is often fascinating, and something arcane can spark an idea, but it has to be playable and sustainable through a rehearsal process. No one can stand at the side of a performance space and clarify an anecdotal, footnotal description. We're puttin' on a show here, folks, and we're tryin' to make it work.
>
> Sometimes the idea is usable, but it still has to be translated into the performance process. A lot of research material out there is not usually about performance. It must be very difficult for scholars to see a play when they have such high expectations, because in the theater, you cannot sit there and ruminate and ponder. It's a bit like looking at a Beethoven score and saying, "I'm just going to consider this first measure . . . hmmm, extraordinary!"

As part of an outreach program with the New York Shakespeare Festival, Kline arranged to invite John Barton for actor workshops on speaking Shakespeare. Kline was gratified to find the well-known teacher/director confirming his own beliefs about speaking Shakespearean verse: "The greatest gift Barton brought to American actors is that he disabused them of the notion that there are *rules*. Folks would say, 'But here's a feminine ending—what does *that* mean?' He would reply, 'It just means there is a feminine ending.'" Kline also praises Barton's important distinction between poetry and other language modes in Shakespeare:

The other great thing that he pointed out was that Shakespeare is not all poetry . . . He said to actors, "Don't poeticize something that is in fact rather straightforward. Especially, don't intone in some elevated mode of speaking if the language is prose."

The language varies from banal to exalted, both in its dramatic content and in the words that express it, as in, "How does your Lord this many a day?," which is really a "Pass the salt" kind of phrase.

Prose is a different cue for the actor. After four acts of some of the most brilliant, heroic, earth-sweeping, inspired rhetoric— suddenly Henry is relegated to prose with Princess Katherine. When Benedick speaks prose, you can do more jagged shifts of thought: "This can be no trick: the conference was sadly borne . . . they seem to pity the lady . . . I did never think to marry." Prose allows slightly more stream-of-consciousness than verse speaking, because of its structure. Prose is much more like conversation, in a way. It's not poetical. The thoughts can bounce around, can jam one idea into another, and you can backtrack. Prose is more like real thoughts cascading. It's a little freer.

Verse seems to be a more measured progress of thought, qualifying the next thought, building on it, and then closing with a rhymed couplet at the end. At its most structured, it is relentless, inexorable—iambs divided into five feet, with lots of variations on that theme, but the theme is prevalent.

Kline notes that Barton's single most important "tool" for the actor was *antithesis*, and he opines, "For the actor: If you are not aware of antithesis, you will never make Shakespeare's language clear, because he uses it constantly as a rhetorical device. It's wise to be aware of it." Antithesis is the setting up of opposing ideas in the text, which gives the line dramatic energy. It seems simple, but with many of Shakespeare's language strategies, Kline emphasizes that it is also complicated:

There is antithesis, double antitheses, internal antitheses [within a single line of dialogue]. In the workshop, Barton worked on the sonnets because they represent entire exercises in antithesis.

"Was ever woman in this humour *woo'd*? / Was ever woman in this humour *won*?" or "I'll *have* her but I will not *keep* her long," are both examples from *Richard III*. Two ideas which contest and contrast each other. Hamlet has them in "In action how like an *angel*, In apprehension, how like a *god*." Also, the famous "To be, or not to be" and the lines that follow it develop ideas in opposition, in contrast. My God, it's practically all Isabella uses in *Measure for Measure*!

Barton told us, "Look, here's a *rhetorical style* here that Shakespeare is writing in." *Rhetoric* is not a bad word, and Shakespeare's language is not naturalistic conversation. Much of it is poetic. There is alliteration, there is assonance, there is onomatopoeia, meter, metaphor, simile, even rhyme. Use them.

Look at the structure of Shakespeare's scenes. They expand and contract—there are intimate scenes and suddenly you have a larger, more public, scene. The same way within a speech—sometimes you get this simple naturalism, and then there is exalted, feverish poetry. You must find an acting style that allows both, that's always real, that always embraces and includes the audience.

Barton warned about actors getting a wonderful feeling from the words while the audience was being deprived. He said, "Don't overcharacterize it with self-savoring—don't show me your appreciation for the sound."

Kline paraphrases Hamlet as he adds important perceptions to handling language in performance:

Don't mouth it. Be not too tame, neither. Don't overdo it. Don't underdo it. Let the language be there. The French say *juste*. Give it its due, no more and no less. Rather than making a meal of it, clobbering it over my head and shoving it down my throat, let the audience get the goose bumps and the orgasms as opposed to watching the actor do that.

It's very hard for me to do Shakespeare and sound natural. You can sound immediate, but you cannot sound contemporary.

Nobody talks like Shakespeare is written—nobody ever talked like that. It's blank verse, so it's either metrical blank verse or a highly distilled compressed kind of language. Small bits of it are naturalistic, but it's not naturalism throughout. There's no play that's naturalistic. Plays are crafted.

The tavern scenes in the *Henry IV*s were a breakthrough in that direction, closer to how people talked in pubs. Although I don't think anyone could have been as witty in real life per square minute as Falstaff was. If you can make the language sound contemporary without making it sound overly conversational, more power to you. There's a balance to be sought and found here—you speak as if the words were natural to you and the audience still understands them.

Kline notes that there are differences between Americans acting Shakespeare and the English acting Shakespeare:

It's the way the English use language. Americans don't use it in the same way. We don't punctuate with language. We punctuate with hands or arms, with a physical gesture. Whereas the English on that tight, little, overpopulated island have to punctuate with a word. (Also, they consider certain gestures, like pointing, to be bad manners.) Americans are more postural, more emotional, more direct.

Occasionally, when some English players play, we get the sense that they are talking to the audience rather than to the other actor. There are no sparks flying between two actors but rather between one actor and his own speech.

As Americans, we often finish a line and then pause and at that point show everyone how we feel after we've said it. We need not to fall into the trap of conjuring up a feeling during an endless pause that one ought to have felt *on* the line rather than *in between* lines.

The Shakespearean line carries the content of the line along with a subtext of how one feels or thinks about the information.[14]

Kline uses one phrase repeatedly: "You have to develop an appreciation of the language." Such stylized, supercharged language does need to sound natural in the mouth of the player:

> There is something that every actor doing Shakespeare has to come to terms with: What is poetry? What is verse-speaking? Jane Howell said (when she was directing me in *Richard III*), you are talking, but it happens to be poetry, as opposed to—you are speaking poetry and it happens to be drama. There's a subtle but crucial distinction being made there: one is *acting*, and the other is *recitation*.
>
> I wish I could say that there is one way to do Shakespeare: it requires something beyond what other dramatic forms do, because it is poetry. Notions about speaking Shakespeare are subject to convention, public taste, the actor's sensibility, and any number of other variables, but it *is* something unique. Some actors have a natural ear for it.
>
> Another thing an actor learns from doing: not only suit the action to the word, but suit the preparation to the project. Each role and each production requires a different kind of preparation. A smart actor knows when to just leave himself alone, to roll out of bed and show up on the set and shoot the scene. Other projects require lots of research, both of a scholarly nature and of a self-searching nature.

There are truisms about actors that are quizzical, that will remain sealed within the gifts of each artist. Kline talks about the elusive quality of the art:

> There are some actors who "observe" nothing and are neurotically self-absorbed. Some actors have great concentration and discipline—all the skills that Stanislavsky talked about and that conservatories teach. Yet there is something else, something intangible which all of my favorite actors share. I call it "presence." Somehow, I am riveted.
>
> You can't teach presence. It's about "being in the moment"— that special essence when an actor connects with the play and with

the audience at the same time. Some actors remove themselves and give you a taste of it and show you the form of it, exactly how Shakespeare and that character and this play should sound like and look like. Yet the audience is thinking, "Why am I bored? Why don't I feel anything?" It's because the actor isn't *there*.

You can be that in life, but not onstage.

I asked Kline what he knew now about acting Shakespeare that he didn't know when he was a young actor. What kinds of observations would he have for novices?

I feel if you let two or three years pass without playing Shakespeare—well, you begin to discover that *it uses a different muscle group in your head.* You cannot say after a long hiatus, "I think I'll go do some Shakespeare." I found, just in the casting process for *Lear,* that some younger actors are still struggling with the verse or the style or the character, basic things they got in drama school. Shortly after that, they go off to LA to do a movie. They have not had enough time or exposure to Shakespeare plays to get a feel for it. Whereas an English actor like Richard Easton has done six or seven *Henry IV*s or *King Lear*s—Shakespeare is not something you've done only one time over there. You need to steep yourself in it if you are going to feel free of mere technical considerations while performing.

Furthermore, many actors think Shakespeare is *something else,* it's not really acting—which is how it feels until you've worked through that.

Experience delivers a whole new set of insights into acting Shakespeare:

When you are younger, the newer you are at a thing, the more you try to abide by the conventions and rules of the game. Then you find out—oh, I am using way too much muscle. The first time you learned a sport, your legs are sore afterward because you over-worked them. Same way with acting. You learn economy. Not only do you learn "Less is more"—that's a very general maxim—you learn what you can *leave out*, which is just as important as what you put in. You realize how many rules can be broken.

This is difficult to clarify, but you learn what you don't have to worry about—those things that concerned you when you were first starting out. When you first start doing Shakespeare, you want so terribly just to be understood. Later, all that comes intuitively, so you can think about larger things that need more attention.

There are always bigger monsters, new mountains to be climbed—you might think Lear is easy once you've done Hamlet and some of the other colossi: it really isn't that easy, but your focus has changed.

Kline's strength is that he moves with the shifts in theater practice, maintaining a critical curiosity about it. Like Hamlet, he is a constant student of the art, testing new ideas from new theories, never arresting but always refreshing the growth of his own acting process.

I once had a director who said in opening remarks to the cast, "Good morning. My single rule is you only breathe at a full stop or colon. No breathing on the commas or "semicolons." Well. Everybody was hyperventilating for the first two weeks of rehearsal! After the second rehearsal, I said, "I'm going to do all that at home. When I come in here, I'm going to rehearse, okay?" The director was kind of appalled.

Some guys feel that the more constricted their canvas is, the more creative it forces them to be. But I can't be thinking about breathing on schedule.[15]

A number of the earlier roles on Kline's wish list were granted by a man who was vital to New York and vital to the idea of bringing Shakespeare to the people—Joseph Papp. Papp sensed the deep potential in Kline and worked constantly to draw him into the New York Shakespeare Festival productions where Shakespeare was performed free to large audiences in Central Park. Kline's great sorrow was that Papp had planned for him and for Raúl Juliá to alternate Othello and

Iago for the New York Shakespeare Festival. Juliá died before this dream team could be matched.

> I really miss Joe Papp–he was like a paternal taskmaster. On the opening night of *Henry V*, for example, he'd say okay, now, *next*. Next summer you're going to do such and such a part. He would exact a commitment from me. Then and there. Woe to him who made a commitment to Joe Papp and then backed out. You could be offered *Lawrence of Arabia II* with David Lean directing, and you'd have to say no because you'd made other plans.
>
> However, I've never regretted turning down movie work to do Shakespeare. Why would I do that!
>
> I remember being asked once by a journalist who seemed concerned about my career: "Why are you working off-Broadway after you've just had a box-office success with a film? Isn't that a step backward?" I said, "Excuse me—I'm playing Hamlet. In New York City next spring. An actor's career doesn't get any better than that."

In 1994, four years after acting and directing his second *Hamlet*, Kline was at the Globe Theatre, the replica of Shakespeare's theater built on the South Bank in London. The actors were rehearsing *Henry V*. He moved around and sat in a number of the seats to check out the sightlines in the "Wooden O." Then he was invited to test the acoustics. He went up onto the stage; it was in the middle of the day—he couldn't help himself. He cried out, "O for a muse of fire!" and delivered the rest of the speech. Fulfillment. Bliss. Heaven.

A decade later, Kline assayed Prince Henry's corpulent companion, Falstaff. He'd seen the Dakin Matthews conflation of Parts 1 and 2 of *Henry IV* and loved the idea of getting the story of the friendship of Falstaff and Hal in one sitting.[16] This 2004 production was a transition for Kline, out of the earlier heroic and romantic roles:

> People told me "You're too young and too thin." I ignored that, and I'm glad I did. Only in *Richard III* had I such a total transformation into a different body and metabolism. Falstaff's pretty

much inebriated the whole time, so it was nice to get into a different physical, psychological, spiritual, and moral skin. I've never been so afraid of doing a role. The fear of *folie de grandeur* later emboldened me to play Lear. Still, I'd rather fail in an interesting way than never to have done it.

Kline did some ranging through the available research about Falstaff but stayed mostly with the text as he felt it:

> I'd read various things along the way—Harold Bloom and Frank Kermode and W. H. Auden's lectures, which I absorbed with interest. I looked at the Orson Welles' film *Chimes at Midnight* and knew I didn't want to head into somber and melancholy. What interested me was Falstaff's dialogue. He doesn't have one bad line, and I liked saying them: "I am not only witty in myself but the cause of wit in other men." I've always been attracted to mean humor, nasty humor—W. C. Fields and *Fish Called Wanda* humor. His attitude toward life in the recruiting scene—pulling in any warm body who could carry a weapon. Stabbing Hotspur's corpse to get some blood on his own sword. He is not a fuzzy, cuddly guy. I loved his Rabelaisian appetite for life. I even read a bit of Rabelais, who is always funny in his variegated horror.
>
> Falstaff is very resourceful. He can talk and maneuver his way out of every situation, a great survivor. He never dies until Hal breaks his heart. I wanted him to be funny and not melancholic. I saw at the first reading around the table, "We should go for the humor here"—and that corroborated my gut feelings.

The director, Jack O'Brien, was one Kline had always talked with about doing a show, and so the comfort level was very high, which is always auspicious for a project of this size:

> Jack had done the Dakin Matthews version with great success in San Diego and was keen to do it again. He let me find my way, is generously freeing, loves actors and the process of collaboration, and he never forced us into something that had worked before.

When I wanted a change, I had both the director and the dramaturge right there—the conscription scene was originally done offstage, and I needed it back to show that horrible part of Falstaff where he is just earning money and is careless of other people's lives, so that was reinserted in an abbreviated form.

The big mountain, of course, was Falstaff's body, so eloquently and thoroughly described by his fellow rioters within the play. It was an Everest for Kline himself:

> The hardest thing was the fat suit, back-breaking, enervating, but brilliantly made by the folks who made those skating characters' costumes for the Ice Capades. There were several trials, because it had to be big without my head looking like a little pin on top. We were teasing out my hair and beard to a fare-thee-well to get the proportions right. Now the arm's too short and the leg's too skinny. They made a kind of shell that was very lightweight, but the problem was that it indented when I rested my hands on my belly, so I had to stuff a pillow in there and use dry ice on my chest and stomach because every other kind of coolant melted.
>
> One member of the cast who had played Falstaff before (in Central Park) did an experiment there and put a raw chicken inside—it heated up so much during performance that it actually baked! I was losing pounds and pounds, but the fat suit was keeping its girth. Once you put on leather pants, a wool coat, and the big swords, it was *hot* in there.
>
> When I wasn't onstage, I folded down the front part of it and took the sleeves off, just letting it flop so I could get some air around me. It pulled down on my shoulders like a backpack, so I had to be relieved of the weight between scenes. I worked out with my dresser how long it would take to get the thing zipped back up and the makeup retouched (broken blood vessels and scars), because I had sweated it off.

Three years later, Kline was back in mountaineering gear, deciding to climb *King Lear*.

I thought, HUH! King Lear. It will kill me, I'll die. Everyone said, "You are way too young." Actually, I am too old! Gielgud was fifty-four when he did his third and final Lear, Brian Cox was forty-five, Paul Scofield was forty-five. Olivier said the irony is that when you are old enough to understand what it is to be four score and upward, to have children and grow old, you don't have the stamina nor the memory to play it. It's a young man's part. I was fifty-eight when I did it, and I found it exhilarating, even fun. It takes a lot out of you, and I felt better on some nights than others. I *survived*. And I actually learned a lot about the play.

The intimate performance space was a definite advantage. The Public/Anspacher Theater has a small, bowl-like arena with very good seats.

I like doing Shakespeare in a space of around three hundred seats. That means that the fustian, the bombast, can be there, but a little will go a long way. You have a more subtle, nuanced, and psychological performance because you can see the audience, and everyone can see everyone else's face. It's more like what you do for a film camera, only on a larger scale. On "I did her wrong" [about Cordelia], I could ruminate and the audience could hear me.

Also, [James] Lapine gave me the creative freedom every actor needs—the ability to change from night to night. Not just blocking, but also speaking different levels of lines like "Howl, howl, howl. O you are men of stones." Some nights it was as if I were saying—if I had your tongues, I would use them so that the bowls of heaven would crack. All that had to be coordinated around the sound and light cues as well, so I tried to modulate between thunder claps or right on top of the noise.

The cast was supportive. Some casts whine, but this one felt free to experiment. They said, "Wow, you did that a whole different way tonight. I loved that when you grabbed me—you've never done that. That was so different when you said it quietly."

That kind of optimism and flexibility assures that the production will be different and fresh each night. Everybody stays on their toes, because they have to react and adjust to the rhythms that come into play. It's not to every actor's taste, but this happens on nights when an understudy does the role—the other actors are on hyperalert. It was enjoyable to explore and create a flow and a drive to scenes because new ideas kept emerging. You could choose each night where to address certain lines.

The discoveries about Lear accumulated quickly as Kline scoured the text:

> You could say that Lear's bursts of anger and sudden changes are symptomatic of Alzheimer's or dementia of some kind—the dividing of the kingdom, the impulsiveness with which he banishes Kent. It's all intensively about the king rather than his role as father—the king no one has ever opposed. Add to that the results—the loss and passing on of potency, endowing your children with the power and resenting it, giving it all up and yet not giving it up—that tension, then that fall into "nothingness."
>
> Many scholars dissect Lear's madness along these lines. However, it's one thing to be a scholar who pores over the various quartos and folios and analyzes foul papers and historicist points of view—it's another to put together a coherent persona who has entered something near a psychiatric breakdown and to perform that. Those are two different experiences.

Kline goes inside the play to begin dealing with the reality of what happens in each scene.

> It's more interesting and more playable to look beyond court cases and scholarly generalizations. It's more interesting when two daughters are pinning the old man down, diminishing the number of his knights: "Dismissing half your train, come then to me." / "What! Fifty followers?" / "What need you five-and-twenty? Ten? Or five?" / "What need one?"

Still his response is, "O reason not the *need . . .*" He means *because I say so.* So much of his character is about will: It's your will against mine, and I am the father.

Kline also found fascinating the number of levels available to the actor in the play:

> I originally put my hand in Goneril's crotch, right where her womb was, yelling and screaming at her. Another night, I told myself to just enjoy the curse, and I said it with relish, really simple and calm. A vicious speech doesn't have to be yelled, "Dry up her organs of increase . . . If she must teem / Create her child of spleen . . . And it may live to be a thwart, disnatur'd torment to her!" You can say hateful things quietly.
>
> Some of the vengeful cursing is talking more to persons "above," in the heavens, rather to anyone on earth. You can take it very rhetorically and dramatically [he does so]—"That she may feel how sharper than a serpent's tooth is a thankless child." But it gets tedious if you rage continuously. Not just for the audience, but for me doing it.

The actor also has to decide from which of these seeds comes the impending madness. Your mind has to go there to make the scene seem real; your actor self has to have that journey:

> So much of it is about "I am your father. Tell me how much you love me" (in the first scene), and then later, it is about trying to retain love from one or the other of the daughters. "Oh, no, Regan—you are tender-hearted, you are not capable of what your sister Goneril has done." Later he realizes and admits—"They've never loved me. They hate me, they despise me." There is a kind of clarity in admitting that: "I don't know who I am. The truth is I am weak and infirm and loathed by my own flesh and blood. Where does that leave me?" Madness can be a breakthrough as well as a breakdown.

Although it may not work for another actor, what was a revelation to me was that playing Lear's madness was so much about clinging to his sanity. First, "I know what I'll do—I'll stage a trial; that will keep me level." You are desperate and losing it, struggling to hold on to yourself, your identity. Finally, this other revelation on the heath, during the storm: "I don't know who I am anymore!" That was the question he asked at Goneril's house: "Does any here know me? This is not Lear."

Playing it is very freeing. Everyone knows it's Thursday night and I am playing Lear, but for an actor to just let all of that go and not know who Lear is—when it is the actor's job to know who Lear is. Trying to find that place in your gut that puts you up against the wall when everything you've built your selfhood around no longer applies.

Many things in this narrative of Lear reflect Kline's tried-and-true opinions about performance and theater practice. There is the element of sampling the research to stimulate one's imagination. There is the knowledge that an actor cannot cogitate for pages on the meaning of a word or phrase—he must choose one and then be specific about it onstage: he has to internalize textual information onto a performance self, remaining true to a text and also to a character template within himself. He needs the freedom to move around inside a production, making shifts and changes and choices that are not the same each night, a point of view that is more resonant with late twentieth- and early twenty-first-century actors. Rehearsal is to find a structure; performance is to "play" within it. These are not merely words on a page, where you sit and pore over them for years, nor are they unperformable, as Charles Lamb insisted about King Lear. The dialogue is meant to be actualized, enacted, made life and breath.

Just to demonstrate that Kline did not wind up in a storm, naked, uncomprehending, inside a fiction, I add a story about his daughter at school. It exemplifies the shifts in pedagogy in teaching Shakespeare through performance that began in the late 1960s and have now found their way into American classrooms:

What was done in my daughter's school was *not* "Read Act I for tomorrow and we'll discuss it in class," but the teacher showed scenes from the 1968 Max Reinhardt film of *A Midsummer Night's Dream*, as well as the Peter Hall version from 1968, and also the one I was in, directed by Michael Hoffman in 2003. Then the students were asked to write a paper on *the differences in how Oberon was performed* in each version! They had to write a paper on the way the actor interpreted a role! Then they actually acted a scene in class, and my daughter played Oberon.

She was so worried: "How am I going to memorize these lines? I am so worried that I am going to forget them." So, we sat down and read it together, and I said that the lines are so beautiful, so unforgettable, this maiden sitting on a promontory . . . And she answered, "You're right—it's beautiful." And my mind was screaming, "Yes, you get it!" I was so excited about her understanding that Shakespeare is the greatest achievement in expressibility in the English language.

We took the kids to see *Romeo and Juliet* in Central Park, and she'd read it beforehand, on her own. I asked, "Are you reading the one that shows the little translations on the right hand side of the page that paraphrase it?

And she said, "No. I like the real one."

More fulfillment, more bliss, utter heaven. To pass the torch in real life.

KENNETH BRANAGH AS RICHARD IN THE 2002 PRODUCTION
OF *RICHARD III* AT THE CRUCIBLE THEATRE IN SHEFFIELD, UK.
(PHOTO BY IVAN KYNCL)

2

Kenneth Branagh
Fretted with Golden Fire

In a conversation about actors memorizing lines, Kenneth Branagh said that he learned the role of Richard III while playing Gilderoy Lockhart in *Harry Potter and the Chamber of Secrets*: "I can't think of anyone on that set who didn't have to hear me run my lines—from Harry Potter on upwards." Shortly after acting that flamboyant loony, he performed Richard III onstage. Branagh is also the film director who created the twenty-first-century blueprint for putting Shakespeare onto film, having directed a half-dozen pictures in all.

Branagh was born in Belfast, Northern Ireland, the son of a carpenter. He decided to become an actor after seeing Derek Jacobi's Hamlet on his first trip to London at age sixteen, and he applied for a scholarship to enter the Royal Academy of Dramatic Art at age eighteen. Principal Hugh Cruttwell was a significant mentor.

By the age of twenty-four, Branagh had performed a couple of leading roles at the Royal Shakespeare Company (RSC); however, he had more pressing aspirations. He formed his own group, the Renaissance Theatre Company, assembling a cadre of talented and convivial colleagues, including Richard Briers, Patrick Doyle, and Brian Blessed. By the age of twenty-nine, he was persuading major film companies to finance the movies that put his Shakespeare spurs on the wall. The creative work is both the means and the end—the more he does, the more he discovers, and the more he achieves.

The scope of Branagh's projects summons comparisons with great actor-managers from the past, like Garrick, Gielgud, and Olivier. To the list of acting, directing, writing, and producing, one is bound to add the fine art of entrepreneurship. Not only is Branagh the most audience-savvy of the auteur filmmakers vis-à-vis Shakespeare (*As You Like It*, 2006; *Love's Labour's Lost*, 2000; *Hamlet*, 1996; *Much Ado About Nothing*, 1993; *Henry V*, 1989), but he has played several Shakespearean roles onstage and in other people's productions as well, including Hamlet for the Royal Shakespeare Company in 1992 and Iago on film in 1995. Add to this Coriolanus, Berowne, Peter Quince, Edgar, Touchstone, Benedick, King of Navarre, Romeo, Laertes, Henry V, and Richard III.

It is the sheer array of unique projects that dazzles—from the officious supervisor in *Rabbit-Proof Fence* to the Woody Allen knockoff in *Celebrity* to the numbing heroism of *Shackleton* (his first Emmy nomination), then *Warm Springs* (another nomination), and an Emmy for *Conspiracy*. Branagh is continually developing ideas—like his early smaller movies: *Dead Again*, *Peter's Friends*, *Swan Song*, and *In the Bleak Midwinter*. His list of awards includes four Oscar nominations, BAFTAs, Critics Circle Awards, the Golden Quill Award, and more. His output is due to an ability to inspire, to lead, to administrate, and most important of all, to network.

Branagh comes to the interview prepared; he has thought about his craft and learned to describe it in a thorough way. The material is easy to write about because it is so opulent. Rich, you understand, not gaudy—plus it is delicately peppered with irony. The spark of Branagh's industry permeates everything he says. "The work" stimulates him to take on novel challenges, including an imaginative adaptation of the opera *The Magic Flute*:

> One's enthusiasm for it, particularly in that central part, the creative part, I particularly like. What you are talking about in this book, the *process*. The process I find fascinating. I don't really think that I understand it, but I am happily on that journey and very happy to know that I will never arrive.[1]

Branagh began to develop his vision of acting Shakespeare at a juncture when he and fellow students were involved in a dialogue about choices:

> It didn't take long to be disenchanted with what appeared to be very attractive, the ability to declaim Shakespeare in a loud and clear voice. It seemed like an impressive thing to do. Yet I felt early on that this could be a rather passive and unemotional tableau of passionate thoughts recollected in tranquility with some sense of predictability. Because of the quality of the writing, often in verse, that in itself was not a bad experience. Well done, it was a pretty effective way of hearing some great human truths as observed by Shakespeare.
>
> In terms of a live theatrical and dramatic experience, what was even *more* thrilling was if that level of understanding and intelligence and clarity was also allied with a sense of it happening before our very eyes. Where the superficial elements of technique (such as a clear voice and diction—and no attention being drawn to them) were present as well, *then* the overall effect was dynamite. A real live person acting and reacting before us in the moment, simultaneously allowing us to *experience* words (rather than just hear or understand) that have an impact on us via their poetic character. That could be a transformative and even a transcendent experience—with everything working at once.
>
> I also realized that it was a very, very challenging thing to do.

Drama school training is for developing an idea about what the art form is and supplying a foundation of technique; rehearsal is for discovery and clarifying undertext; performance relies on all of these. Drama school is also the place where you practice technique—crafting a flexible and clear voice and body that are at your command, and where you are constantly critiqued on it. Branagh states that you must shelve and store all that information for later use:

> Henry Irving, when asked how classical acting happens, said, "Be natural and speak up"—which is a way of summing it up. I've

discovered that some evident technique is a pleasurable part of the audience experience. However, I do not want to be aware of it until *after* I've left the theater. I do want it to be *there*, because it is a marvelous way through which the character and the play can be communicated.

Basically, the removal of a declamatory style, or anything else that is not authentically and passionately felt, was something that I was being headed toward, from drama school and from Hugh Cruttwell, who was quite influential on me and on a whole generation of actors. It was clear that you had to do *everything*. You have to be brilliantly clear, technically precise, and then you have to be unaware of that as you absolutely experience, moment to moment, the journey of the character. When all that coalesced, it could be rather marvelous. That's what has stuck with me.

From performance to performance, whether it's a film or a play, that is the goal. From whatever your latest understanding of what the playing position is—what some people would call "the dramatic action of the character" (people chew it up in all sorts of ways) or "What does my character want in this scene?"—you walk into the scene, knowing all the lines and having researched all of the moves. Thinking from that central focus, the lines come out the way they come out.

The lines are always affected by what the other actors say and how they say it. That is always changing, and that is good. So the temperature of a scene might change quite dramatically from performance to performance, but somehow it is all linked to whatever your latest assessment of what the *center* of that scene is.

That is what happens across the run of a play—for example, saying in broad terms, "I love my mother, but I love my father more," as opposed to going onstage and saying, "If I go over this way, I'll get a laugh, and then I move over there and then I shout this bit . . ."—very consciously resisting as much as possible *fixing* the delivery of the performance from night to night.

A look at Branagh's comments about acting *Henry V* at the RSC, his numerous encounters with *Hamlet*, and a lengthy discussion of his 2002 performance in *Richard III* follows, revealing how layers of experience accumulate through an actor's career. The discussion demonstrates the kinds of research Branagh has done for different roles. He started out by reading the standard critical works and then took a fruitful sidetrack:

> With Henry V, I read the intro in the *Arden Shakespeare* version (these are often challenging) and studied the footnotes, in that case pretty fully. I went to authors who had something interesting to say. That was my introduction to the Dover Wilsons and the Quiller-Couches and the Kenneth Muirs, and yes, I would go and pick up *The Wheel of Fire* and *Shakespeare Our Contemporary*, for example. That was a time when I gave myself a more general sense of some of the academic approaches to the play.
>
> Also, I spoke with Prince Charles [the Prince of Wales], and it was a sort of scavenging about the play. I found the visit very valuable. I carried away a sense of atmosphere in talking with someone like that. It was a search for the internal qualities of princeliness, a question of being aware of his deportment, of his gravitational weight, what he thought and how he considered things. He was very distinct from other people up close and tangible, and it had to do with carrying the burden of responsibility and of service that must at times feel excessive. All that affected my body language and the look in the eye and so impacted me greatly when I performed the role.
>
> I wanted to meet Prince Charles because there was this separateness, an isolation or loneliness or melancholy that seemed also to be absolutely *right through* the lines in the play in direct or indirect ways. I needed to find out what I could bring on a human level that is also promoted by the text.
>
> Anyhow, it was very helpful for me. I go through the same process to discover the inside of a character.[2]

At the RSC, where Branagh's first Henry V was played, there were very good assistant directors who did more individual coaching. In that situation, Branagh could take advantage of being able to narrowly focus on just a few lines in a speech, or on a difficult and problematic passage, spending exclusive time in a helpful and specific way that could not be done in a long rehearsal process with large-cast plays.

Hamlet was, of course, a horse of a different color. He played it first at RADA (the Royal Academy of Dramatic Art), then in Birmingham under the directorship of one of his mentors, Derek Jacobi. He later returned to the RSC to play the role. He directed himself in his own film and also recorded it on BBC Radio. He notes changes in each of his portrayals:

> Inevitably, the part of Hamlet provides so much to discover. First of all, there is the intellectual challenge, trying to understand as much as you can each line, each scene, and what the whole play says. You start with the production and where it is set, what ideas the director may have, how much of yourself you bring to the role.
>
> It's a role where you discover that the process of playing—whether across a run or through a number of different productions—is a changing entity. Your views develop. They amplify (if you are lucky) when your consideration of the role and the depth of the production is good, and so both intensify. You might decide Hamlet has a mother fixation, and then weeks or months into the run you might decide he has a father fixation. You might change the emphasis on different kinds of scenes. Across the sweep of acting it several times, what becomes important to you can shift dramatically.
>
> Derek Jacobi describes it as "the greatest straight part ever written." It's a personality part in a way that is distinct from most other Shakespearean heroes and characters. The audience expects, the tradition suggests, and you are invited to bring as much of yourself into the role as possible. It's one of the reasons why people go see my Hamlet and then go see someone else's. The two are going to be completely different by virtue of our different personalities.
>
> That may not be as true when the character on the page has more particular circumstances, say Henry V, which define a nar-

rower world more affected by his journey through the play—for example, the events that lead to Agincourt.

Some actors appear to find one way to play Hamlet and then simply stay on that key, so to speak, perhaps because the play is such a high mountain to climb. Branagh suggests why:

> Trying to fix on a particular way of playing it is perhaps a comfort in the midst of feeling what otherwise can be a wash in the face of a trillion ways of doing it.
>
> If you are an actor who goes the literary route, you could spend a year and not miss a day which offers a book describing a completely opposite interpretive route—what lines mean, how the actual text should be shaped. These are often equally convincing. You'd be reading Ernest Jones one day, Jan Kott the next, Granville-Barker after that—all eloquently persuasive and enthusiastically argued.
>
> Many actors do have very dogmatic views about playing the role. As well they should—because that informs their commitment and the quality of their performance. They often feel they have actually discovered something that no one else has.
>
> However, *is* there a definitive way of playing a line like, "Nymph, in thy orisons / Be all my sins remember'd"? It could be played as a question, or as a reflective, private, internalized thought prior to speaking to Ophelia (making it a question of "Hello—are you reading your prayers and are you remembering me in them?"), which provides an alternative dynamic for the scene that follows. I've played it both ways, to be honest.
>
> If a new reading inflects something different—or affects that scene or an upcoming scene—I'm happy to try it. I don't feel proprietorial about the way each scene or line should be performed. The more you explore it, the more possibilities you have.

Only a handful of actors have had as much experience with Hamlet as Branagh has. Gielgud acted in it four times, occasionally directing

himself—he also directed Richard Burton in the role. Kevin Kline
played it twice onstage and once on television, directing himself on
two of those occasions. Derek Jacobi played it for 379 performances
and directed Branagh in it as well. There is a deep well of wisdom to
be found in actors who have returned to the play several times:

> In our film of it, when Hamlet is being pursued by Rosencrantz
> and Guildenstern and various guards, he goes through one room
> after another and one door after another. You feel that playing
> Hamlet is like that. You make a breakthrough, you open a door,
> and there is another vast hall for you to cross through and look at
> and consider, so that there is limitless potential in your attempt
> to understand your engagement with the role. The challenge is
> to maintain that sense of exploration.
>
> The landscape of Hamlet is vast, and the history of its produc-
> tion suggests that it can be interpreted in a million different ways.
> So, that's true for an actor as well. I think the role has limitless
> possibility across any actor's engagement with it in a lifetime.
>
> Gielgud said that with the hundreds and hundreds of times
> he's played it, it was still a new experience each time. Even as he
> finished a radio recording of it in the 1950s, he continued to find
> new things in it.

Branagh's characterization of Hamlet in the 1993 RSC version
was very like that of a young CEO, troubled about family affairs and
attempting to manage a situation gone awry while holding himself
together as well. The same sort of small-family-corporation milieu
shoots through the 1996 film version. One wonders if these kinds of
administrative overtones are intended in either version. In any case,
they do parallel what he can "bring to the film on a human level"—
young executive manages large artistic enterprise.

When the actor's attention turned to yet another role, the stage
production of *Richard III*, Branagh described the research he tackled,
some of it decidedly literary, some experiential, some textual, all of it
feeding a central pool of invention:

I suppose I read about as much as I could absorb in terms of academic criticism. I am sure it was only scratching the surface of what was out there, but in view of the incredibly contradictory views and ideas, one could become pretty confused.

My goal was to focus on the historical character. My tools were the play itself and some historical biography. I tended to avoid seeing other productions, even though I am a great fan of Olivier's 1948 film of *Richard III*, particularly for a performance which I think is wonderfully magnetic and his best performance of Shakespeare on film. It is so sexy and intelligent and charismatic and thrillingly executed. However, I didn't want to see it right then, because I didn't want to be affected one way or another, intimidated and cowed by what I already knew was absolutely brilliant.

I simply wanted to get a strong sense of the historical Richard, within two or three books, so I would have a sense of perspective in going to the play itself, thinking about how and why Shakespeare might have diverged from what was a pretty complex man in real life. There was much conjecture about the nature of his character and the actual facts of where and when he did things, particularly regarding the princes in the Tower of London. The general assessment of whether he was a good man or a bad one rests on those actions.

A book I reread was Josephine Tey's *Daughter of Time*, a crime novel, basically, which breathes authentic atmosphere and is very charming aside from the matter and substance of it.

Branagh warns against reading too much criticism beforehand:

I try to narrow the process down rather than gathering a million books. Simon Callow makes a good point in his book *Being an Actor*. He talks about the totemic value of biographies and books, often kept by actors' bedsides. They are stroked and held and photographs looked through but not necessarily in any detail— their very presence, borrowed from a library or sought out and purchased, as graphic evidence that the actor is researching. In most cases, people use them quite quickly and then drop them.

Research can sometimes be a handicap when you come to a scene and are trying to prove or illustrate a point that you believe to be some kind of revelation. It's often a problem for you *to just do that with the words that are there at your disposal.* You suddenly find yourself in a contest with what Shakespeare has written, because he simply isn't giving you the one sentence that explains the brilliance of your connection to an insight you found in a book! This can lead to some tortured time in rehearsal as you throw a few red herrings in the way.

Branagh finds again that the quality of the preparation and research heightens if one varies the sources of inspiration:

I visited the Tower of London and found that very interesting. In a way, you are looking to spark your imagination. More and more, my character preparation involves simply engaging with the play, trying to understand the play text as it is written—with quite a lot of investigation into the nature of the text and how corrupt it's believed to be. Not so much to come down with a definitive decision—you can't. But if there are alternative readings, alternate lines, lines from another edition or quarto or folio, I think it's fair enough to look at them if they are related to the way you are considering the character. I have no bones about bringing that material in.

Look, it's part of the general amount of material that *is* this play. If we don't fully understand the absolute truth of this artwork— which is a nebulous thing, *because it changes in performance so that's something we will never definitively know*—then it's fair enough to sort of jigsaw your text together. If you've threaded your way through all the footnotes in the debate about Hamlet's "sullied" or "solid" flesh, those nuances have quite important consequences for the internal process of the actor. So, my work is pretty much text-led, with supplementary ignitions of imagination provided by other material.

Branagh entered the field early with good fortune and fairly quick fame. He's had the luxury of performing a great many major Shakespearean roles, an array of plum parts that most actors might wait a lifetime to re-create. His insights give us a glimpse into a privileged realm of performance preparation and show what an actor can glean from this vantage point.

In the case of Richard III, there was ample time to explore character. Branagh's textual starting point for discovering the inner workings of the character was an important soliloquy near the climactic point of the play, when Richard is alone in the tent near the battlefield and gives a speech very different from his usual self-assured discourse:

> I've had the luxury, in the last few projects I've done, of having a significant gestation period, which I asked for when I agreed to do *Richard III*. I knew about it a year in advance of the start of rehearsals. In engaging with the play, perhaps any Shakespearean play, you are looking for the moments of great questioning and doubt, the parts of the play which have been subject to the most conjecture and debate. You might discover them yourself, if they are already deep in the culture—"Is Hamlet indecisive?," for example.
>
> Our process with Richard started with the question "Who was the man that spoke the words on the night of the Battle of Bosworth Field—who was that man in the tent? For a while, put aside the dazzlingly, flamboyant actor manqué who goes through the first part of the play, the ruthless killer, the marvelous politician. At issue in that play is how all of those roles marry (if they do) and whether they are required to be consistent psychologically with what later appears to be a guilt-ridden man as he contemplates the battle, his possible demise, his potential route straight downward into hell. In the tent is a man who hasn't really talked *that way* throughout the rest of the piece.
>
> So, then, where is the *central problem*, where is the bit that scholars haven't answered, where is the common link that tells me here is a difficulty to solve with this character? Right there in the middle of the text, not from a biography or a film or a trip to

the tower, but right there on the page. Do I need to believe that this is the same man? Do I need to explain it in any way? *Or is it just there*, and the audience can intuit what they wish from what other people seem to find a psychological inconsistency?

When Richard later wakes up from that awful dream and says, "Give me another horse! Bind up my wounds!," the consideration of whether he's a killer, these voices talking inside his own head that discuss what might happen and his own culpability—that was something I could take at face value. That capacity for guilt, that capacity for self-examination, that capacity for doubt—I tried, in some sense, to infuse it into every scene that came before. Once I'd decided if the man was capable of *that*, well, I worked backwards from there.

It's finding the balance between wanting to *explain* a character (which can be a dull process and can even work against text in some ways) and *working instead to feed the inner life of the persona*, the psychological substance of the character.

The point Branagh makes here about the inner and outer self of the character and which to emphasize—or better yet, how to make them *work together*—is especially significant. There was an outer component to the character that was obvious—a striking visual clue that registers with the audience immediately, the reason he is called Richard the Humpback. Branagh tells how he integrates this aspect into the inner core of the king:

> Another hugely important factor in working on that part was to take at face value what Shakespeare says about Richard's physical disability and then to discover what impact that difficulty had on his behavior, which can be a crucial part of the interpretation. In broad terms, the dialogue suggests that he felt very much abused, disregarded, ignored as a result of not being considered able-bodied. That was strong emotional fuel for the kinds of amoral behavior that punctuated the play, a sort of revenge on the world for the injustice that had been visited on him. Or, if you like, for the *lack* of love that he received.

All these cues are used in creating the personality of the man who goes onstage. Once inside this casing, the actor has the freedom for a variety of gestures and vocal intonations, which may differ from night to night, depending on how the performance goes.

> As I worked on the part, it was those kinds of things drawn out of the text—a man who has more doubt in him than appears to be the case upon first examination, and then someone for whom the disability he dealt with had a profound impact.
>
> There is more of this building up of the inside stuff, the psychological model, *the thing from which you play when you then go onstage every night.* As I mentioned, I generally feel that my intention is never to fix a performance, not to have a set of pre-inflected lines. The basic goal is to re-create every evening from that truthful psychological center. So that the end result is that the lines will come out the way the lines come out. Hopefully, they will surprise you and they will surprise the other actors.
>
> Part of that ultimate aim is that they have an improvisational quality. You are trying to get to a point where it seems as though you don't know what you are going to say next. So that the *audience* receives it as if the thoughts are developing before their very eyes.

Branagh emphasizes that the Richard III experience was unique and that he was lucky to have had it. Moreover, actors work in different ways at different stages within their acting careers:

> Various factors affect how you act a role—the age you are, the way you meet it in your life, the director and how you get on, how closely involved with him or her you are. Especially if it's the director presenting a very vivid idea of playing the play or offering some staging coup so that you are both off on a roll in an interesting direction.
>
> Lots of actors don't want to discuss their role preparation much. Sometimes, they come in with a great *wodge* of strong feeling they have about the character. Sometimes it lands absolutely in

the center of what the part requires, and sometimes there follows a process of realization that acting requires another step. It's not enough to say, "I have a son just like that who gets angry all the time." That's a broad way of declaring you have a background of experience that will be useful in the perception of the role. But the ultimate return to the text demands an active imagination. *You are going to have to go there.* You're going to have to imagine what it is like to commit murder if you are going to play the Scottish king.

Actors forge all kinds of unique relationships with their directors. Branagh describes an ideal collaboration in working with Michael Grandage:

During the year before the *Richard III* rehearsals, we met many times and were able to talk about the larger picture and quite small details, sometimes in rambling ways. This was about working the ground of the project. It was helpful because it happened well in advance of design deadlines. The logistics of meeting design schedules, once that construction process begins, can cut a few things off at the pass in terms of the development of your imagi-nation. You can also get a lot of your own stupid ideas out of the way when you begin talking early on!

Christopher Oram, the designer, was in on the discussions, so we could sit with pieces of paper and do drawings. It was enor-mously enjoyable, and I can't imagine not having a long-term advance relationship with the director before major decisions are made about the way you play the role. The idea of just showing up in the rehearsal room is less attractive to me now, because I have discovered the importance of a long-term *marinating* pro-cess. You sort out the wheat from the chaff, you develop a way of shorthand communicating, and you get to talk about the ways you like to work.

Working on a project with this much time for collaboration is a rare gift. There are major benefits in terms of clarifying details and extending what is usually a four- to eight-week rehearsal time.

Much of this preparation is not to set specific ways, but it's really to do with *trust*. It's important that people are not intimidated by my track record with this kind of work, not frightened to say things, whether it's a substantive or imaginative issue in the performance. Or even if it's something smallish and technical, such as "I can't hear this" or "Why do you gabble that?" or "Why do you do that funny thing with your head?" A certain amount of honesty and openness is mutually beneficial.

The thrill was that the director agreed and welcomed it as a chance to do more work on the play. The process was more like a continuing conversation about our approach, and so some of the curse of the opening-day formality was reduced.

The same thing happened at the National with Edward Hall directing me in David Mamet's *Edmond*. I felt we had somehow stolen another seven or eight weeks of rehearsal because of conversations we had about scenes. Things heard out loud surprised us in reading the play together. It was invaluable.

What it does is start the rehearsal process early. With two months yet to go, you feel different in reading a scene. You get further down the road on day one as a result of having done the former.

The experience of working with Michael Grandage also yielded a fresh insight about memorization. The technique of memorizing is very individual—how one does it and when—and there are shifts in preference in theater practice. Most actors nowadays memorize as they rehearse, not beforehand.

The director was keen to have the play learnt before we got there, something actors and directors occasionally resist. Since we'd had that extended conversation, I was very happy to do it. Some actors think, "How can I possibly learn it if I don't know what I am doing?" I feel there is an enormous onus and responsibility on the actor *to work out what you are doing*, to have worked out some ideas ahead of the rehearsals. Memorizing beforehand does not imply "setting your performance" or presenting the other actors with some immovable version of how you will do things. It provides a familiarity with the text from a position of confidence that it can still be very malleable in your hands. It also removes a psychological barrier: that can be a really difficult moment in rehearsal when you put the book down and start to walk-the-tightrope-look-no-hands. You can waste a week in rehearsal while you are simply trying to remember your lines.

In future, I would like to be as familiar as I possibly could, up to and including learning the whole thing, fully confident that it would not involve me learning it in some wrongheaded way—where I would get locked into inflections or a certain approach to a scene. It's more about being able to discover it as it goes.

Memorizing ahead of time clarified some of Branagh's ideas about what he might require in future productions, an instance of his thinking as both actor and director.

It takes a rehearsal of a scene to see what's working, and then it's important that you feel free enough to let that version go and be affected by the current stage of the process, where another revelation is provided, or by another actor's input into the scene which could shift it in some important way.

In the case of *Richard III*, we were in a regional theater [Sheffield], and we had four weeks with the whole cast, which is no time at all. I began to think six weeks' rehearsal is what you need for a Shakespeare play. Not nine or eight or four, but *six*, from my point of view, to provide the best achievable, most practical number of weeks, especially given the cost of things. Then you are in pretty good shape.

One more thing about lines: in performance, an actor travels along parallel universes, where one part of your awareness is in what's going on onstage, and another track is fidelity to the character. One track is remembering the lines, another track is thinking about what you might possibly have for dinner that night. Somehow all of it melding together.

I asked Branagh if he ever was consulted about who would be in the supporting cast when he was playing the title role:

> Yes, I did in *Richard III*. I was in all of the auditions, but I had no veto power. I simply wanted the experience of reading with people. I wanted to say the lines out loud. The more you do, the more natural it becomes and the more a part of you. You're somehow *in the lab*. Also, it was important to me to get a sense of how the atmosphere is with another actor, what the level of trust is, how the connection and intuition work, and to be able to express an opinion about that.
>
> In any case, it's better for the actors if they act with someone while auditioning Shakespeare rather than doing it alone as a kind of party piece. Performing with someone who is already in it gives a better account, rather than its being a sort of prize-day speech, which is awful for everyone and doesn't tell you much except how the actor responds to stressful situations.

One of the continuing issues in acting Shakespeare is verse speaking. Everyone has theories, some voice coaches having honed the endeavor into complicated interlocking rules. Branagh has had a broad range of experience with both stage and film actors, and he has reached his own conclusions:

> I resist fixing precepts about subjects like this. You develop what you can and you do what you can in any given situation. I think it is dangerous to declare that there is a set way of speaking the verse. However, there has to be a very sophisticated *understanding* of the line underlying the execution of it in performance. We are dealing with a language that is now over four hundred years old and which has particular challenges in its delivery and in what is required to understand it and then to convey that in performance. Once one starts to break it up and talk about verse speaking, when the ultimate aim is *a delicate combination of truth and reality*, one risks disintegrating something that should be integrated.

You cannot have the feeling that technical ability is separate. Discussing verse speaking by observing line endings—that is a tool on the way to achieving the proper marriage of language and characterization. The greatest exponents of verse speaking in Shakespearean acting have always been people with a perfect understanding of the rules of classical acting—people like Jacobi, Dench, McKellen—and they are also in a position to bend them.

Jacobi once said to me, "I always play fast and loose with the punctuation because we cannot be sure if it is correct on the page, and so the notion of a very dictatorial way of speaking the verse line does assume that we have a perfect playhouse copy of what's intended. We know for certain that is *not* the case, so we can, in rehearsal, debate the merits of individual cases."

Branagh hints that it is not folly to know what a phrase means ahead of one's performance, but that it might be foolish to plan how it will come out of one's mouth. The actor needs to understand (in the sense of *fully comprehending*) what he is about to say and, of course, his reasons for saying that dialogue. However, the actual speed, pitch, and quality of the vocal sounds get tempered by what his fellow actors feed him onstage:

> Even the most scrupulously honest performance of certain lines, filled with the greatest integrity, cannot be totally controlled. *The true issue is*—is there an exciting tension in the theater between the actors? If Shakespeare has placed a wayward line in the middle of a highly charged atmosphere in order to change the direction and the tone of the scene, then the actors need to know that the goal is to allow the audience to sufficiently switch temperatures when the line comes up.
>
> Adrian Noble told me about Gielgud doing Prospero's "Our revels now are ended" speech at a memorial service. He said Gielgud broke every single rule of verse speaking in that presentation, and he was absolutely brilliant. I think that supports the idea that in the hands of the very, very expert few, the capacity to make it mean exists without a set of hidebound rules.

Branagh repeats that the goal of speaking Shakespeare's verse is that it must sound natural, as if the actor is *not* attending to a set of rules. The actor's preparation in craft and technique has taught him to speak well, but that quality must not distract from the meaning of the words.

> I am phenomenally picky about diction, about clarity, about breathing toward the end of the line, about being faithful to the punctuation we appear to have. Yet I want at *all* times to *believe* what the actor/character is saying. I don't want to break it up into something dry and rarified. I don't want to be, in the theater audience, overly conscious of the way the language is crafted. It should seem effortless and natural.
>
> Both technique and naturalness can inform one another. Spending an afternoon in rehearsal purely, dryly, observing the technical requirements of a speech can sometimes give you a clue to the emotion of a speech, because you can focus—hear a rhythm, or hear a vowel sound that is more open or more closed. Somehow there is a taste of the emotional texture inside the phrase that can be sensed and revealed and thus inhabited more by an actor for whom the words are somehow in the way of the release of feeling, when in fact *those words* have to become necessary to say. When it's all achieved, it's pretty exciting—because doing both together is difficult.
>
> In the end, if any given set of rules does not support or effortlessly produce meaning for the audience, the performance will stick out as "a presentation of the text." It might be more precise and more faithful to the poetic experience, but in terms of life and the reality of the theatrical experience, it can be *uninvolving*.

Branagh now has the he-can-do-anything reputation among stage and film and television directors, who will postpone the date of a project to wait for him to join it. He is known to tackle difficult jobs on offer and turn in a performance that puts him in prize-winning categories. His reputation is due to the expertise he has gained as his vision widened via directing in a number of art forms. No matter what has preceded, he now sees acting from the point of view of a director. He talks about the daily act of rehearsal as paramount to the entire process of performance:

> The cliché applies. Gary Blair, this marvelous South African golfer who's won many tournaments, was told, "You're very lucky, Gary." He replied, "Yes, the harder I practice, the luckier I get."
>
> I've worked with a great many brilliant actors—no matter how early you get to the rehearsal room, they will be there before you. They will be doing whatever it takes to concentrate on the work and use that time well.
>
> A lot of actors dodge rehearsing with a ritual of avoidance— chitchat, unnecessary explanations, lobbying for a particular idea—which defers actually engaging. There's no substitute for tasting it, kicking it around, just getting up and doing it. There is often unnecessary caution because in the end, it *is* bloody scary. Might as well throw yourself at the fear at the outset. Relish it.
>
> I have some pretty strong views about a general sense of discipline in rehearsal, in relation to punctuality, concentration, that sort of thing. I find it tedious when people don't turn up on time and are not absolutely ready at ten o'clock. It surprises me sometimes that there are people who just don't get that. *You do all your work there.* It has to be a sacred place. It can be a practical place as well, but its purpose is to focus the work. Rehearsal is such a key part of the whole process.

For Branagh, most of the work is done in the rehearsal room, and if any is done in his leisure time, it is mostly subconscious attention:

> If I have a full day or a full weekend off, then I might look at notes in the margin (most actors do this) or read the scene again. I might think of something I remembered from rehearsal and wanted to try next time. Sometimes the physical act of writing it down allows your system to absorb it in a different way.
>
> On the whole, the mental energy used in rehearsal is surprisingly fatiguing. Over the course of a week or so, it is quite valuable

to switch off. Work your socks off while you are there, and then go home and be surprised at how exhausted you are. You need to veg out. A zombie-like feeling takes over in the evening and makes for a restorative emptiness where the subconscious can work if it wants to.

Rehearsal processes are very invasive in the psyche. In working on *Richard III*, most of us were away from where we lived. You might have dinner and a pint, and inevitably you'd talk about it and there would be a sort of ongoing chatter between folks who were in scenes together. Questions would get asked, people registering how they felt differently about a scene or a character, which is a helpful process. Genuine time away from it is also good.

One of Branagh's major skills is surrounding himself with strong casts. His group of loyal supporters was built up with some astute networking in his salad days. On the other side of the coin, he is unflinchingly steadfast to those who work hard. That kind of reciprocity goes on giving.

I continue to be excited and surprised by the work of other actors in rehearsal and also by other directors in their productions. One of the advantages of getting older is that you can unreservedly admire your fellow actors. My sense of wonder for this category of performers increases year by year: Maggie Smith, Derek Jacobi, Judi Dench, Antony Sher, Ian McKellen, and in my own generation, Simon Russell Beale, Mark Rylance, Greg Hicks, Ralph Fiennes, all sensational actors and a thrill to watch. I am not trying to put myself into the same category with these people, nor being falsely modest, either, but I do come away from their performances with a sense of awe at how effortlessly they do something very difficult. Watching work on that level is a real delight, a pleasure I seek out. It is good to see strong ensemble work from the whole cast, all up onstage at the same pitch.

Another thing that goes with these greats: a kind of absolutely natural, unaffected modesty, a genuine disconnection between their abilities and their awareness of it. In both Derek's and Judi's cases especially—they don't seem to recognize their own ferocious intellectual ability. On their level, there is no luck involved, only successful artistry.

In Judi's case, I think it's a determination not to let that "mind" part get in the way of her intuition. She is much more actively in search of "the mysterious" than other actors. She seeks to put herself in the vulnerable and endangered position of truly discovering *anew*—and that means actively attempting to abandon your intellect. Which in her case is considerable, never mind that she is very self-deprecating about it. Both she and Jacobi have given me moments that are absolutely transcendent, where your very being is transported. Derek under the balcony as Cyrano: that was actually like communing with Rostand. He is an incredible vessel who seems to use his heart and his soul. I was uplifted and deeply, deeply moved, totally aware that this was an experience I would never have watching film or TV or even listening to a piece of music.

Although an ideal kind of acting style is very difficult to describe, most actors know it when they see it. There is a community response to those people who do it best, taking the audience along in the story and providing some spectacular moments of theater. For Branagh, as for each of us, that definition comes with time, with preserving one's openness, with usage, and what develops is an educated sense of taste:

I like Shakespearean acting to be *effortless truth*—that is what I am after. It's very hard to do, but to do anything well is difficult. I am more excited when I see it and more disappointed when I don't, and I am much more aware of the differences in it. It has certain rare qualities.

Nothing can be casual: no line, no characterization, no piece of staging. There can be nothing that isn't considered and worked to death—and then *all that work taken away*! The wonderful flying thing that emerges has all the support in the fabric of its being. Everything in the production is felt and has depth and weight and intelligence behind it. But moment to moment, the audience is caught up in a compelling unfolding of the story that is real and theatrical at the same time. If that is not a contradiction. When it's achieved, it's pretty thrilling.

I always want the Art That Hides Art.

The point of view of an artist is extremely revealing. Branagh comes in from having worked in various media. Here, he presents some angles on the work from what is now a honed and experienced vision. When I asked him what he knew now that he didn't know as a young actor, he summed up:

What I think has been absolutely consistent. I don't really have theories about the work. I realize that there are things that one can do, that a great deal of hard work is required and always will be. But I have by no means arrived at conclusions about things. I know that I want truthful moments, and that if those provided within the work of a man like Shakespeare, where the end result for the audience will be quite spectacular because of what he provides us with—by way of his intelligence and his wit and his insight and humanity—then that is enough.

DEREK JACOBI AS MACBETH IN THE 1993 ROYAL SHAKESPEARE
COMPANY PRODUCTION OF *MACBETH* IN STRATFORD UPON AVON.
(PHOTO BY MARK DOUET / ARENAPAL IMAGES)

3

Derek Jacobi
Sweet Prince

Oh, I adore all actors . . . I'm just in awe when I go to the theatre. Good, bad, or indifferent, because . . . I know how difficult it is and what it takes to get up there [onstage] . . . It's a great club to belong to, and I like actors as a race of people very much. They're very generous with each other . . . [1]

This speech is typical of a man who channels all of his energies into the work, eschewing most charity causes, talk shows, and social events. He has referred to himself as "a placid soul,"[2] although his stage persona has been described as a "typhoon in action" in the role of Hamlet.[3] Royal Shakespeare Company director Terry Hands calls him "the most complete actor we have on the English stage, able to move effortlessly from comedy to tragedy, full of steel and an icy intelligence which often masks his . . . easy boyish charm and friendliness."[4]

Though Jacobi has the best-known Shakespearean roles among his classical theater credits, he sees himself as "an old, kind of jobbing company man really. Rehearsing one thing [in the daytime] and doing another show at night. That's really what I've been doing most of my life."[5] An actor of tremendous versatility, he is often singular, not always in a company, a bit aloof, not grand but certainly savvy, who makes considered decisions about his career.

Jacobi's Shakespearean roles include Hamlet (in the UK, on world tour, and on BBC), Prince Hal, Benedick, Prospero, Richard II, Richard III, Macbeth, and Malvolio, as well as supporting roles in the 1998 film version of *Hamlet* (Claudius), *Othello* (Cassio), *Timon of Athens*, and *Antony and Cleopatra*. He has played the title role in many stage successes, including *Peer Gynt, Cyrano de Bergerac, Kean, Hadrian VII, Uncle Vanya, Breaking the Code, Becket, Don Carlos*, and *A Voyage Round My Father*. His television career introduced him to a wider English-speaking audience and included *I, Claudius* (which received a BAFTA award), *The Pallisers, Philby, Cadfael I, II*, and *III, Breaking the Code* (on BBC), and Emmy-award-winning performances for *The Tenth Man* and an episode in *Frasier*. His film credits include three with Kenneth Branagh—*Henry V, Hamlet*, and *Dead Again*—as well as *Day of the Jackal, The Odessa File, The Medusa Touch* (with Richard Burton), *Little Dorrit, The Fool*, and *Love Is the Devil*. More recently, he appeared in *Up at the Villa, Gosford Park, Gladiator, Nanny McPhee*, and *Adam Resurrected*. One hears his distinctive voice narrating numerous radio and television programs, and he shows up on the occasional *Miss Marple* or *Doctor Who*. His list of awards includes the Golden Quill and literally fills pages, and he holds knighthoods in both Britain and Denmark.

Jacobi was a cherished only child, born in the East London suburb of Leytonstone. His parents, neither of whom was involved with the theater, made every effort to expose him to performance and to encourage his dramatic inclinations:

> When I was about five they took me to the theatre for the first time, to see *Cinderella* at the London Palladium with Evelyn Laye as Prince Charming and Noele Gordon as Dandini. We sat in the very front row and at one point Miss Laye came down into the audience and ruffled my hair, took my hand, and led me up on to the stage; and I got a balloon and a bag of sweets.
>
> It was only years later that I learned that my parents had gone without so they could give me enough. I was spoilt rotten . . . [6]

> I joined the local library players when I was six and the first
> time I was onstage was a dual role in a Christmas play called *The
> Prince and the Swineherd*. I played in the street with my friends,
> I imagined scenarios, I dressed up in my parents' clothes.[7]

One favorite adventure was to take the Underground to Marble
Arch, then get a taxi and be driven to the Palladium, where a knowing
doorman would allow him into the lobby to look at the photographs
and posters. He greatly enjoyed school because the class took day trips
to the theater to see such greats as Richard Burton. An English teacher
from Leyton County High School encouraged his interest in acting and
for years afterward wrote extensive critiques after each of his pupil's
performances. Jacobi also performed with the National Youth Theatre
and played his first Hamlet at the Edinburgh Festival at seventeen.

He went to St. John's College, Cambridge, on a full scholarship and
read history, but the studies were often fitted in around the performances: "Cambridge was just like being in rep. Everyone acted all the
time, some directed, the blind led the blind, and by the end of my last
term, all my friends already had agents." For the Marlowe Society at
Cambridge, which was invitational, he performed Edward in *Edward
II*, Prince Hal in both parts of *Henry IV*, and Iachimo in *Cymbeline*.
Subsequently, he was influenced by George (Dadie) Rylands: "Rylands
was very much of the 'beautifully spoken' school—his great god was
Gielgud—deeply into iambic pentameter where Shakespeare was concerned." Among Jacobi's acquaintances at college were Trevor Nunn,
Ian McKellen, Corin Redgrave, Eleanor Bron, and Peter Cook.[8] At this
point he realized that one needed good health and lots of luck to be
an actor—talent came third.

After graduation, he got an audition with the prestigious Birmingham Repertory Company. This tour of duty placed him in line for
inheriting leads at the Royal Shakespeare Company (RSC). He was
invited to meet the then directors at the RSC—Peter Hall, Peter Brook,
Michel Saint-Denis, Clifford Williams, John Barton—who wanted
him to audition for the part of Ariel. Being neither forewarned nor
forearmed, "I did it in my best light fairy voice, sounding like a sick

choir boy."⁹ The reading did not go well, and he was not invited to join up.

His luck continued, miraculously, because he returned to Birmingham Rep, where he was offered three major classical roles—Henry VIII, Troilus, and Aaron the Moor. These performances introduced Jacobi to his most significant mentor, Sir Laurence Olivier, as the younger man moved through the formative years of his acting career. The first time Olivier took notice of him had a certain prophetic quality—Jacobi had just finished playing Henry in a matinee when the word went out that Olivier was backstage. Jacobi was already out of his padding and wig, ready to grab a bite to eat at the local café, when the great man arrived at the dressing room Jacobi shared with the actor who played Wolsey. Olivier said, "Well done," to Jacobi and effused over Wolsey. Then he left. Shortly, he was back in the dressing room, saying, "*You* played Henry," pointing to Jacobi. The two locked eyes and Sir Laurence boomed, "*Well done!*"

A few days later, Jacobi received a note from Olivier inviting him to join the Chichester Festival Theatre company, the core group that later moved to London to open the National Theatre. He worked there between 1963 and 1971. He observed the aristocracy of the British stage at work—John Gielgud, Maggie Smith, Albert Finney, Robert Stephens, Colin Blakely, Max Adrian. He made his London debut as Laertes to Peter O'Toole's Hamlet, and he went on for Olivier as Tattle in *Love for Love*. He understudied Michael Redgrave in *Vanya*. Directors there included John Dexter, Peter Ewing, and Olivier himself, plus a burgeoning crop of playwrights like Peter Shaffer.

Consequently, Jacobi described his tenure at the National as offering more than drama school ever could have: he was never without work during the first eleven years of his professional life and had an amazing set of mentors and role models. His colleague Edward Hardwicke described working with Jacobi during that period:

> The whole rehearsal period of *Othello* [at the National] remains in memory as sharp as yesterday . . . The first time I watched Derek working with director John Dexter on the Reputation scene . . . was a revelation. I had never seen Shakespeare made as accessible and

real, or examined with such understanding and humour. I remember thinking how lucky I was to be part of such a company.

Derek became Laurence Olivier's S.A.S. Whenever there was a
crisis—an actor ill, or missing, Derek would be rushed to the scene.
His prodigious technique, concentration, and ability to learn texts—
I have never known anyone faster—were taken full advantage of.
Sir Laurence always knew a good thing when he saw one.[10]

The incident that propelled Jacobi into the public eye and onto
the feature pages of the British press was landing the role of the Em-
peror Claudius in the famous 1977 BBC series. The part made him
a household word and won him a long list of honors, including the
British Academy of Film and Television Arts award and a Variety Club
award for 1976 TV Personality of the Year. He then played *Hamlet*
with the Prospect Theater Company (including a world tour), which
garnered him that role in the BBC "Shakespeare Plays" production.[11]
John Trewin wrote one of his rare laudatory columns about the
performance:

> Jacobi was, and is, among the best Hamlets for years . . . . He has
> always been a particularly touching actor. At the Vic now, one is
> aware of this quality and also of the princeliness that is so often
> absent from the part today. . . .
>
> Jacobi . . . restores our faith in Ophelia's [words]:
>> The courtier's, soldier's, scholar's, eye, tongue, sword;
>> Th'expectancy and rose of the fair state,
>> The glass of fashion, and the mould of form. . . .
>
> He speaks with an unself-conscious rightness of tone and
> phrasing. This is a relaxed and truthful Hamlet.[12]

Olivier played Hamlet in Kronberg Castle at Elsinore in 1937, Gielgud in 1939, Redgrave in 1950, Burton in 1954, and Jacobi in 1979. That
placed him among the literal and figurative royalty of the classical stage.
He had done a great deal *despite* not yet having appeared at the Royal
Shakespeare Company. His trajectory shows how a strong career is
forged, stone on stone, no steps backward.

Jacobi defines acting in a very particular way and has no illusions about the job. His ideas surface in a variety of interview commentaries:

> Displaying what it's like to be an actor . . . [is] not what it's about. Let's take an actor's talent proverbially. Let's say, all right, you're an actor. You can act. You don't spend the evening convincing me of that. You use that to take me on a journey . . . to make me think thoughts and feel feelings that will surprise me or that I haven't thought or felt for a time . . . [13]

> [The actor] imagines himself in a part—in performance, he imagines his way along—and acting is about pretend, so it's artificial in that sense.[14]

> Theatre is a machine for emotions. A world of pretend that's nevertheless recognizable. Minds and lives on offer, emotions experimented with and put into perspective. To do this, we as actors keep one foot in the cradle. We must be open, like a child, and retain naivete.[15]

> Theatre is trickery. A bit of performance works and you gloat to yourself. You *know* how you managed to carry it off—and it's a moment of pure private pleasure, knowing you'd succeeded . . . Ask any actor. He'll know what I mean . . . [16]

> An actor has to be totally absorbed in the part—not withholding anything . . . yet he must also project an ego or a double of himself into the auditorium, which will constantly monitor his actions. If you are an actor, you must act and watch yourself simultaneously. You split up. You put yourself in the position of the audience, think what they'll think.[17]

An actor cannot be so totally involved in the part that he loses track of stage reality. Even if the actor as Cyrano is spouting romantic poetry and making heroic promises, he has to problem solve. Jacobi describes a dilemma with a broken ladder in the middle of a performance:

> I thought to myself at the end of the speech, are we going to have the stage manager come out and say, "Ladies and gentlemen, there's been a technical problem. We'll bring the curtain down while Mr. Jacobi gets off his chandelier?" But you, as an actor, are responsible for that, and so are the other actors, *during* the performance, during the portrayal. I still hopefully *stayed* Cyrano, but I was Cyrano thinking, "How the hell am I going to get off this chandelier?" in a purely technical way as an actor. That did not take away from my commitment to the role, my absorption in the role. You've got to create your own safety nets, and one of those requires you, as the actor, not to lose yourself.

That split consciousness has always been necessary for the craftsman onstage. When asked if he made use of his own personality in a role, Jacobi said yes, that was part of the acting process:

> It's got to come from within. So the imaging, the fantasy, has its own kind of realism; it's made up but authentic at the same time . . . [It's] not as easy as donning a costume and wig.[18]

> There are actors whom you know how they are going to act something because they always take it *to* them, always play themselves in the guise of the character. Other actors actually transcend themselves and seem to become somebody else. I find that more interesting, as a matter of fact.[19]

> Acting deals in the world of the imagination, acting is imagining and pretending—the magical *if.* If I am Macbeth, I see Duncan lying there asleep and I think, *if* I were in that room, what would I do, what would it be like, what effect would it have on me, given that I'm full of doubt anyway before I go in there. I do "image" in that sense.

"The magic 'If'" is a Stanislavskian term introduced by the early twentieth-century Russian who recorded his acting theories as he worked them out with his acting company. Its essence is that the performer must be able to completely and totally imagine himself into the world of the play. About methodologies in general Jacobi states:

> Sometimes I think that the rules we have made for the performance of Shakespeare have actually gotten in the way of the communication of Shakespeare, because many directors and commentators have decided that there is a "way to say Shakespeare" from which we must not waver. I don't believe that. I think that one of the reasons the plays *live* is that they are totally contemporary now; they deal in universal situations and universal emotions.

Jacobi constantly emphasizes that it is the actor's responsibility to communicate the text in its entirety. A scholar's work has to do with finding one meaning and arguing for its unconditionality. An actor openly admits to several performance possibilities for meaning and selects one, through trial and experimentation, that lives and functions within the production he is working on. The actor knows, nonetheless, that *in performance* Shakespearean language has a fluidity and adaptability that can fluctuate and move within the theatrical context. In that way, Shakespearean language can be "alive."

Thus Jacobi acknowledges methodologies but refuses to be boxed into one or to encompass his creative impulses with inflexible rules. He is a creator, yes, but he is aware of the potential for re-creation—at another time, at another place—of any given text:

> I have no theories. I try to work truthfully, I try to make the text live, I try to make the text *not* based on any method. In the Stanislavsky method, he really tabulated what most actors do quite naturally and instinctively, but the work must be entirely based on the text.
>
> The most important person in the theater is the writer, without whom I can't act, the director can't direct, the designer can't design. To be truthful to that play, to find out what that play

is about, to find out what your part in it is about is the be-all and the end-all—*not* to use it to show off whatever talents you possess, but to use them in the service of the play, to make *it* shine.

When Jacobi expresses the notion of the primacy of the writer, he means that all the necessary clues to analyzing and realizing a character onstage can be found in the play's script. There is no right way—there are several right ways. Because the character is built from the composition of the actor's personality conjoining with the words of the text, a number of possibilities can be shaped from the playwright's work. Each time, it is Jacobi's instinct to plunge into the written dialogue and to ask particular questions about this created self that he seeks to embody:

> What is he thinking, what is he feeling, what is he saying, why is he saying it, and what effect is he trying to make by saying it? Is there something that some other character said that occasioned his saying this? I don't use the words "motivation" or "intention"— although those are the words for what I do. I use more active phrases: "What does he want?" or "What does he what to do?" or "What is he trying to do?" It is common to actors—actors all the time question who and what and where they are onstage.
>
> If you don't do that, the lines are just words. It has to be logical. It has to be real to you.

These questions are not just Stanislavskian but are common to any basic dramatic analysis of theater texts. Jacobi believes that "the Stanislavsky method" has shortcomings. For one thing, it is not helpful for an actor doing eight performances of *King Lear* a week. It does not account for the kind of grueling performance schedule a classical actor is subjected to in the midst of a run of a major play, yet it could work very well for film actors. He feels that American actors have submerged themselves in Stanislavskian ideas so thoroughly that they are often a "little too inward-looking" and not focused enough on the audience. Jacobi holds strong opinions about communicating with an audience—that if one does not, the performance becomes "masturba-tory," a performance for only oneself.[20]

Jacobi points out that Shakespeare's words are all you have to go on in character building. Many actors use the phrase "It's all in the text," a guideline that can sound ephemeral and mysterious when, especially in Shakespeare, there *is* so much text and there are so many kinds of it. Ian McKellen called Derek Jacobi the best verse speaker he knows.[21] Jacobi says:

> I think the most important thing is *to go for the sense of the line.* Don't begin with the meter. Aim for making it accessible for the *audience* to understand the meaning. Do not give the impression that what you are saying is not your native language, not the way you would naturally express your thoughts. All verse speaking is potentially a barrier to actually speaking your thoughts, because there is the danger that you will get into a pattern and the audi-ence will stop listening. *Or* they will have to listen so hard that they cannot understand what you are saying. You've got to make the language absolutely real and believable.[22]

Jacobi's insistence on the reality of a character, absolutely and totally believable even though four-hundred-year-old language emanates from his mouth, is something he exemplifies each time he takes the stage. He does not speechify or orate. He delivers the language in whatever mental and emotional state the character inhabits—with few flourishes, naturalistically, coined from the center of a vital and animated persona. When asked if he subscribes to the notion of not taking a pause when a thought ended midline (so as to not disrupt the iambic pentameter), Jacobi answered:

> I wouldn't subscribe to that at all, because such rules prevent any newness of interpretation, any imaginative leap on the actor's part to "new mint" the thoughts and the words so they come out truth-ful. Which sometimes happens if one approaches the punctuation slightly differently from how it is marked, but it also happens if you approach Shakespeare the way you approach any other play.

The trouble with most actors (and with a lot of very, very good actors) is that in the presence of Shakespeare, all their instinctive techniques and skills seem to desert them. They put on *a voice*, they put on *a walk*, they put on *a manner*, and it all starts to *go classical*. Everything goes wrong. All the things they would do normally in a play, a flesh-and-blood modern play, all that reality, all that imagination, all that talent, all that theory, all that re-creation of a text seems to vanish. They think they're reading the Bible!

Directors and voice teachers encourage this, I think—"the voice" school, the "classical" school. In a modern play, the voice is informed with tonality, you can hear the comment on the lines in the voice: you can hear someone say, "I love you," knowing that they *hate* the person they've said it to. So if you speak the line "de da de da de da de da de DA," or if you assume an artificial voice, you cannot do any of that *expressing*.[23]

When questioned about whether or not he actually "scans" a line or counts iambs, he replied:

No, not at all. There is that school that does it and knows the exact end of the line. I think I have the healthiest disrespect for scholastic punctuation. If you want to make a full stop, to make it mean something specific when a punctuation mark is not there and it needs one to make vocal sense, then by all means do so if it makes the text alive and much clearer. Face it—we don't know exactly where the commas came, so I say, what the hell.

The genius of the writing is that it has a poetic bloom. Even the worst verse speakers in the world can never wholly mangle the verse, because the actual choice of words is inbuilt into the line. The thoughts expressed are extraordinary, so I'm all for mucking about with the punctuation.

When I directed *Hamlet*, I gave some of Polonius's lines to Gertrude and some of Claudius's lines also. Perhaps scholars will be aghast.[24]

Jacobi does not research a play in the sense of reading what critics before him have written about it. Such background knowledge, for him, is the purview of a director. He will read a scholarly edition, but he does not think these are always terribly helpful:

> I'm reading the Arden *Richard III*, and occasionally the editor makes such crass remarks about the plays in performance. For example, several people enter here in the folio, yet they enter over there in the bad quarto, and what this means in production is . . . All this is so mind-numbingly boring, and usually something you couldn't *show* in performance even if you found it curious enough to be interesting.
>
> When you *really* want them to tell you about—the meaning of a strange word in a strange context—there's no explanation about it at all! Not a word![25]

On the other hand, Jacobi does research the *text*. A few talisman-like words can stimulate his pathway in to character:

> When I first read *Macbeth*, I was very struck by the repetition of certain words. I went back through it and circled words like *blood* and *night* and *fear*. That's the word used more than any other in every scene and many, many times about himself. *Fear*. Macbeth saying, "I'm afraid."
>
> I wanted to give him a journey where he was the brightest of the angels when the play *starts*. He's a golden boy—saved his country, killed everybody, won ten gold medals at the Olympics, came back loaded with honors and praise. Of course he's ambitious, and of course he's contemplated what it would be like to be king. Lady Macbeth pegs him absolutely: "Thou would'st be . . . not without ambition . . . holily . . . play false." By the end of "If it were done," he's talked himself out of it. Then she goes for the jugular, says he's not a man and has no courage, the two things that are guaranteed to make him say, "I'll show you!"
>
> Look at the dagger soliloquy—full of self-doubt, full of knowledge, full of premonition, full of *fear*. After he's done the murder,

he comes out of that room a madman. *She* had no idea that it would do that to him, because she lacks his imagination. But *he* sees murder continuously—the damnation, the consequences. His journey is one through madness, to an almost catatonic state at the end. In the "Tomorrow and tomorrow and tomorrow" speech, he is totally aware of what he is and where he's come to, aware of the futility of it all.

Jacobi thought it was important to take a new look at the role and give it a fresher interpretation, a different character arc from the traditional approach:

> We've acquired a stereotype of Macbeth. In every production I've seen, he begins as a killer and remains one—so there is no drama, no tragedy, no development, no human problem, no journey. He has nowhere to *go*, and Lady Macbeth has no function in the play.
>
> By the end, you see, he really should be a fallen-angel figure. That's the more interesting choice.

Jacobi is vitally focused on the text as his most important tool in the process. He enjoys the detective work in rehearsal that helps him ferret character out of lines, feeds his own creative process. "I love trying to find out new meanings for lines, meanings that are attractive mentally to me, that are stimulating."[26] He gives this example of newly minting a line, one that Kenneth Branagh used in the film of *Much Ado About Nothing*:

> There are places in the text where the punctuation is open-ended. At the end of the gulling scene, Benedick comes out of hiding, and there the actor has his full bent. "Love me? Why, it must be requited"—If you get rid of that comma after *why* and add a question mark—"Love me? Why? It must be requited!" the audience laughs, it's funny, it's *of* the situation, it's what Benedick *would* say.

Certain discussions about text are irrelevant or too subtle for actual performance, for example, this one from Hamlet's first soliloquy:

I did Hamlet in Peking and Shanghai, and there was a lovely old professor who came to see it . . . and brought this twenty-five-page thesis about why it should have been "sullied" and not "solid" flesh. . . . [Afterward] he said . . . "In the performance you said the word and I understood the word, whether it was *sullied* or *solid*. It doesn't matter in the context of the whole because you were showing me your feelings, and I was receiving your feelings . . . I was understanding what you were saying." . . . The great debate only applies in the confines of a study, or a classroom, or a library. In the theatre, the impact, the communication, is immediate.[27]

Jacobi's goal in studying verse speaking "comes from a great desire to make the play accessible to an audience."[28] He feels that often at a Shakespeare play, audiences do not understand the lines and are there in spite of themselves. They are *spectating* but really bored throughout: "My aim is to try to discover a way to share the play with them just as if it were a modern play."[29] Appropriately enough, this goal has made him a better player. As John Andrews describes him in an interview, "He's one of the few actors I've seen who manages both to get the sense, all the emotion, and at the same time retain the meter."[30] Generously, openly, Jacobi asserts that audiences train *him*—one of the positive benefits of constantly working to communicate with them.

He is a great believer in technique, those skills actors need to heighten the effects: a clear and adaptable voice, a body that moves well on command, good timing, summonable energy, and a trained memory (his is almost photographically correct). Technique work begins early in the career and continues throughout:

There are occasions when, as Gielgud said, "You send technique on." . . . You can't fly every time; you can't be inspired every performance. . . . It's an impossibility. So for that lack of . . . inspiration; for that lack of . . . total commitment, when the mind wanders, or the body wanders, or something wanders, which is bound to happen over the course of a week in eight performances, technique fills in; and from a distance the painting looks wonderful. It's only if you go terribly, terribly, terribly, terribly close that you see one tiny bit of the canvas wasn't covered.[31]

Although Jacobi had some voice training as a young actor at Cambridge and voice lessons at Birmingham when he could afford them, he was obviously at work cleaning out his regional accent early on:

> My great chum . . . was the local pharmacist's son; they were a marvelous family and quite well to do; and because of this, and because I acted in all the school plays and read the lesson each morning, I developed a voice which was not wholly tied to a district. But I was sent up rotten at school because I seemed to be speaking "posher" than anybody else.[32]

He nonetheless persevered, because accents onstage are very limiting, and one must be able to do a great number of them and not be confined to just one. Also, the voice must be lithe and supple:

> If you listen to young actors approaching Shakespeare, they don't inform the language with any kind of vocal cleverness or vocal interest. They tend to find a pitch and to stay on it. You've got to be able to play more than one instrument; the voice has got to be orchestral. It's not a question of music and certainly not of pronunciation—it's a lack of variation, a lack of strength, a lack of putting into the voice the *thought*, as you have to do in Shakespeare: let the voice do more of the work, because Shakespeare is about *the words*. Words come through the mouth, out of the mouth comes the voice, so the voice needs to be flexible enough to make those thoughts understood. . . .
>
> Of course, the voice also tires. So you have to stroke it and nurture it.
>
> It's what we used to call *expression* that the audience reacts to—because it corresponds to their own sounds in their own heads. If the audience doesn't understand, they'll be bored.

Jacobi had a providential encounter with a man who became a fan and a guide. He had seen Richard Burton onstage, of course, when his English master took the class to a production of *Hamlet* during the year Burton was playing it along with Henry V, Caliban, and Coriolanus at the Old Vic. Later, when Jacobi was playing Hamlet at Cambridge, the production was taken on tour to Lausanne, where Burton was living. The star came around to the dressing room later and introduced himself, and when Jacobi returned to England, there was a letter waiting that said two things: one, that if he wanted to become a professional actor, he should contact Burton, who would help him. And second, that Jacobi had a slight shortcoming that Burton had wrestled with, as well—his voice was too mellifluous and should be "roughened up" through voice lessons to make it more interesting and less beautiful.

Years later, the great actor appeared at the dressing room door when Jacobi played Hamlet at the Old Vic. Burton invited him out to dinner but first wanted to walk out onto the stage of the Old Vic, the scene of his earlier theatrical triumphs. They spent the evening talking about theater until 4:00 a.m. There can have been no more validating experience than to be the acknowledged colleague of this esteemed Welsh Shakespearean and to take advice from one of the masters on the subject of voice.[33]

Jacobi is equally specific about use of the body, which needs to correspond with the words. In theater, unlike film or television, the audience sees the whole body all of the time. He noted that Chekov is difficult to play because the feet and legs are often saying something that the head is not. In Shakespeare, the body should complement what the voice is saying in order to clarify Renaissance language, which is occasionally unfamiliar to an audience.[34]

One very striking quality during an interview is Jacobi's intelligence. He has a remarkable intellect, including an innate sense of taste about theater, an ability to articulate and develop a point far beyond what the question requires, a ready wit, and an astonishingly concrete vocabulary for describing ephemera like the experience of acting.

His descriptions of Shakespearean plays are unrivaled; he recounts them through performance, from an extraordinary sense of having experienced the center of the storm. His talent is coupled

with a gift for narrative that colorfully develops his arguments. His
mental acuity obviously helps to digest difficult scripts like *Breaking
the Code* and to understand complicated, ironic characters such as
Francis Bacon in *Love Is the Devil*. He is particularly adept at finding the essential key to unlocking each character and to providing a
broad, general outline for the necessary detail. There are a number
of good examples.

When Jacobi played Cyrano in the early 1980s, he began with the
facts about the Gascon warrior, his nose and his heroic imagination,
building the character's psyche with "all the doors that ugliness closes,
all the doors that beauty opens."[35] Jacobi imagined the soldier as a
youngster who grew up compensating against the taunts of his peers
by developing many skills:

> [Cyrano] is a fully rounded, gifted, talented man who has this
> burden of what he feels is a physical deformity. He has the mis-
> fortune to fall in love . . . an enormously believable and attractive
> character . . . very difficult to play . . . to walk the line between the
> braggadocio of the character and the actor showing off. It has to
> be him showing off, not me.[36]

Terry Hands said, "When I saw Derek doing Cyrano on Broadway
eight times a week I was utterly in awe. It was like watching a supreme
Olympic athlete. There [were] actually five Cyranos: the clown, the
poet, the soldier, the lover and the victim. [Ralph] Richardson managed
two of them, Derek did all five."[37]

When Jacobi played Alan Turing, the shy mathematical genius in
Hugh Whitemore's *Breaking the Code*, there was a predominant color
in the final portrait:

> The key to the role for me, the word that kept recurring in Andrew
> Hodges' biography, was "boyish"; it was also the word that many
> of his friends and his brother, whom I contacted, used. A kind
> of Peter Pan quality, and a sort of ability to cut one's self off—
> because of an interest in pure thought—from the consequences
> of everyday life.[38]

Cast as a medieval monk in an ITV mystery series, he also quickly outlined the character's essence in a few strokes:

> Cadfael is a delightful creature . . . because in a world of con-
> templation and discipline he has spent two-thirds of his life out
> in the big, wide world killing people. . . . he brings that into the
> abbey with him. . . . Life was violent and uncomfortable then . . . .
> The way Cadfael deals with violence is pre–forensic science and
> pre–car chases. . . . All his detection is done by smell and touch
> and intuition and knowledge—not only of the world and of the
> human character, but also of plants and animals and nature. That's
> how he solves the puzzles.[39]

It was, above all, this sense of shrewdness and sagacity that defined the quintessential Cadfael persona. Early on in his career, film producers dogged Jacobi to play Hitler (in *The Third Reich*), but he resisted because he could not picture himself in the role. One last appeal won him over: "They said . . . we want somebody who can play a man who is acting. And that interested me at once."[40] This uncanny ability to locate the central facet of the character is paramount to his stage and media successes.

Despite a number of wise career moves and having played several parts that appeared to be tailored for him, Jacobi insists that he needs a director. He credits especially Toby Robertson, who directed him as a student at Cambridge and then later in *Hamlet*. He has developed some distinct methods of negotiating:

> I'm one of those actors who need a director, oh, indeed, but rather
> than argue, rather than confront, I'll say, "Yes, that's not going
> too far." I won't say, "I don't want to." *Or* I'll go ahead and do what
> I want, what *I think* is correct, and then say to the director, "Is
> that what you mean?" He'll say, "Yes, yes, it's coming," or he'll say,
> "No, you didn't do what I told you." Then I'll say, "Yes, oh! But I
> thought—all right, I see, okay." You play games. And directors play
> games, too. If you really feel that what they've got to say wouldn't
> work for *you*, by all means try it first, but then forget about it.

I'll often see an actor do something absolutely from left field, and the director will pick up on what he's done, and then tell him to do it, and then the director will reject it—so that the rejection comes from [the director], so that the actor can save face for having done something wild and irrelevant. But it's all based on *trust*.

A mutual trust is obviously the first step in collaborating, and often actors have learned this the hard way. It has much to do with wanting direction but also wanting to be treated well:

I don't like the confrontational type of director who terrorizes a performance out of you. You end up really only acting to please the director, to get his approval, to stop him chatting at you, to make him be nice to you. I hate that kind of director.

What I'm saying might imply that I go my own sweet way and do what I want to do. That's not true. I do desperately need an eye I can trust plus judgment and knowledge and a level of culture and intellectual grasp that are greater than mine.

Terry Hands is wonderful that way. He has a marvelous knowledge of the text and an intellectual breadth which is a marvelous rock to have in the maelstrom of rehearsal.[41]

Jacobi prefers to dig in and make good use of the rehearsal time rather than discussing things overly much:

I'm all for working on the move, working on my feet. I'm not a good talker . . . I want to *do* it. I want to demonstrate, and show, rather than say, "Look, if I did this . . . and what about me trying to do this?" I'd rather say, "Look, watch this . . . Is this what you're talking about?" Rather than talk myself into a performance, I'd like to be able to feel myself into a performance. . . . By making mistakes, I mean being embarrassing and awful . . . but always on my feet. . . . I think I'm mentally and emotionally alert. I'm mentally quick; I'm emotionally quick. I feel increasingly, as I'm getting older, that I'm tapping in, I'm plugging in quicker to the center . . . of my feelings.[42]

Finally, Jacobi no longer reads reviews and critics in the newspapers. He used to, but it upset him so much that he stopped.[43] He finds them limited and unhelpful:

> What actors put themselves through—emotionally, physically, mentally, psychologically—doing the roles onstage is wearing enough. To actually have to *add to* that the spiritual upheaval that critics can cause in an actor's breast when it can be avoided by not reading them. You get to know what the critics have said very quickly . . . in people's faces, and you can tell by the tone of their voices . . . Even friends will ring up and say, "Oh, marvelous. Congratulations on the reviews. Whatever you do, don't read *The Times*." . . .
>
> My distrust of the critics . . . [is that] they write for a certain public. The critic from *The Express* sees the same show as the critic from The *Times* but will write a slightly different slanted review because his readers are different. They are also furthering their own image as reviewers. Nowadays most of the columns have a cartoon or a photograph of the critic attached to it, so they are becoming big stars themselves. . . . They praise for the wrong reasons. They throw brick-bats for the wrong reasons . . .
>
> The critics come to a very special, highly charged *un*—if there is such a word—*indicative* performance. There are, on a first night in London, something like four hundred people out there. Perhaps a third to a half of the audience are [critics], doing their work. They are observing and they are commenting at the same time. They cannot participate, because they've got to have one eye on what they're doing . . . what they're going to write about. . . . It's the most uptight, nervous, and unrepresentative performance that [the actors] will ever give. When [the actors have] worked into the play and they know more about it, the critics never see those performances. It's so unfair.[44]

Jacobi's successful rise to the top of the ranks of classical actors has appeared easy, golden, uneventful, and fraught with neither adversity nor challenge. One night in the late 1970s, during a performance of

Hamlet in Sydney, he thought for a moment what it might be like to forget "To be or not to be." Later that night, as if his thoughts had jinxed him, he in fact dried (forgot the lines) on the soliloquy. Like a domino effect, he began to fear that this would happen every night because he had, just once, doubted his own abilities.

His schedule permitted a brief, sheltering hiatus into film and television work for about three years while he contended with the worm of doubt. He emphasized that the experience was a condition of "mind-numbing and body-paralyzing terror."[45] Later on, an offer came, fortuitously, from the Royal Shakespeare Company to do a series of truly remarkable roles—Prospero in *Tempest*, Peer Gynt in *Peer Gynt*, Benedick in *Much Ado*, and the lead in *Cyrano de Bergerac*. This time, of course, no audition was necessary. He faced the trauma head-on, not fearlessly but deeply and knowingly: "I battled through."[46] If he had not accepted that challenge, his acting might have been cut off in its first lovely flowering. Like Olivier, he locked eyes with his devils, he struggled, and he clearly bested them.

Just prior to an evening's performance, Jacobi sits quietly in his dressing room, surrounded by mementos that have guided him in the past and that he has with him wherever he goes: small birds, rabbits, bears, a pencil sharpener with a skull on it—each one associated with a time and a place and a play. Sometimes he steams his throat. Eventually, everyone is politely dismissed so that he can concentrate. Of his love of acting, he says:

> You know that at the end of every day, something extraordinary is waiting for you. It could be horror, it could be joy, but at 7:30 every night, you are going to be given the opportunity to do something that most people . . . experience fairly rarely in their lives.[47]

Once a photographer told him, a bit embarrassed as the picture was taken, that he had never photographed an actor who appeared to be in a state of grace. With a certain amount of humility, with a touch of stage fright, with credulity and incredulity, Derek Jacobi enters that place.

STACY KEACH AS LEAR IN THE 2006 GOODMAN THEATRE
PRODUCTION OF *KING LEAR*. (PHOTO BY RICHARD HEIN)

4

Stacy Keach

Sweet Are the Uses
of Adversity

"I like being able to play Hamlet and Mike Hammer at the same time,"
Stacy Keach announced.[1] Who would have thought that in the foothills
of Hollywood—nestled in an office next to Art Deco department stores
and red convertibles flashing by rows of palm trees—would sit a badass
sheriff, cowboy desperado, private dick, and tough-guy warden once
again brushing up his Shakespeare? These surprising personas mesh
well, because Keach is a take-no-prisoners actor who gobbles up the
Bard with the same voracious appetite with which he jumps into the
cab of an eighteen-wheeler and tools on out to New Mexico.

Toss in a dollop of scholar and musician and you have that rare
performer who talks about earning his spurs in Shakespeare and then
uses a musical analogy to develop the idea:

> It follows that if you are a great classical pianist, you can play
> jazz. But the reverse doesn't always work—you can be a great jazz
> pianist, but that doesn't necessarily mean you'll be able to play
> classical, because you haven't studied it. It requires work. One of
> my favorite professors at Berkeley told me *if you can act Shake-*
> *speare,* you can do anything. Just like—if you can play Beethoven
> and Mozart, you can play anything. What I am hoping is that

young actors will understand that the diligence and persistence
in studying Shakespeare is worth it because of the exhilaration
and the achievement they feel when they actually do it.

Keach had major allies during his early training, but he also girded
for battle against those who felt he was wasting his time. His parents
were behind him, because his father, Stacy Keach Sr., left teaching
theater in a community college in Savannah to accept an invitation to
join the Pasadena Playhouse. The younger Keach succumbed to the
lure of drama in high school; however, his father forewarned him that
classical acting would feed the soul but probably not the family.

Perhaps because Keach's parents both had graduate degrees, he
felt the need to educate himself in the classics. His college career was
interspersed with experience in performing, and that activity kept him
hungry for and interested in dramatic literature.

At the University of California, Berkeley, he took courses from stellar
professors Mark Shore and William Oliver, who not only recognized
his talent, but made it clear that knowing how to read and understand
play texts was his strongest weapon. Professor Marvin Rosenberg's
research interest was the documenting of stage business in hallmark
productions of Shakespeare. From him, Keach learned how long a
tradition and how much baggage there was in a play like *Hamlet*, and
consequently how challenging it was to make one's own mark on it.
He used Rosenberg's *The Masks of King Lear* (which details how actors throughout history interpreted important moments in this play)
in forging his own 2006 Lear at the Goodman Theatre in Chicago.
Keach played his very first classical role at Berkeley, De Flores in *The
Changeling*—"a Richard III kind of character who allowed the actor
to 'let the stops out'"—and also roles in O'Neill, Jonson, and Molière.

Keach's time at Yale was not so rewarding. His acting teacher's
ideas collided with his own views. His fellow students agreed with
him, boycotted her classes, and began their own class, which Keach
taught. Even though he wasn't in tune with particular Yale perspec-
tives (and flunked his two acting courses there), he won the school's
performance award for best acting, concluding, "That was my own
paradox of acting."

The next key event in his early schooling was winning a Fulbright scholarship to attend the London Academy of Music and Drama (LAMDA) in 1964:

> Roland Fuller was the most directly influential teacher in my classical training. He was curator of the British Museum and later dramaturge at the Old Vic. He came to teach at LAMDA, and the students would sit around him as he held forth about Shakespeare's life and Elizabethan times in first person, as if he were a member of her court! It was the most extraordinary experience, and it personalized for all of us the historical ramifications. He simply narrated how *he* thought Shakespeare worked.
>
> He was not a proponent of the Marlovian or the Baconian or the Oxfordian school but felt that Shakespeare was really Shakespeare. He speculated that Shakespeare took off to Italy during those seven or eight lost years when we can't account for his movements. Fuller said that the Italian plays were written with such specificity that the playwright must have lived there for a time.
>
> I've had the argument many times about who Shakespeare was, and the Edward de Vere possibility [the Earl of Oxford] does stimulate my imagination. The dynamic of suppositions like this encourages you to go deeper into the period and to form your own opinions—plus you learn about the culture as you go.

London was a rich and exemplary place to be in 1964-65, because a world theater festival was in full flower in the city. Keach saw famous groups in action: Israel's Habimah Theater, Jean-Louis Barrault's French company, and the Berliner Ensemble—a great feast of international actors at work. Furthermore, Laurence Olivier was acting in *The Master Builder*, Albert Finney appeared in *Black Comedy*, and Robert Stephens was the lead in *The Royal Hunt of the Sun*. Keach already had favorites among the more naturalistic of the English Shakespeare actors—Alec Guinness, Finney, and Ian Holm—whose detailed and modern portrayals he wanted to emulate.

LAMDA posited the idea that playing Shakespeare is a compulsory cog in the acting wheel:

The great advantage of being able to study in England was the tremendous boost it gave to my self-confidence and security. There, acting Shakespeare is an expectation, a given. If you are going to achieve the status of Dench or Mirren or Jacobi or Kingsley, you have to be someone who does it all, who devotes time and energy to the classics.

Keach's current tally of Shakespearean roles is twenty-odd or more. When I asked him the perennial question—Why Shakespeare?—he said he really got a powerful taste for it in his salad days at the Oregon Shakespeare Festival (OSF). In these summer trips to a regional festival, presenting plays in a bowl-like outdoor theater in southern Oregon just over the border from California, the motto was "Stay four days, see four plays." It was the ideal adventure for a young actor in training and carried with it the 1960s brand of rough-and-tumble Shakespeare, perfect for a college student having summers off and looking for something exciting to do.

Keach was in his junior year at Berkeley when he went to Oregon and walked into the history of Ashland's Tony-awarded repertory company, played out on the foundation stones of a Chautauqua tent, one of the early educational and entertainment arenas for turn-of-the-century Sunday school teachers. A tribute to the founders of the Oregon Shakespeare Festival today is the near-perfect proscenium-arch stage, the Angus Bowmer Theater, one of three operating there. Keach was directed by Bowmer and tells the story of his wife, who had a photographic memory:

> Gertrude Bowmer was an extraordinary woman. On the first day in early June, once you had deposited your luggage in the housing accommodations, you went off to the first session. She would go around the room—some forty actors in all at that time, plus tech crews and administrative staff—introducing each person, giving a little fact or two about each, without a single note in her hand. She welcomed everyone to the season. Angus Bowmer himself was a larger-than-life character with a great sense of humor.

Another Ashland icon was Margery Bailey, a professor from Stanford who taught a Shakespeare Institute there every summer [her donation of books founded the Margery Bailey Renaissance and Shakespeare Collection at the Hannon Library on the Southern Oregon University campus]. She seemed to have every word of Shakespeare captured in her brain. I met her only once and sat in on a class she was doing. She had presence and authority. Alas, the actors never had any verse training from her; rather, we did that work with the directors. It wasn't as extensive as it is today.

Auditions were held the next day, everyone remembering Gertrude's ability to memorize, and I landed Antipholus in *The Comedy of Errors*, Westmoreland in *Henry IV, Part 2*, and a senator in *Coriolanus*. The following year, I looked forward to returning and was given Mercutio in *Romeo and Juliet*, Berowne in *Love's Labours*, and, very fortunately, the title role in *Henry V*, directed by Jerry Turner.

In the summers of 1962 and 1963, one play was rehearsed in the morning, a second in the afternoon, and a third in the evening. They opened like a chain reaction, one on the heels of another. At Keach's age, playing this level and quality and quantity of Shakespearean roles was nirvana. He had to create three distinct characters (in different genres, from each of Shakespeare's great periods of writing) and get the lines down very quickly. Such challenges allowed him to stretch his performance choices and to develop as an actor:

To this day, I still feel that repertory is the best training ground for young actors and for audiences as well. The cost is high, the shifting of sets is expensive and time-consuming, but for actors, it's ideal. The key benefit is being able to remain flexible, to be protean in the best sense, to "change shapes with Proteus for advantages."

I remember getting together with one of the other actors, who was also a playwright, and going down to the Marc Antony Hotel to do another play there. We were just kids, and we had gargantuan appetites. We did a modern play at lunch at the hotel, and then we'd go over to the outdoor "Lizzie" [the Elizabethan Theater, the only one existing then] and knock off a Shakespeare at night. We were in heaven!

In those days at OSF, an occasional period play might be added, perhaps one by Ben Jonson. Presently, the repertory runs to a dozen plays a year (a third of which are by Shakespeare), has over a hundred in the acting company, goes from February to November, and includes other classical American playwrights as well as a rich selection of new plays. Shakespeare sits happily inside this plan and might well have insisted on it if he were here today.

In an odd way, an alternating strain of encouragement and discouragement runs through Keach's career. Living with that, and seeing its ultimate positive results, has given him the essential strength to be able to take criticism, to pull out of adversity some valuable lessons, and to attack the next project with energy and gusto. When he eventually got to Hollywood, he was told by a well-known agent at Creative Artists to come down from his ivory tower and to forget about acting Shakespeare. No one, she said, is casting for *King Lear* this year— in fact, nobody cares. Keach adds, "I am talking about *the business* now—I am not talking about the public. Because Shakespeare is the pinnacle of expression in dramatic literature in the English language, there will always be an appetite for him." (A side comment—in 2006 and 2007, four nationally prominent *King Lears* were in production, one of them Keach's.) He commented on the odd coincidence that the American Shakespeare industry includes one-hundred-plus regional festivals, not to mention a Shakespeare theater in both New York and Washington, D.C.:

> We don't encourage classical acting in this country. What we encourage is "Get your nose fixed, get your boobs fixed." It drives me crazy. In Los Angeles, it doesn't mean a lot to be a great Shakespearean actor. Well, it means something to me, even though I hear my agents and managers tell me I am going to lose money if miss this movie or that movie. What they cannot articulate is what I am going to gain. In terms of what it means to me personally, money cannot buy.

> Young actors are going to hear a lot of professionals discourage
> it. Most classical actors in the United States have encountered this
> dilemma. But if you want to be someone who does it *all*, you have
> to devote time and energy to it. There are a number of American
> actors who are making a name at both—Christopher Walken,
> Kevin Spacey, F. Murray Abraham—and the group of actors you
> are talking to in this book.

Notably, these events and this attitude have worked in Keach's favor. He has an edge as an actor. He gives every performance his all, but in Shakespeare he is like a whirling dervish. Few actors match him onstage in terms of energy and commitment: his work aims for the pinnacle. Although there is a shadow of rebellion and defiance in his strength and power, he's not cast to type particularly, yet he does get the big, showy roles where an actor has the opportunity to strut and fret. He moves swiftly between comedy and tragedy, television and film, all based on tools he gained from an early track record onstage.

Keach's stage credential began early and remains astonishingly fruitful. He performed at Lincoln Center and acted roles on both coasts, snagging an Obie for his work at Circle in the Square with *Macbird!*, a gutsy satire of the Johnson administration during the Vietnam war (based on *Macbeth*). He played leads in *Marat/Sade*, *The Lion in Winter*, *The Three Sisters*, and *Enrico IV*, and he won a Tony nomination for portraying Buffalo Bill in *Indians.* Then he acted Cyrano, then Hughie (in *Hughie* at the National Theatre), then played Marc in *Art* at the Wyndham in London, and followed this by winning a Helen Hayes Award in *The Kentucky Cycle* at the Kennedy Center. His credential includes musicals as well: the lead in *The King and I*, King Arthur in *Camelot*, the title character in *Barnum*, and General Waverly in *White Christmas.* Added to this is lots of sitcom and serials work: *Titus, Mike Hammer, Prison Break, ER*, and other guest shots.

Once the Shakespeare credential lifted off, he continued in lead roles on PBS, at the New York Shakespeare Festival, the Long Wharf Theater, the Shakespeare Theater in Washington, D.C., and the Goodman. He's played three Hamlets—the third at the Mark Taper in 1973—along with Brutus, Kent, Feste, Autolycus, Coriolanus, Falstaff, Edmund, Richard

III, two Macbeths, and Lear. The term *working actor* is an understate-
ment in his case. Along the way, he has developed a work ethic that
includes the ability to pull himself out of challenging situations, dust
himself off, and march toward the next achievement—tenacity and flexibility that cannot be taught but that are absolutely necessary personal
qualities for anyone who chooses the acting profession.

Keach used the first decade of his career to train and polish technique and his ideas about verse speaking. He discusses some of the
practices that he remembers and retains:

> Along the way, I was given articulation drills as warm-ups. Some
> I still use "Red leather, yellow leather" said very quickly. Running
> up and down the scale vocally. When I was at LAMDA, they
> were very specifically teaching about two centers in the body, a
> physical one at the base of the spine in your back, and the other
> emotional, at the solar plexus. All the practical work was about
> trying to strengthen, loosen, and elasticize those areas—lying on
> the floor and making loud "HA HA" sounds, a part of Alexander
> technique. Generally speaking, when actors first encounter a line
> in Shakespeare they don't understand, they tighten their bodies
> as opposed to relaxing and letting the line flow out of them. One
> forgets when you've been acting as long as I have; those practices
> took a long time to learn.
>
> Michael McGowan was our text coach at LAMDA, and he
> was a master. We studied verse extensively there, particularly for
> clarity and meaning, but also he imparted tricks to us. Generally
> speaking, when you are saying a line in Shakespeare, the *verb* is
> the activated part of the sentence, rather than nouns or adjectives.
> It was a way of teaching Shakespeare that made younger students
> begin to look for important words to emphasize and, most of all,
> to slow down the pace of the key parts in speeches.
>
> Once you are in performance, those things may shift. You
> know the old joke about "To be or not to be"—it all depends
> on where your head is at on that particular night. *There is no
> one right or wrong way to do it.* There are better and worse, but
> it has to do more with the emotional condition of not only the

character, but the actor at that particular moment, in terms of what is emphasized in the line. I certainly found myself doing it all sorts of ways.

LAMDA's philosophy was provided to the students on their first day there, a notion that proved all naysayers shortsighted:

> I remember the head of LAMDA quoting Granville-Barker: "The success of an actor rests for a short time on his appearance and perhaps for a long time on the sound of his voice and perhaps for a longer time on the characters he's playing; but ultimately the success of an actor is totally dependent on who the actor is." . . . So we would . . . develop an aptitude for expanding one's own horizons, to visualize all the potential things you could do. Of course, much of that had to do with Shakespeare . . . the roles that most of us who were there aspired to play.[2]

Keach also took instruction from voice teachers:

> In New York City, I met a man through Judy Collins named Max Margolies. He taught not only voice, but *process*. He had us approach a great work of art by interpreting it and expressing it, an avenue that worked for both the actor and the musician. I happen to be both, so I really identified with this method.
>
> His objectives were always clarity, clarity, his final goal. To achieve that, there were little tricks again. After I'd read a line, he'd say, "Can you pitch that just a little bit higher and be a little bit clearer, without forcing it, mind you—so that it becomes easier to understand?" It was fascinating that when I pitched something a few notes higher, up here, rather than down here [he demonstrates] in your chest, it becomes easier to hear.
>
> He was always working on getting what he called a "head voice." Later, when I came out to California, I began studying voice for singing. I'm not a singer and haven't a vibrato. Nonetheless, I studied with Seth Riggs and he said the same thing: "Get the voice into the head." It emanates from the emotional center lower

down, but get it out of your chest and throat and up into the head. He had me use a visualization technique to enable me to get my voice unstuck from my throat and out of my chest, freeing it considerably.

I remember Olivier saying that when he was training to do Othello, there was so much physical work because it was breath, breath, and more breath. Also, learning to *stop* within lines. Young actors tend to get caught up in them, and then they cannot make sense of the stream of consciousness of Shakespeare's words in order to help the audience. In the great performances I've seen, the actor gets inside the character's mind and the audience is not aware of the words but rather of what is going on inside the performer—it just flows out of him and makes sense.

The soliloquies are like this. They are born out of an emotion in a situation.

Although Keach understands counting the beats in the lines, his goal is to make language natural and unfeigned as it generates from within the man:

My focus is more on the behavioral state of the character. It's hard to separate the speaking of verse from the actual performance text. From whatever the emotional reality of the moment is, you do the verse according to how that instructs you. It's got to be clear, but it's got to come out of a real person in a real situation.

The big question that I wrestle with is, when you count out the iambic feet, do you stress words strictly according to the meter? For example, is it *opposed*, or is it *oppo-sed*. Is it *banished* or is it *bani-shed*. For me, it depends on the moment onstage. If it catches your ear in the wrong way, and you become aware of it, I think you should say the word the ordinary way. That whole British thing of "How well I speak the verse," where they faithfully follow the meter, occasionally drives me crazy.

Some American actors assume an English accent when performing Shakespeare:

I do not. I think it is important to do what we call "Mid-Atlantic speech," which is not British and not American but does use some softer vowel sounds like you might have heard from Fred Astaire onscreen. "Cahn't" instead of "kehn't," for example.

Furthermore, I think it doesn't work to ignore a midline period and run thoughts together with no caesura or vocal stop. I realize that the punctuation in the plays was added and tampered with by many, many editors after the first printing of the folio, and possibly there was some hanky-panky in the printing process. Nevertheless, you have to try the phrases out in performance a number of times, a number of different ways, until you find out what works for you.

It is robust energy that appeals to an audience. Whether or not the dialogue is spoken on or off the beat is low priority.

Always work on the text *aloud*, even if you make mistakes. Then do it again and again, which is much more valuable than intellectualizing about it. You learn all these techniques in drama school as your tools. Then you get rid of them. In performance, they must not show.

Given the extent of Keach's experience, he has worked with a great many directors. His favorites exemplify where his preferences are in this important partnership:

I really liked working with Gerald Freedman, with whom I did *MacBird*, Hamlet, Edmund, Falstaff, and Peer Gynt. I admired not only the breadth of his knowledge about the plays, but also the fact that he always had an idea about how to do something. The bottom line for Gerry was always the humanity of the characters, getting to their core and what makes them tick, so that all of that technique associated with Stanislavsky's method comes into play. It's not as if because you are doing something classical, something "Shakespearean," you forget acting essentials—the character work continues to be all the reality. Gerry also had a great sense of humor—absolutely essential. I am always looking for that in the characters as well, because it humanizes them.

Robert Falls is one of the best actors' directors in America right now. My friend Brian Dennehy has worked with him as well. Falls and Freedman truly understand the actor's process. Their job is to inspire the actor to take chances and to go places where he has never gone before.

Keach added that both men love actors and acknowledge their "childishness" at times. It is a profession where one is continually asked to go into playtime mode and one's ego is on the line. A smart director has many skills in protecting and polishing this duality in an artist—the need to be open and inventive, and the need to be noticed.

Keach made a particular statement about Michael Kahn, artistic director of the Shakespeare Theatre in Washington, D.C.:

> I loved working with Michael Kahn on *Richard III*. Not only does he stimulate the imagination, he also gave me the confidence I needed to tackle Richard III. His passion for Shakespeare has inspired actors and audiences alike. I am very proud to be a small part of his retinue and look forward to returning there in June 2009 to reprise my King Lear. In my opinion, the Shakespeare Theatre in Washington, D.C., is close to becoming our national American Shakespearean institution.

Keach's acting process began to develop when (after playing Marcellus, the Player King, and Fortinbras) he played Hamlet at age thirty. He and a fellow student at Yale, Arvin Brown, had formed a close friendship as they collaborated on a script celebrating Shakespeare's four hundredth birthday in 1964, to be performed at a college in California. When Brown became artistic director at Long Wharf Theater, he approached Keach and said that the readiness was all; it was time to play *Hamlet*. Brown offered to direct:

> That first one, in 1970, may have been my favorite, because the theater was small and intimate, unlike the later two. The pressure was also on because young actors see a good Hamlet as the whole objective and goal of their careers, so just getting over the

intimidations of the role—even just memorizing the horrendous number of lines—was a huge challenge.

In fact, everyone asks me about that, and I always respond with a comment Mark Shore made in class at Berkeley when someone asked him how do you write? He said, "Apply the seat of the pants to the seat of the chair." There is no secret beyond that, I have discovered. You go over it and over it and over it until you get it. It's like the juggler with the plates. He gets one plate going and then the next one and then you get all of them going. You just sit down and do it.

By the time I got to the second production, I had learned so much during those six weeks in New Haven that I was raring to go and couldn't wait to do it again. The same was true with the third production in Los Angeles. In a funny way, you never feel like you get Hamlet *right*. You don't play it, it plays you. And since you are always changing, *he* changes.

It's like golf. You can get two birdies in a row and then get a triple bogey in the next scene. You can never take anything for granted in Shakespeare, because he gets the whole motor going, that's for sure.

As that *Hamlet* closed, Keach was approached by Joe Papp, who wanted him to play the role in the Shakespeare in the Park series in New York, a developing project that brought Shakespeare free to the populace. This was indeed a plum—Papp promised and delivered a stellar supporting cast: Colleen Dewhurst as Gertrude, James Earl Jones as Claudius, Raúl Juliá as Osric, Sam Waterston as Laertes, and Bernard Hughes playing Polonius. Keach was learning momentous, life-changing methods of working during a fertile growth period:

> What surprises young actors—and is very important to learn— is that when you are in a scene with someone, the other actor's performance will influence how you play a particular moment. At times other actors are shocked when you imbue the scene with totally different behaviour, without altering the text or the block- ing. Part of the rehearsal process is to find as many alternative

ways of playing the scene as possible. Then choose one. Or *not*. When that moment comes during the evening, the performance will then be spontaneous.

Remember, I had a sterling cast of New York's finest supporting me. So, I cannot tell you how many hours I spent before going on, writing down all of my premeditated ideas in a journal (which I still have), getting them out of my system, so that I would *not* go onstage with "an idea" of how I was going to do anything. When I actually was onstage, I would not know *where* I would be, because I had already "expressed it"—so wherever Colleen Dewhurst was or James Earl Jones was, that was where *I was* when I reacted to them. My mind was not on the gesture or the movement. It was busy stalking them.

That is what I want. No premeditation, all spontaneity, alive at that moment, never been done before or since. When a director comes up to you and says, "It was so much better the way you did it *yesterday*," I don't remember what I did yesterday—I have no idea!

What Keach is describing here is something that contradicts general notions of what the rehearsal process and the performance process is—partly because for almost all of our earliest experiences of being involved in the theater, rehearsal was to do it again and again until you got it right. The professionals are working for something far more edgy and spontaneous.

Always, always, actors are guided by the text first and take all their clues from the essential dialogue provided by Shakespeare:

When we meet Hamlet in that opening scene, a lot has happened. His father has died, his mother has married his uncle, and he's bitter and angry about that. That's what we know. The quality of behavior has to go beyond that color. It's how you deal with *that*. Are there glimpses of madness in the scene? Is there laughter? You start thinking—hmm, laughter. Should I make this gesture (or phrasing) or that?

But all that pre-planning has to go out the door. One thing I've always felt about Hamlet is that he is not someone who is sitting around trying to find which direction to move in. Instead, he moves in one direction and it is wrong, and then he moves in another which is wrong. Yet those are *active* choices, as opposed to becoming frozen or immobilized and saying, "Which way should I go?" Always active. Only one of the soliloquies is inner-directed—the others have the energy directed vitally outward.

The whole Hamlet experience, which happened in a fairly close sequence (Long Wharf in 1970, New York Shakespeare Festival in 1971, Mark Taper in 1973), was seminal:

Yeah. It freed me. It enabled me to just "be in the moment."

It's hard, very hard. All of the things you are taught come into play in some form or another, even simultaneously at times. Visualization, observation, emotional recall: all these concepts are important, but they all have to be forgotten, to be gone from conscious self and somehow still present in your muscle memory. That's why training is important. Things are now lodged somewhere you don't have to think about. They have to be there as part of your apparatus, but not at the forefront.

One of Keach's pet peeves is the opposite of spontaneity and explains why his favorite Shakespeare actors are more contemporary than the Gielguds and the Redgraves of the earlier twentieth century. He proclaims: "One thing I always resent when I go to the theater is when an actor of great technical virtuosity shows you *yesterday's performance* and how well he's rehearsed it."

Next to Hamlet, the big role for most Shakespearean actors is Lear. Keach's history with this monumental play began with playing Kent in drama school and then acting Edmund early in his career to Lee J. Cobb's Lear in 1968 at Lincoln Center. Although the role did not gather the praise for Cobb that *Death of a Salesman* did, it was a

portrayal from which the younger Keach could begin his own collection of research notes about the performance of the role. A novice
actor learns from watching another master onstage and mentally notes
what operates and what needs close attention within another actor's
performances—a subtle mentorship where the information is absorbed
into the observer's storehouse.

Keach felt in 2006 that ripeness was all: "There have been many
Lears who were astounding in their twenties, prodigious mimics with
great technical ability, but the life experience was not there. Things
onstage are said with looks, so that knowing and hard usage has to
ooze out as well. I played it at exactly the right age—at sixty-six you
are still physically strong enough to do it."

First came his favorite task. He declares, "I love research." When
he performed Hamlet, he read the available documentation of Booth,
Irving, Macready, Barrymore, and Olivier performing the role. His
process during *King Lear* was an illustration of the kind of background
digging he likes to do:

> I've been researching Lear for about twenty years. I start with
> Shakespeare, the playwright, and I look at the places where he
> drew his sources for the story of the play, such as Plutarch or *Ho-
> linshed's Chronicles* [the accepted history from which Shakespeare
> drew plots]. These introduce me to the images and ideas, and I
> can see where the plot differs from the original and get a feel for
> the historical context. It's important to know the period the play
> source was written in, the period and place that Shakespeare's
> play was set in, and the probable dates Shakespeare's company
> performed it.
>
> Shakespeare depicts a pagan culture for *King Lear*, yet there
> are many Christian overtones—forgiveness and redemption are
> huge themes. I like to know if there was anything going on in his
> personal life. For example, scholars have thought that *Hamlet*
> might have been associated with Queen Elizabeth's death.
>
> I've seen the play many times onstage. Also, I like to look at all
> the manifestations, beginning with some of my earlier exposures—
> Innokenti Smoktunovsky's *Lear* filmed in Russia in the late 1960s,

and then more recent ones like Olivier's, Michael O'Sullivan's, and Ian Holms's, which was my favorite because of its detail and specificity. Both the director, Bob Falls, and I scrutinized and discussed these.

I had a year to do research, and I think it is important for an actor to do that *early on*, so that one has enough distance from the actual production. In fact, I don't think you can do too much of it. *Then* there comes a point, generally speaking for me, a couple of weeks before the first day of rehearsal, where I throw all that stuff away and just deal with *text*.

I finally believe that with this preparation, you give a richer performance. Performances are nothing more than layers of expression, and the more detailed they are, the more engaging they are. As long as you hit the big moments, the genius is in the details, which will flow from knowing what those words mean.

Keach's orientation is unusual. Many actors are disinclined to look at other performances, because they don't want to be influenced by them. He prefers to go into battle with full armor: "I say give me all the research I can get, because I am ultimately going to do it my way anyway. I am richer by having seen what I don't want to do."

Keach also had that lucky break that leading actors dream about: being able to ruminate and cogitate with his director ahead of time. Ordinarily, the director and the lead have had an idea and have spoken for about a week together. For a year prior, e-mails flew back and forth between Robert Falls and him, so Keach knew what the sets and the costume designs were beforehand. He also talked periodically with Gloucester in the production (Edward Gero), who had played Clarence in Keach's *Richard III* and Banquo in his *Macbeth*. These kinds of discussions before and during rehearsal move the process forward quickly and ensure that everyone is on the same page.

Keach set the bar high on a couple of issues, a gesture that immediately focused the whole rehearsal process on the task at hand:

It is important when you are playing a role like Lear to come to the first rehearsal with the lines learned cold. You've got to know the music of them, because until you get the script out of your hands, you cannot begin to play it. That's how we started.

This was difficult, because we were adding and cutting lines in the ebb and flow of rehearsal, but I like to know the text before I set foot in there. Many actors cannot learn lines out of context, because they need to know where they are standing onstage and what their relationship to the other actors will be. So the cast was astounded when I came in without book on the first reading.

Within two or three days, they all knew their lines.

One of the great things that acting in TV episodes teaches you is that you have to work fast. There is oftentimes no rehearsal. You do it once in front of a camera, and then it is on film for immortality. I apply those same principles to theater, particularly Shakespeare. The sooner you get your head there, the greater your chances of finding more varied interpretations of the play you are embarking on.

Here, Keach is mentoring, without noticing that he is delivering good policy to less experienced actors in the cast. His background in a variety of performance arenas taught him about expediency and doing the homework beforehand. Teaching by example broke through some other notions as well:

We spent a short week around the table reading and discussing before we got on our feet. Once we got on our feet, we were performing full-out *every time* we rehearsed it, no holds barred. You have to learn the *amount of energy required* to find the level of reality needed for each moment. The only way you can do that is by committing yourself in rehearsal, rather than sitting back and looking at it and being tentative, which is no way to discover anything about a scene.

In rehearsal, you are looking for the variety of different ways you can say those lines and also attempting to build an emotional structure that lets you express the character in a number of ways without compromising the staging.

He talks about one of the most difficult things for all actors, keeping the performance fresh for oneself and for the audience, even when rehearsal has turned up some gems as options:

> The hardest thing for younger actors is that they find something in rehearsal and they glom on to it. They won't let go of it because they are a bit insecure. When it goes "off" [no longer works], and it will, they cannot understand how to get it back. Because they try to get back what they *had* rather than what they didn't have. It's what you *didn't do* that you are trying to achieve. It's a paradox.
>
> Is there a right formula? It's like an alchemist trying to make gold. You take some lead, you put it into a pot, you stir it without thinking of the word *hippopotamus*. If you can do that, you have found the magic recipe.

Inside rehearsal, discussions about adjusting the dialogue continued. Director Falls was more of a relativist and Keach more of a textual purist. Even though the production was contemporary in design, Keach wanted to retain Lear's line "Gather my horses." Falls said there would be cars onstage, and the actor replied that it would sound ridiculous to say, "Gather my automobiles." They compromised with keeping the original line, allowing the audience to make the connection about horsepower under the hood. However, Edmund's redemptive moment in the play, where he sends a soldier (too late) to stop the hanging of Cordelia, got cut, and he died quickly with a gunshot and no preceding comments. Keach insists, "People take issue with me, but, generally speaking, I do not believe in altering the text to satisfy the production concept. You do it the other way around—*you alter the production concept to illuminate the text.* I respect the director's concept—I just don't always agree with it." These are sometimes sensitive moments in rehearsal, but one negotiates them.

The mission statement of this groundbreaking production was to explore how the play and its characters would reverberate when set in one of those seriously unraveled communisms like the ones in Romania or even 1970s Cuba. A despot rules in rubble-ridden decadence, and grasping, violent characters surround him, more like gangsters and aging pop stars who indulge every sexual whim and feed their greed with no thought of consequences. There is a barbarous energy about such dictatorships, and Falls depicted it with shock and gusto. His vision was admired by one critic for its consistency and clarity in a culture growing used to crassness:

> [Falls reimagines] . . . the worlds of Slobodan Milosevic or Nicolae Ceaususcu or the fall of Baghdad . . .There are narrative liberties taken here that will have Chicago's tragic purists spitting nails in the Goodman Theatre's direction—[yet] this is a carefully wrought directorial vision expressed with such intensity and detail that it envelops its audience in a small-time world of expansive scale. Falls' *Lear* is a show that deserves to move beyond Chicago, and it will set people talking wherever it lands. And at least half the room will be arguing that it doesn't have much to do with Shakespearean tragedy.[3]

No character was left untouched. Albany was unbound by any moral fetters, Edmund chilling in his casual criminality, and even Kent (dressed as a skinhead) intended to assault Goneril's servant with a tire iron for insulting the king. Edgar had a drug problem, and the two ugly daughters were unnatural in their rapacity and gluttony. As brutal as it sounds, the picture drawn dripped with the bloody events the audience read about daily in the media, from the digital blur of Gitmo to the wriggling coverups of politicians.

Lear himself was flamboyant in a light blue suit and pointy-toed shoes. His insecurity and insensibility were obvious as he craved the level of fawning he richly deserved. So, too, was the kind of ride the audience was in for once the scene opened on a dirty set of urinals with Gloucester and the boys sharing ribaldry. One critic called it a "Boschian tableau,"[4] where one atrocity after another jarred as the preceding one numbed.

Then the king was feted at a vulgar and lavish retirement party in a huge hall, a gigantic portrait of his younger self hanging above the festivities, where a handheld microphone was passed around for guests to pay tribute. He then explained his "darker purpose," slicing up a gooey cake that represented the parts of his realm:

> Know that we have divided
> In three our kingdom; and 'tis our fast intent
> To shake all cares and business from our age,
> Conferring them on younger strengths, while we
> Unburthen'd *draw toward death.*

On these lines, Lear pulled out a gun, made as if to shoot himself, decided, "Noooo, I won't do *that*," and shot the ceiling instead. Plaster fell down. With that gesture, as Keach says, we know he's somewhat wacky. The question is how much, how often, and when does he show that in performance:

> He's just demonstrated that he's a practical joker. If you can get the character's vanity right then, the overwhelming need for attention and for love, you have laid the groundwork. I felt that he was terribly eccentric. He is disposed toward and has a penchant for madness. He is not so much *gone mad* but is certainly unpredictable.
>
> There were other touches of humor in the first scene. Gloucester was snuggling with the cake lady, and Lear doesn't appear to know the difference between his sons-in-law, Cornwall and Burgundy ("What says our second daughter, wife to, uh . . . Cornwall"). That kind of erratic behavior gave me the *platform* I built the character on. Shakespeare really takes care of the rest of it. In the scene with the Fool, you get a glimpse of his complicity into the full-on crisis of his life, an awareness of what he's done. He says, "I did her wrong [when he banished Cordelia], I did her wrong"—and this is what drives him over the edge. He knows he went too far.
>
> But is he mad from the beginning of the play? I gave up on answering that question. If you start very high on Lear, there is still a long way to go in his journey. I can't stand it when Lear is played as completely off his rocker at the outset. He gets there soon enough,

and by the time you get to Lear at the end in the reconciliation in the scene with Gloucester, he alternates between second child-ishness and keen awareness. That level of him was interesting to perform, because he's so free when he's in his dotage.

Keach talked about Lear's stability in the program notes as well:

> Under his motions we are conscious of the guilt that begins to creep into his emotional world . . . It eats him alive. It eats at him and he can't deal with it. He pushes the guilt aside yet it keeps coming back at him. So he begins to create his own world, the fantasy played out in his mind. He's totally full of contradictions. I just love the imagery and the non sequiturs in Lear's [post-storm] scene—it's just heaven for an actor. It becomes like a virtuoso performance.[5]

> I had an idea how to create it so that you see, without any speech at all, Lear enjoying the storm—to get rid of that problem of actors screaming over thunder. And then the storm subsides, stops. So that "Blow winds and crack your cheeks" becomes an exhortation to the storm. It comes back, and then he has to deal with it because it is in his mind—that's where the tempest is.
>
> However, I'll never do eight performances a week again. It's barbaric. I wanted two intermissions, but Falls insisted on one. The intermission happened deep into the storm after one hour and forty-five minutes, but it worked.

Occasionally, audience members walked out. The Chicago school system carefully weighed whether or not to bus students in to matinees. The critics were fascinated, many praising the audacity and craft of the directing. Some argued that Falls's concept overshadowed the larger humanistic landscape of Shakespeare's design and left Lear forlorn and uncomprehending, a Beckett character in a Shakespeare play.

Given the last two acts of *King Lear*, the director does have to come to terms with the title character. In Falls's production, the civil insurrection and the chaos of the country were well advanced when the play began, and the show explored how or if anyone could halt that country's spiral into chaos, atrocity, and destruction. In Shakespeare's script—where Cordelia's command of one-third of the kingdom might have offered a mitigating influence in governing the land—that possibility is eliminated by Lear. His decision becomes the inciting incident that results in the country being turned over to daughters who surprise him and destroy it through their own lust and greed. Falls's premise makes Lear the sole cause of chaos. Shakespeare allows Lear (as well as Edmund, Edgar, Albany, and Kent) a measure of redemption. Lear asks particular forgiveness for wronging Cordelia; Cordelia forgives her father; Edgar takes heroic responsibility in saving Gloucester; Kent remains a stalwart supporter against great odds; and Edmund seeks to save Cordelia as he is dying. Even a Good Samaritan soldier pops in to aid the good guys here and there. Most of these actions, with the exception of Edmund's attempt at self-redemption, remained in the Chicago performance.

These are not so much differences between a traditional and a contemporary point of view but rather differences in how the playwright constructed the play and how the director reshaped it. Ultimately, every artist has to release his or her work to a wider audience. One always wonders what would have happened to Shakespeare's plays had his family been able to control the copyright after his death.

In any case, the cast was obviously skilled and working well, and the spectacle was well worth the price of the ticket. Lear was praised, even if some of his thunder was stolen: "Keach leaves everything he has on the stage, as he mixes emotional rage, sardonic wit with comical asides, and his perfect diction and eloquence combined with his graceful physicality gives complexity, strength, and truthfulness to the aging Lear . . . . [He] leaves us wondering if Lear is really crazy or crafty."[6] Both Lears, of course, are in the text, both the titanic and the temperamental, as well as the tragic and the defeated. That is the quintessence of Shakespeare's skill in characterization.

Finally, Keach describes pre-performance rituals he carries out. When he was performing Lear, he liked to come out of himself a bit and go to the other actors' dressing rooms to wish everyone a good show. He wanted to extend himself and communicate that they were all in it together and the power of the performances depended on

their collaboration. Before his performances of Richard III, he felt
that his colleagues might have been intimidated by him because of the
unpredictability of what he might do onstage, so he kept to himself in
his dressing room.

Macbeth was its own special case:

> I used to keep a candle for each of the three witches in my closet
> in my dressing room and also at home. I'd heard many stories, one
> from Ben Iden Payne. He was directing the weird sisters' scene
> at the Oregon Shakespeare Festival and, as he was backing up,
> fell off the stage into the pit and nearly broke his neck. I learned
> that you must respect those women and pay homage to them at
> all times.
>
> I firmly believe that you do not mention the name of the Scot-
> tish king in the theater. If you do, you have to stand up, spit three
> times, and turn around three times.
>
> I came *firsthand* to learn how true the superstition might be.
> The very last night, the very last performance, the very last blow
> in the fight between Macduff and the king—he cut me right open.
> I didn't need stitches—they put that skin gauze on—but it was very
> close under the eye, so I was very lucky. I was bleeding throughout
> the curtain call.

Somehow, one thinks, neither blood, guts, thunder, pounding rain,
nor failing crops would keep Stacy Keach from taking that bow.

ZOE CALDWELL AS CLEOPATRA IN THE 1967 PRODUCTION OF
ANTONY AND CLEOPATRA AT THE STRATFORD SHAKESPEARE
FESTIVAL. (PHOTO BY INGE MORATH, COURTESY OF THE
STRATFORD SHAKESPEARE FESTIVAL ARCHIVES)

5

Zoe Caldwell
Her Infinite Variety

Rarely equivocal in delivering opinions, Zoe Caldwell declares, "I must tell you that if there's any doubt in anyone's mind—should they be an actor or should they not—then I would say *not*. It doesn't leave room for doubt."[1]

Her forthright conviction is bolstered by a remarkable credential in classical and modern drama. Caldwell began her professional stage career in her native Australia with the Union Repertory Company and the Elizabethan Theatre Trust in her youth. In 1958, at age twenty-five, she was invited to England to Stratford-upon-Avon to perform with the Royal Shakespeare Company, where she played Bianca in Paul Robeson's *Othello*, Cordelia in Charles Laughton's *King Lear*, and Helena in *All's Well that Ends Well* with Dame Edith Evans. She then performed in *The Changeling* at the Royal Court in London. Soon after, she was invited to join the Stratford Festival Theatre in Canada, playing Rosalind in *Love's Labour's Lost*, Lady Anne in *Richard III*, Mistress Page in *The Merry Wives of Windsor*, and Cleopatra to Christopher Plummer's Antony. The only non-American invited to act at the Guthrie Theater in Minneapolis, she acted Ophelia in *Hamlet*, Millamant in *The Way of the World*, and Grusha in *The Caucasian Chalk Circle*.

Caldwell won her first of four Tonys in Tennessee Williams's *Slapstick Comedy* in 1966 (followed by *The Prime of Miss Jean Brodie* in 1968, *Medea* in 1982, and *Master Class* in 1996). In 1970 she was awarded the Order of the British Empire, concurrent with a successful Broadway career that included leading roles in *Colette, Lillian, Dance of Death,* and *Long Day's Journey into Night.* She won a third Tony acting in Judith Anderson's *Medea.* Her fourth Tony was awarded in 1997 for a masterful performance of Terence McNally's *Master Class,* which depicted opera diva Maria Callas teaching and reflecting on her life. In 1998 she received the Golden Quill Award for excellence in acting Shakespeare. She was also given an honorary doctorate by the University of Melbourne.

Caldwell's directing credits include productions of *Richard II* at the Stratford Festival; *Othello* with Christopher Plummer and James Earl Jones; *The Taming of the Shrew* at Stratford, Connecticut; *Macbeth* in New York; and *Vita and Virginia* performed in New York by Vanessa Redgrave and Eileen Atkins. She has considerable television credits on CBC, BBC-TV, and American television, as well. She has held the Eminent Scholar Chair at Florida State University.

Caldwell's overarching view of theater is utterly classic in its definition and scope:

> I would say there are only three things that are necessary in the theater: the playwright—someone to write the text—the actor, and the audience. With those three things, you can make theater. If one of those is missing, you can't make theater.
>
> Everyone else is an appendage. Each of the three had better serve the play, or each will become an unnecessary appendage. That includes the director. The theater is a collaboration, and we are all, *all,* to serve the playwright. When any of those collaborators becomes too potent and takes up too much of the oxygen, bet your bottom dollar he is not serving the playwright. He may win a prize, but that's not what theater is.
>
> We have a lot of theater now where the director is serving the director's *concept,* or the lighting designer is serving his own concept. Everyone needs to serve the playwright. The best do automatically.
>
> After the rehearsal is done and you've explored and finished exploring, always serving the text—see, I don't believe actors are

artists. The real creator is the playwright. Actors don't create. We
are a sort of funnel through which the play reaches the audience.
That's our job—communicating the play to the audience.

This notion is becoming downright iconoclastic in an era of concept
productions where not only directors but also designers have charac-
teristically imposed a point of view over the playwright's words. The
time period of the original play may be tampered with in a production,
the gender of the characters may change, and a director may highlight
or capitalize on certain themes to the exclusion of others. In truth,
the actors are not usually the initiators of the concepts that dominate
Shakespeare productions.

Even more visionary is Caldwell's notion that acting makes her
"weller" as a person. She claims that practicing the art form has a
beneficial influence on the practitioner:

> You know, if I didn't act . . . I might not be a very good member
> of society. . . . If [my energy] weren't channeled off somewhere,
> I'd be an aggressive woman. Or possibly a bad mum. I need to be
> an actress to exist peacefully with myself. I think everyone needs
> something like this.[2]

Clearly, Caldwell believes in following her heart when it comes to
her profession. She offers this explanation:

> I had small-motor-skills disability as a child. I didn't know I did
> *then*, but I know now because my son has the same. It doesn't
> mean that you're crippled or in any way inferior to anyone else,
> it just means that your strengths are not the same as everyone's,
> nor are your weaknesses. And you should go where your strengths
> are.
>
> As for me, my large motor skills were fine—speaking, moving.
> However, I cannot write. Taking a pencil and actually doing that
> is very painful. But all human beings need to communicate, and
> if we could only discover how every human being is best skilled
> at communicating, I think we'd have a lot less crime.

There is a strong sense of inevitability about Caldwell's entrance into the acting profession. She found her vocation early, and this single-minded sense of focus never wavered. Her life in performance was abetted by parents who adored the theater and actively encouraged it in their daughter by taking her to everything possible in Australia:

> We were very poor, but my mom and dad saw *everything* they could in the theater: vaudeville, Shakespeare, musical comedies. Everything. We did go to ballet a couple of times, but I didn't dig that.
>
> Mother would pick me up from school, and we'd go to the theater in Melbourne. We'd stand in line at the box office, and Dad would finish his work (he was a plumber) and get dressed and come and stand in line with us. By that time, we would be very near the front of the queue. We'd get our tickets and we would run-run-run-run-run to the top balcony, where we'd have our tea and sandwiches and milk. If the show was a success, there wouldn't be single seats up there but only benches. Then they had what they called in Australia "packers"—a man with a short-handled broomlike thing that had a padded piece on the end. He'd come along the row and ask you to move in, and you'd move in and in.
>
> There was something marvelous about seeing a show like that, because you looked down from the top balcony. It had to do with the same kind of theater that began in Greece, where they sat on long stone benches, and only the people who paid money for the production had arms on their chairs. I had the experience of the theater at Atticus and Epidaurus from the age of five on up! When a singer or an actor would look up to the top balcony, it was such joy.
>
> So when I perform, I always play to the people in the top balcony. (It's also good for the chin!)

Caldwell's instruction did not cease. This was the era of "culture training," when a polished presentation of self, in both voice and movement, was part of the education of children and was greatly valued:

Although you can start old, I think it's better to start young, only because the sooner you start getting your instrument worked upon, the better it is. So. I was in my first dancing concert at two years of age. I was trained in toe-tap, ballet, eurhythmics,[3] physical culture, and also what they used to call *elocution*, which is speech and speech production. Placement of the voice and all that stuff. I do think dance is very important to learn, anyway, and if you can sing, that's fine, too.

Caldwell refers to some of her mentors as "Jean Brodies,"[4] a reference to a role she played and understood very well. Her first important teacher was an Australian who offered weekly training to the talented youngster without requiring tuition:

When I was seven, Dad got £500 from an old aunt in England and we moved up, real grand, to a suburb in Melbourne.

Mum took me to a woman called Winifred Moberly Brown, who taught elocution. She was a married woman, but she was childless (and I remember she had enormous breasts!). She auditioned me and gave me training weekly from the age of seven to the age of eighteen. I was a sort of surrogate child to her, I suppose, and because my parents were poor and it was during the Depression, she took me to art galleries, gave me books to read, and generally filled in the part of my education that my parents would have if they hadn't been so busy making ends meet.

When young people ask me, "How can I have a voice like yours?," I tell them about my training throughout those years in placement of the voice and in diaphragmatic breathing.

I realize now why I've never had any difficulty with Shakespeare. It was because I started so young and she gave me such appreciation of the text. There were kids in elocution training at the competitions who-spoke-things-like-that. Mrs. Brown was too classy and would've hated that. I was asked to delve into what *the author* was saying and thus requiring the performer to do. Wasn't I lucky?

Mrs. Brown's husband, John Alexander Brown, was a very well-known singer who would put on his white tie and black tails and go to these various events and sing. I would go along and *entertain*. I don't mean bawdy songs—but I'd work at birthdays and wedding anniversaries from the age of twelve on, doing Stephen Leacock type of things. I'd come home from Methodist Ladies' College and take off my gray lisle stockings and gray hat and get into my silver or gold lamé and go out entertaining. Also, I was always in radio and had my own news-and-interview program at age eleven.

Other role models came onto the scene as Caldwell began the early part of her career, which coincided with the development of professional theater in Australia. There was a theater sitting idle at the university in Melbourne, and local officials brought in a man named John Sumner from England to put together a group eventually called the Union Theater Repertory Company. Caldwell was one of the original members:

It was fortnightly rep, which meant you rehearsed for two weeks, playing one play at night, and then you began rehearsing another in the daytime. On the next Sunday night, you changed over. On Monday, you dress-rehearsed and opened on Monday night in the second play. So you were literally rehearsing all day and playing at nights.

You did not sit back and say, "What role would I like to play next week?" You were given roles. Sometimes I played the leading character: Jeanette in *The Lady's Not for Burning*, or Viola in *Twelfth Night*; or I might play Elvira, the old Irish aunt in *The Holly and the Ivy*, who had four lines. You got to play a host of roles that you were not nearly ready for, but you had to *find a way*. That was the most valuable—three years of the most terrific training.

There was an older Czechoslovakian actor with the company named George Pravda. He gave me one piece of advice which I thought was very good: "You must always, Zoe, when you have a sad character, find the moments she's happy. When you have a happy character, for God's sake, find the moment when she's sad."

During her time in a repertory company, Caldwell absorbed every tidbit of information that came her way, always observing colleagues from the wings. She mourns the loss of the tradition of young actors watching skilled older actors work during the apprentice years of performance training. She says that students who have a future in the theater "are those who are *watching* when others are off in the corner knitting or reading a book—the ones who say, 'If the stage manager has to go to the bathroom during rehearsal, I'll prompt.' Nothing, nothing is too menial."

One of those who taught Caldwell life-related lessons as well as artistic lessons came back to her native country to do a tour of *Medea*. Caldwell described this period in her own life:

> When I felt I really must stretch and go further, they opened the Australian Elizabethan Theatre Trust, which was based in Sydney although the actors played all over Australia's major cities. Dame Judith Anderson opened as Medea and I played the Second Woman of Corinth in that cast.
>
> By observing her, Anderson taught me a hell of a lot. Primarily, that I mustn't just have acting as my life, I must also have a life with husband and children, as well. Otherwise, it's too much to lay on a career—if something happens to it, you are decimated. I found that out by watching her, how lonely she was and how angry she was when things didn't go right. That was an important guideline: one's life must support one's career.

Like a number of the other top classical actors, Caldwell formulated a general operative to take the next job that came along. She advises that novices never ask whether or not the next part offered is the right part—the more important question is "Are you *in work*?" She warns, "If you say, right, I'll be there—then you get to work a lot." Early on, Caldwell was practicing what agents today call "name recognition." Being seen, having one's talent on display in a variety of venues, promotes one's career. Work begets work. Caldwell says she actually auditioned only once, and that was by mistake. She showed up to read for Annie in *The Miracle Worker* on the day the director was auditioning for *The*

World of Suzie Wong. After unsuccessfully trying to persuade him to audition her anyway, she never went back.

She has developed a method of studying for roles that is neither totally logical nor totally instinctual but rather a kind of immersion process. Once she is cast, the first step is to get as fit as possible: physically, vocally, and mentally. Since she has played a great many roles based on actual historical figures—such as Colette, Lillian Hellman, and Maria Callas—she finds her habit of extensive background study essential. In fact, she emphasizes that she studies character every moment of the day from the moment she awakens:

> I do as much research as is possible to do, an enormous amount. I read everything I can read about the subject. I also try to meet with people who knew the person, if possible.
>
> I learned everything about Medea before I played Medea. My husband, Robert, and I did a little university course at home (now it's all gone from my mind because you study for a reason). I learned about the matriarchal society in which Medea was born. I learned about goddesses, particularly her goddess. I learned about life in Calchas, as opposed to life in Greece. I studied physical movements and postures as shown in the ancient Greek vases.

Caldwell is equally thorough in this self-saturating approach when she prepares to perform Shakespeare: "You'd be amazed when you learn a new piece of information about somebody. It will not only affect the character, it will also affect something that happens to you physically."[5] A prominent aspect of Caldwell's acting process is her need to physicalize, to find the ways and postures in which the character's body works. Caldwell herself is very physical when she makes a point in conversation. She often fearlessly slides close to the listener to illustrate a point or stands up from her chair to demonstrate her story. That full, expressive quality carries over into the way she creates: "I guess I *always* have to find out how people move." Without actually professing to embrace a particular theory of acting, it is clear that the telling detail does not escape her attention.

When she was working on *Master Class* (her third Tony), she interviewed Maria Callas's pupil Sheila Nagler for three hours. Just at the end of the conversation, Nagler said, "Of course there was the way she *strode*." Since Callas had heavy legs, she had developed a characteristic way of striding when she walked. Here was a distinct, usable, physical detail (advantaged by the wide skirt in the costume designed for Caldwell) that helped to create the authority and command evident in the character of the great singer. Caldwell added, "Nagler told me that when [Callas] approached you to tell you something, you felt like backing away because it was like a wild animal walking toward you."

Caldwell states that she also uses the designer of the production as a research resource:

> When Tanya Moiseiwitsch designs a play, I want to look at what she puts in her costume drawings, because she was very careful. Tanya would give you a little purse held in such a way, and I would always find a moment to hold it exactly like that because there was always a connection.
>
> Ben Edwards is the most sophisticated and civilized designer in New York. On seeing his work, you're never saying, "Oh, isn't that interesting the way that back wall went up and came down with a bang, that was exciting!" Meanwhile, whole acres of the play might have been skipping by you. Costume is the same way. Costume is not to show itself off but to serve whatever the character needs. With any luck, it won't look like a costume but will look like *clothes*.

This idea of what the character wears relates to Caldwell's sense of personal discipline and also to her faithful adherence to theater protocol. She unfailingly enters her dressing room from the stage door, because that is what professionals do; she says that a factory worker would not return to his tools via the administrative offices. Then she performs a particular ritual. Before she applies her makeup prior to performance, she strips stark naked. That way, she has made a complete transformation from herself to her character's persona and clothing.[6]

In 1967 she played Cleopatra to critical acclaim at the Stratford Festival in Shakespeare's famous tragedy *Antony and Cleopatra*. She read Edith Hamilton's studies of early Greek mythology and traditions. She collected useful details in the work of Greek historian Herodotus:

> I read about clothing and makeup and that Cleopatra had put henna on her hands. In that time in Egypt, if you were a member of the lower classes, all the hair was removed from your body, because people got lice in it. The higher classes were prominent for having much more hair on their bodies because they had servants and slaves and baths and water and they could afford to be clean. Cleopatra was very proud of her long, oiled pubic hair, also hennaed.
>
> Cleopatra wasn't beautiful, she really wasn't. Romans who came to see her were shocked at how unattractive she was. She had prominent teeth, a bulbous nose, pendulous breasts, but a beautiful voice, a great command of many languages, and *wit*. She most certainly didn't look like Elizabeth Taylor or Vivien Leigh. But you see, that makes her a much more remarkable woman. If you are already gorgeous, of course Caesar's going to be enchanted; Marc Antony would also be quickly won. But if you are *not* . . .
>
> People would be with her for ten minutes, be captured by her charm and intelligence, and they would come away saying she was the most beautiful woman in the world.

Walter Kerr especially praised this production, in which director Michael Langham emphasized the performance that lovers and emperors give to one another—which constituted great portions of both their public and private lives. Shakespeare, of course, had already threaded the theme of seeming versus being (acting versus being real) throughout this masterpiece. Kerr commented on Caldwell's command of character and text:

> It is a real tribute to the actress' cunning that she has not been trapped into the velveteen languors and imperious self-control that have cushioned and concealed Shakespeare's mercurial

wench. . . . Miss Caldwell has a nasty eye and a lizard's tongue; she sees all that is coy and funny and feminine and cruel in the magnificently contrary queen Shakespeare did write.[7]

That rare and sensitive interweaving of text and research characterizes Caldwell's working method. She is always conscious of the play that Shakespeare crafted and how she, as interpreter, can use it:

> A friend said to me that the only time he'd ever heard the "barge she sat in" speech of Enobarbus done correctly was when it was done cynically (as actor Bill Hutt hinted at when he spoke the lines). He gave the "Age cannot wither her" speech with a slight pause before "infinite" [in the phrase "infinite variety"] as if he'd seen all her tricks, heard all her scenes. He insisted that Enobarbus doesn't like the fact that Antony is with her, and so he wouldn't have given the speech as glorious praise. I replied that that is the whole point of his lines: "You want to know who Cleopatra is? *I'll* tell you who Cleopatra is." That tone, that attitude is there. It's in Shakespeare's text. And it makes *both* Antony and Cleopatra huge people.

Ronald Bryden recounted how Caldwell had swept away prior interpretations of the Egyptian queen as a grand diva concealing kitten's claws:

> To an extent few Cleopatras dare, she played the royal harlot: sexy, foul-mouthed and funny, itching with desire. . . . But she was royal, too, with the same animal unselfconsciousness that made her wanton. As her Antony's head fell back on her arm, she launched into Shakespeare's lament for the withered garland of war [Antony dying] in a crooning howl, like a wolf baying at the moon. The theatre throbbed with wild, furious desolation. Had Lear been a woman, you felt, she could play that, too.[8]

An important strategy is the way Caldwell relates to the characters she plays. She does not linger on the notion of separating the character from herself. She plunges in and submerges herself:

> If you're going to play a character, even an evil one . . . to play the
> part well you must have a feeling of *love* for the character, under-
> stand the pressures that have shaped her. The author, the director,
> and ultimately the audience will make all the moral judgments.
> The character *herself* will speak through you. After all, it's only
> when you really get to know someone—when you've seen her
> washing her hair or sad or beaten—seen her in all these facets,
> that you can really love her.
>
> It's the same thing in building a character. You reveal, reveal,
> reveal, and suddenly it's all there—the whole! Cleopatra was a
> great part for me because I really got to know her, plus I got to
> *be* her—violent, arrogant, vicious, beautiful, but always superbly
> womanly. A wonderful role![9]

Despite the attention and care played to reading, listening to vid-
eotapes (if the character was a modern persona), and interviewing
acquaintances of the character, Caldwell emphasizes that her "homework" eventually gets set aside, at the ready if needed.

She transfers into the next stage, into rehearsal, with an open mind:
"*Now* I'm going to have to respond to this particular acting partner
playing Antony, as opposed to another person playing Antony. So what
is happening between him and me, what is happening *between*—is
terribly important."[10] She acknowledges the vital importance of interaction, action and reaction, the particular chemistry that gets created
when one actor is catalyst to another.

There are other habits Caldwell has developed for herself over the
years, all parts of a coherent philosophy of performance. Foremost
is her attention to the script: "Every day, I read the script, top to tail,
and every day I find something new."[11] Reviewing the playwright's
words daily acts as a self-corrective. If she had added something in a
prior performance, even a bit of punctuation that the writer had not
included, she admonishes herself to stay with the original text, and
that keeps her performance fresh.

Furthermore, Caldwell is occasionally restless and unhappy when
there is a hiatus in the production. She hungers to return to the run

of the play and finish out the stage life of the persona. When *Master Class* was between theater venues, she observed:

> When I was doing Maria Callas, we had time off, and I don't like having time off. I don't like it. Earlier on, in getting the production ready to go into New York, we had a month, but I hadn't discovered her so much, so fully, in Philadelphia. The second time we had a break, I got sick. I wasn't sleeping more than two hours a night. I had a demon inside me and my older son said, "It's Maria, the demon is Maria. You'll be okay once you get back into rehearsal and are playing again." And then I was. And then I slept.

Having acted Shakespeare from a very early age—as a youngster, she played a fairy in *A Midsummer Night's Dream*—she has formulated definite ideas about handling the language: "Of course, doing Shakespeare is good for any actress. He's so challenging that he's a marvelous *stretcher*. If you retain your elasticity, it's very easy to spring back into modern drama."

Caldwell believes that there is one important key to speaking Shakespeare's text, and that is following the punctuation. When she directed Shakespeare's plays at the Stratford Festival, she always began with a reading of the text:

> The whole company read it for punctuation. I said I don't want to read it for acting—*I want no acting*! We read it for about a week, around the table, so that every actor was in on the meaning of *everything*—not just one actor familiar with only his own role. I said, "If you come to a section that Shakespeare has written and you don't understand it, speak up! I will do the same. And we'll nut it all out." Usually, it takes very little time to sort it.

Caldwell does not pay undue attention to the actual beats of the iambic pentameter, nor does she require (as some theorists espouse) that actors pause at the end of each iambic pentameter line. (Indeed, neither did Shakespeare—see Peter Quince's prologue at V.i.108–16 in *A Midsummer Night's Dream*, a parody of an actor vocally marking the end of each line.) In fact, Caldwell is opposed to this prescription, to the idea of taking even a slight pause at the end of each iambic pentameter line:

> It's not meant to be stopped in the text. If one should make a full stop [a period], let it come to a full stop because the punctuation tells you to do that. Let's just take a look at act I, scene I, from *Macbeth*, this particular passage:
>
> > 1. *Witch.* When shall we three meet again?
> > In thunder, lightning, or in rain?
> > 2. *Witch.* When the hurly-burly's done,
> > When the battle's lost and won.
> > 3. *Witch.* That will be ere the set of sun.
> > 1. *Witch.* Where's the place?
> > 2. *Witch.* Upon the heath.
> > 3. *Witch.* There to meet with Macbeth.
> > 1. *Witch.* I come, Graymalkin.
> > [2. *Witch.*] Paddock calls.
> > [3. *Witch.*] Anon.
> > *All.* Fair is foul, and foul is fair,
> > Hover through the fog and filthy air.

Caldwell takes us through this section, giving performance instructions:

> "When shall we three meet again? [she makes a full stop]. In thunder, [partial stop] lightning, [partial stop], or in rain? [full stop]."
>
> It's so quick and easy when you do it with punctuation. I try and find a good clean editor. "When the hurly-burly's done, [partial stop] when the battle's lost and won" [full stop].
>
> And if you read *for the sense of the line*, the rhyme will follow. A full stop is not [the same as] a colon. "Fair is foul, [she leaves her voice up] and foul is fair: [leaves voice up] Hover through the fog and filthy air" [brings voice down on *air*].

Here is her set of definitions for each punctuation mark:

> A comma says keep-listening-keep-listening-keep-listening. A colon says keep listening but this is the end of this particular part (and keep the voice up, not concluding vocally—now wait for the rest of the line). A period [or "full stop"] says stop listening, period, closure, voice down, end of thought. Exclamation points should be louder and more emotional, as in, "There's a banana in your hair!"
>
> What is so interesting is that we get little tunes into our heads: "To be or not to be: That is the question." It's *not* a full stop—it's a *colon* after the word "question"—and if you drop the voice and conclude the thought on the word "question," it's as if you are saying, "Ladies and gentlemen, may I call this meeting to order, because what we are going to discuss is 'the question.'" That denotes someone who is in charge of themselves and older. But if you put a *colon* after the word "question," leaving the voice up, as Shakespeare is telling you—well, maybe we know that Hamlet hasn't got the whole answer in his head.
>
> You can go at quite a lick in that soliloquy, because there are fewer commas or other stops. If there's no punctuation, have the actors go at a good clip.

Caldwell recommends using A. L. Rowse's editions of Shakespeare:

> He's very clean, his punctuation.
>
> He does one thing that I don't think is necessary. Sometimes words that Shakespeare uses are diametrically opposed to modern meanings, and so these words appear to mean the exact opposite of what the passage should mean. Then Rowse will change the word so that the passage or phrase has the same number of syllables and the same feeling. If it *isn't* a very, very, very well-known speech, maybe his adaptations will help the audience's understanding. But if it *is* a well-known speech, you might not want to make the changes Rowse suggests.
>
> What I say to the student is—first of all, speak it with the text and the punctuation of the edition and the editor that we've

decided to use in our production. Now if you find that that edition doesn't work for you, go and examine other texts, but at least you have a starting point *from inside the available texts.* You can then say: "But in the Arden, it's a full stop." Always ask: what does that *mean* to you? What does a full stop *do* to the meaning in the play?

However, if you're floating in the air, you have nowhere to start from. It's no good if the actors are speaking in the most beautiful, lyrical iambic pentameter and nobody in the audience understands a word that's being said. First of all, *sense.* The strange thing about our language—especially with Shakespeare, because he's so supreme—*the sense is also the rhythm.*

If you go for punctuation, the passage not only makes sense, it also gives you great speed. You *can* elide beyond the end of the line. If the period is in the middle of the line, you *can* pause there—because that's the end of the thought anyway, so don't go running on into the next thought.

Caldwell illustrates her point about being faithful to the text with an anecdote about a student:

I taught at Florida Atlantic University for six years. When I first went there, they were performing *Lie of the Mind.* I talked about punctuation in class, and one girl (I could see) didn't go for my thoughts about punctuation at all.

She said to me, "Miss Caldwell, will you come and see *Lie of the Mind* and would you give me a critique on my performance?" and I said, "Sure."

I went and there she was playing a brain-damaged girl, and she was almost turning her toes in to do it! Of course, the performance was impossible. So the next morning she said, "May I have my critique?" So I said, "Yes, you were really, really appalling—because you were *playing* brain-damaged, so I was never able to discover that *person.* I do beg you, if the writer hasn't done it, the writer clearly doesn't mean you to do it. Don't help him." Then I went on and critiqued the rest of the performance, because some of her work was very good.

Two days later she came in and said, "All last night I went through the text for punctuation, and do you know what I found?" And I said, "No, what?" She said, "Two words, full stop. One word, full stop. Three words, full stop. One word, full stop. Now, if the character has only enough concentration and brain power to put two words together to create her sentences, what does that mean? It means something is damaged in her brain. The actor doesn't have to *do anything* physically—doesn't have to *do brain-damaged acting*. The audience automatically understands that there is something the matter."

So, that was good. The student found it of her own accord. *Which is best.*

Caldwell is also adamant about the use of accents, and she articulates a policy that is like the one adopted at the Stratford Festival:

> The historians tell us that Shakespeare was spoken very quickly in his own day. Spoken exactly like Americans, which is why I love hearing Americans do Shakespeare. When I hear them affecting an English accent, I say, "Noooo. No. Use your own voice. You are performing in your own country, so use your own accent."
>
> I suddenly realized that students would whisper and talk to one another in very natural voices. Then when they came to Shakespeare, all of a sudden—[she demonstrates] "theah is this whole othah placement of the voh-ice."
>
> I found out that they were also taking huge pauses and stopping to give emphasis to every other word and so it got *very slow*. No wonder audiences go to sleep in Shakespeare—because they try so hard to follow, and then suddenly they sigh and say, "I cannot follow." The actors have all been helping them so hard, and the director has been helping Shakespeare, and the designers have been helping Shakespeare—*and he's the one guy who needs the least help!*

Zoe Caldwell has collected her ideas and philosophies from several years of performing Shakespeare in a variety of international venues, from the Royal Shakespeare Company to the Stratford Festival to Broadway. She has worked with the best-known directors of the twentieth century. She cites Tony Richardson and Sir Tyrone Guthrie as her most significant directors. She relates a story from her early encounters with Guthrie, who set the bar for Shakespeare early in the second half of the twentieth century:

> I did three years with the Australian Elizabethan Theatre Trust, touring around, so I was still very young, only twenty-four when I went off to Stratford-on-Avon. I won a scholarship, I mean the government paid for me to go there, and I had a contract to walk on and understudy as required. Tony Richardson, whom I adored, had me play the daughter of Antiochus in *Pericles*, and Loudon Sainthill made the most extraordinary costume. I was painted green and dressed in a snakeskin.
>
> After that, Tony Guthrie came and said, next year, I want her to play Helena in *All's Well*. Which was pretty extraordinary, since there is nothing remotely similar in the roles. Maybe he was just being perverse! Whatever he was after, I had no idea who Helena was, no idea what I was getting into. In fact, I hadn't read the play!
>
> In those days in Stratford, Glen Byam Shaw used to invite you in and you had to go up some stairs and he'd give you a sherry and you'd sit down and he'd tell you his plans for you for the next season. He was always a very civilized and gracious man, and he told me that I would play Bianca in *Othello* with Paul Robeson and Sam Wanamaker playing Iago, Albert Finney playing Cassio. And I said that would be great. He said, also Cordelia with Charles Laughton playing Lear, and I said oh, gosh, and then he said Helena. All those heroines are called Helena or Isabella, so I said that's great, thank you. Then he said, *with Dame Edith Evans*!
>
> I came out of his office and everyone said, "What are you playing?" And I told them, and oh, they all fell down with surprise.

So I went off on a trip to Denmark to stay with Ray Lawlor and his wife, and I was just about ready to go back to Stratford when I said, I've gotta read *All's Well*, Ray. So we went into Copenhagen and got a little Penguin edition, had coffee and an early dinner, and they went to bed early and I began reading the play. And I read Helena-Helena-Helena-Helena and again I read Helena-Helena-Helena, scouring through the script, and I ran to their bedroom door and said, "Wake up, wake up! Helena's got *so* many solloquies!" Ray said, "The word is *soliloquy*, and go back to bed."

So I told Tony this tale one day. He loved stories like that. On occasion he would announce, "Right, Miss Australia, we'll have your solloquy now." He was very wicked.

He had rehearsals with me. He was quick, too, which is how I like Shakespeare—*quick* [she claps her hands]. Quick, quick! You don't have to speak slowly.

Neither man (Tony Richardson nor Tony Guthrie) had any fear of directing Shakespeare.

Guthrie wanted his shows truly to be full of life, life, life. He did outrageous things. Always a complete balance between showmanship and the play. Guthrie could not stand to be bored, nor to bore other people, so the audience never was. In rehearsal, no one ever knitted or read because he was always making the rehearsal very exciting.

Caldwell is nothing less than candid on all subjects, so it was confirming to find this nutshell statement about handling directors in her very charming memoir, *Zoe Caldwell: I Will Be Cleopatra*. The comment illustrates her unique brand of problem solving, her tempered diplomacy, and an utter consistency in her philosophy: "If a director asks of you something that you know is not what the author intended, don't make a fuss—just let it get lost."[12]

She summarizes two ways of approaching the acting, a statement rife with self-knowledge and her ability to absorb herself in the performance of a character:

The French have two categories: the *acteur* and the *comédien*. In the first, the role is fitted to the *acteur*.

The *comédien* takes a role and goes inside it. . . . I'm a *comédien*. Olivier (oh, boy, go straight to the top) was a *comédien*. Christopher Plummer is. Edith Evans was a *comédien*.[13]

Zoe Caldwell is known for her boundless energy, for being "a definite creature of the theater."[14] Although she has accumulated a wealth of experience, a collection of clear opinions and solid practice, these do not account entirely for her genius. There is a quality about her that is very difficult to describe but enormously easy to sense in her presence. Part of it is commitment, although that is far too soft and mundane a description for the size of her personality.

Ultimately, she is master of the histrionic gesture. Her years in performing classical drama and the exuberance with which she throws herself into "the work" has taught her to jump for that huge, telling theatrical moment. She understands instinctively that this aptitude could taint a production if it were overused or took up "too much of the oxygen." But she also understands that a great performance requires it and an audience hungers for it. The spectators come to hear the tenor hit the high notes, and Caldwell has the pipes: she has perfect timing, an innate intelligence and instinct about the text, and a huge range. We call that class.

NICHOLAS PENNELL AS KING JOHN IN THE 1993 PRODUCTION
OF *KING JOHN* AT THE STRATFORD SHAKESPEARE FESTIVAL.
(PHOTO BY CYLLA VON TIEDEMANN, COURTESY OF THE
STRATFORD SHAKESPEARE FESTIVAL ARCHIVES)

6

Nicholas Pennell
Words, Words, Words

Nicholas Pennell was my earliest interview. I spent two hours a day with him, in between rehearsals and performances, during a week in August 1994. That summer, he was both playing at the Stratford Festival and doing a lead in a television program about Erik Satie for the Canadian Broadcasting Corporation. Pennell had taught master classes at my alma mater, the University of Michigan, and we shared not only common ideas about literature, but a common acquaintance, Professor Claribel Baird, who was one of my Shakespeare professors. When I sought the interview, he asked only one question: "Are you one of Claribel's kids?" After that, he was an open book, sharing all he knew.

Six months later, he was dead of lymphatic cancer at the surprising age of fifty-six. When I transcribed his interview, there was a sensation of a literary character pacing around my desk, commenting on what he'd told me on tape, adjusting my grammar and usage as I worked. He stayed with me as I completed not only this chapter about him, but a full biography, titled *Risking Enchantment: Classical Actors Speak*. His cherished lines in Shakespeare were from a high point in his career, playing Hamlet—and also that character's final words in the play: "If thou didst ever hold me in thy heart, / Absent thee from felicity a while, / And in this harsh world draw thy breath in pain, / To tell my story." Odd, how his admonition continues.

Nicholas Pennell was English by birth but chose to fulfill most of his acting career in Canada. His first role at the Stratford Festival was Orlando in *As You Like It* in 1972. After that, he played seventy-seven different parts with the company, including the title roles in *Hamlet, Richard II, Julius Caesar, King John, Richard III, Macbeth, Titus Andronicus, Pericles,* and also Stephano and Ariel in *The Tempest,* the Fool in *King Lear,* Malvolio in *Twelfth Night,* Iago (his favorite role) in *Othello,* Jacques in *As You Like It,* Oberon in *A Midsummer Night's Dream,* and Ulysses in *Troilus and Cressida.* He gave hallmark performances of Jack in *The Importance of Being Earnest,* Thomas Beckett in *Murder in the Cathedral,* Jack in *Home,* and Victor in *Private Lives,* and he also created the roles of Leonard Woolf in Edna O'Brien's *Virginia* (which transferred to the Haymarket Theatre in London) and Siegfried Sassoon in *Not About Heroes.* He toured the United States and Canada in his one-man show, giving a special presentation to the Shakespeare Association of America.

Pennell was an inspiring teacher and a passionate advocate of theater. It is typical that in one of his last interviews he worries about the erosion of language on the stage, is concerned about rising ticket prices at the Stratford Festival, and expresses pleasure at the "emergence of a generation of Canadian-trained actors who have grown up with professional theater around them."[1] A recipient of a 1991 Tyrone Guthrie award, he had a large following throughout the United States and Canada and accumulated more than 250 film and television awards, including one for his notable portrayal of Michael Mont in the BBC's first *Forsyte Saga.*

Pennell was born on a farm in Brixham, Devon, England, in 1938. His early years held no sign that he would one day be an actor, yet patterns were forming that would influence his later career:

> I was born during the war, when there was virtually no theater happening. We still had pantomimes, that weird English hybrid, a kind of Christmas fare that was partly vaudeville and partly musical. There was the cinema, of course, although I don't remember too much beyond *Bambi.*

I wasn't aware of any desire to do performance—we used to dress up a lot, but all children do that. I went to kindergarten with a brilliant teacher, and I read very early and still have a passion for poetry and verse. I was sent away to boarding school very early, at age seven. I remember standing on the porch at school and calling to my mother as she went away, "I won't do it again!" Being at school for nine or ten months of the year from that age up to eighteen years was emotionally a rocky situation. The need to portray an emotional state and the life of a character, to project somebody else's existence, comes from a need to be approved of in some way, since I lacked that kind of nurturing in my childhood. That's really cheap psychology, but it's a possibility.

My first play was a Molière, *Le bourgeois gentilhomme,* at All Hallows School in the West Country at age thirteen. Our master was Mr. Horace Lee Hogg (we called him "Hogg-Lee"—he was a very fat man). He wanted to play the big parts while we got the small ones, mostly H. M. Tennant plays. It was an all-boys' school, so even the women's roles were played by boys. We only read Shakespeare but never acted him.

Later on when I was older, I met this wonderful actress Margaret Leighton in London. I was very shy and nervous, and she said, "How are you?," and I said, "I'm fine" and "Oh, it's so good to meet you because I feel I know you already," and she said, "Why is that?," and I said, "Because I've played all your parts." I'd made a specialty of the Margaret Leighton roles at school.

I was lucky in that I had small classes and a brilliant English literature teacher named Thompson, and my housemaster, Stone, was an English teacher, as well. The whole of "A Shropshire Lad" and a lot of T. S. Eliot and the Georgian poets popular then are still with me. When I did *Not About Heroes,* I found I'd read virtually all of Siegfried Sassoon and Wilfred Owen. That's been a great boon coming into the verse plays.[2]

Pennell had no particular memory of the moment when he decided to become an actor. Nevertheless, he decided to attempt entrance into the Royal Academy of Dramatic Arts (RADA), the most prestigious drama school in London at the time:

> I went up to London on a day ticket and auditioned. By a complete fluke, I got in, much to the disapproval of everyone.
>
> Ma didn't think I'd be able to do it and wanted me to take a secretarial course. Then I got a scholarship from the Devon County Council, and RADA gave me tuition money, so with all of that, I gathered enough together to live.
>
> Having been shut away in an English school, I hit London for the first time and didn't do any work at all. At the end of the first year, the principal, John Fernald, called me in and said that my record was very poor and they couldn't continue funding me. He was prepared to get me a job if I would stick at it a while. I was engaged as an assistant stage manager with the Chesterfield Rep at the equivalent of fifteen dollars a week.
>
> Throwing me into that experience at that time was absolutely *key*, because I attained work discipline. I wasn't a member of Equity in those days (you couldn't be until after a year), but I worked sixteen-hour days and got familiar with sets and lighting and props. We did a play a week for about fifteen or twenty weeks, then took a break, then did another stint. The people I was working with wouldn't give any leeway, so you learnt quickly on your feet. I would have been fired if I hadn't.
>
> One of the dangers of repertory was that you could pull out a trick from your bag to enliven a performance. You had no time to investigate character or character relationships, because the week was spent learning the lines and memorizing the moves.
>
> I didn't really know what I was doing, but I had an instinct to produce bits of myself that seemed to be right. I respected the actors I worked with—the leading man was Ronald Harwood, who wrote *The Dresser*. The senior actors were from a prior tradition. For the first ten years in the business, I never called anyone by his Christian name. That would have been rude. The older women even wore hats to rehearsal.

Pennell's years at RADA paralleled an important transition in the history of the theater. He had one foot in traditional theater entertainments and another in the gritty realism emerging from young playwrights during the mid-twentieth century:

A year later, I went back to Fernald. He said, "You've worked hard and the word about you was very good, so we'll give you another chance." This was autumn of 1958. I was doubling parts with Tom Courtenay and in school at around the same time Brian Bedford, Peter O'Toole, and Albert Finney were at RADA. John Osborne had just shocked the establishment by opening *Look Back in Anger*. I was very much an anyone-for-tennis kind of Englishman and found myself in an acting program with this extraordinary working-class power, because the Shaw Bequest had given scholarships to kids with very different backgrounds. I learnt a tremendous amount about the new kinds of plays. We were adapting to a changing society and a new look at class structure in England.

It was an incredible time. I was part of the generation from the late 1950s to early 1960s that formed Peter Hall's Royal Shakespeare Company and the first National Theatre Company. The theater was changing radically, so the work had to change, too. Back in classes at RADA, we did a lot of Shakespeare. Both Peter Barkworth and David Giles (who directed *The Forsyte Saga*) were mentors. Barkworth was a genius who taught a great deal about the truthfulness of acting—not creating theatrical gestures but always looking for the truth within the character and finding how the character's experience paralleled your own.

You cannot become someone else onstage: you can only be yourself. You elevate the characteristics and the emotional and imaginative experiences of your own that parallel the character's. It is the bit of you that is Hamlet or King John that you pump up or heighten. There are also qualities you have to *suppress*—no, that's the wrong word; there are bits you have to *minimize*.

We'd do showcase productions at the term's end, and I doubled Claudio with Tom Courtenay in *Much Ado*. John Broome was the choreographer on the musical. He was later the movement coach for the Royal Shakespeare Company and has worked for years in Stratford [Ontario]. We've known each other for nearly forty years.

At RADA, Pennell had voice training that focused on technique almost exclusively:

> I was very lucky to train with Clifford Turner at the height of his powers—Kristin Linklater and Patsy Rodenburg succeeded him. He put the theory in place so that there was a way of training the voice. His great thing, gone out of fashion now, was "rib reserve," a method of speaking (principally Shakespeare) where I breathe into my rib cage and then I next breathe into my diaphragm: "Now is the winter of our discontent made summer by this glorious sun of York and all the clouds that lour'd upon our house are on the deep bosom of the ocean buried" [this is done on one breath]— and I'm still only speaking on my diaphragm.
>
> What I have *left*—is a full rib cage. Now, the principle of that was that you didn't use the "rib reserve" unless you had to do a very, very long extended thought which required six or seven lines of text spoken on a breath. The most famous example I can think of is in Hamlet's last soliloquy, "How all occasions." If you can speak it on one breath, the oxygen rush you get from that centers *incredibly* the emotional content.

Pennell went from drama school to regional theater. In England, regional theater functions as a kind of apprentice schooling where young actors continue learning on the job, providing important experience and mentors:

> My first job was in musical comedy, the old-style revues, working in Ronald Katz's *Carry on Laughing*, which we did at the end of the pier in Bournemouth. When there was high tide and a rough sea, it hit the underside of the theater and there was so much noise that the audience couldn't hear. Which is probably just as well, because

it was a pretty sophisticated London revue—above their heads water-wise. Joanna Drew recommended me to the director, but I got the job because I looked like Adam Faith, the pop singer.

Revue trains you to always be "in the moment," as we say today. There's an area in acting where you have to do "instant character." It's a very good exercise but dangerous if it becomes facile. You have to be absolutely committed to the person you've chosen to play, even if it's for only three minutes. You cannot just put on a funny hat: you have to find the reality of the persona.

Then I got a small part in *Masterpiece*, about a painter who painted fake Vermeers and sold them to the Nazis. The play introduced me to an actor who was my link to the nineteenth-century European continental theater. He'd played the lead in *The Red Shoes*—Anton Walbrook. He came into the first reading with the skeleton of his character. With absolute precision, I watched him gradually put the musculature onto the bone and then the flesh. It was done with the care of a surgeon and riveting to watch this at my age. He'd been a great actor in Vienna and left when Hitler came to power. He's forgotten now.

Pennell devised his own methods of preparing a Shakespearean role. Many actors read literary criticism, performance criticism, biographies, or production histories as they investigate the background of the play. Some study and examine the history of the role. I asked Pennell what kinds of research he carried out, and he responded with a variety of qualified sources:

> I think the single most important thing to me is *no research*. When I played Hamlet, I made the error of reading Ernest Jones's *Hamlet and Oedipus*. I swallowed it whole and I just escaped from it two weeks before we opened, when I changed entirely how I'd been playing the role. I swore that I would never again read anything to do with the play. The moment you do, you start taking on other people's baggage. It's fatal in creative work.[3]

We live in a profession that tends to want to prove its intellectual prowess. We insist that we're not really silly creatures, so actors come into rehearsal with an awful lot of reading done which isn't of value. Or at least not to me.

When I played Siegfried Sassoon, I read a great deal of his poetry, but I didn't read any biography. The most difficult thing is the director who always brings in a pile of stuff he wants you to read—as if there's going to be an exam later. When he says, "What did you think of that bit in the book where . . ." and then you have to actually pretend that you've read it.

It's very vexed, this question of research, because people tend to misunderstand me. I mean I don't read accounts of the play: Cliff's Notes, there-are-fairies-at-the-bottom-of-my-Arden sort of thing. The Arden's [editions of Shakespeare] jolly handy at translating some of the more obscure stuff, but sometimes it doesn't help at all. Often what happens *around* the rehearsal period governs what you do with a given part—not consciously, of course, but it can cross-fertilize. I am an avid reader of the newspapers and listen to radio news and find that its imagery reinforces what was going on at the time the play was written or the period in which we've set it. When we did a modern version of *Measure for Measure* (Michael Bogdanov directing) during the Falklands war, one saw a parallel in the cynicism, the vulgarity, and the criminal stupidity of the people involved, as one did in the Gulf War. Here are two sources, then: what one's reading—biography or poetry or whatever—and then journalism.

From these gleanings, Pennell got his raw material. The ideas and action of the play then summoned up the images and, together with the script, a logic of character was created. The next step was to embrace language and to keep oneself open:

I tend not to be able to prelearn a part. One forms frightfully bad unbreakable habits if you prememorize before you start rehears-als, because you "set the role" early, and that cuts out the inevitable changes that are going to happen when you come in touch with other people. During the first period—sitting around the table and during the very early blocking—I try not to get in the way of anything that's coming from my subconscious.

When I played Iago, the director said to me at the end of the first week, "I really think it's interesting that you're doing that Manchester, is it, dialect?" And I said, "Pardon?" I was literally unaware that the voice had arrived and that it had come from when I was in the army doing National Service. Our commanding officer had the ability to butter up his superiors and was also sadistic and cruel to the rest of the unit. I had no idea he would crawl out of my memory.

That happens a lot: that one's memory *does produce*. The most important thing we have as actors is *observation*. Consistently taking mental note of what's happening—the way people dress, the way they move, the way they behave, the way they live their lives—is the source of everything we do. Then it comes filtered out through oneself in the work. I never consciously say to myself, "Oh, I can think of somebody perfect (a model) for this role," because then I would be doing a bad imitation.

He introduced a related principle of acting:

Every single clue, for me personally, comes from the text. Everything I know. Then a lot of the work happens in early rehearsals when one is still on book. On that day you've really discovered and achieved some originality or some newness on a character, it's so satisfying. A good rehearsal day is an astonishing gift.

Yet the final thing would be what Jean Genet calls "the wound." It is the ongoing well of experience from which you draw. The artist consistently doesn't allow scabs to form. His job is to pick away all the time at the edge of it to make sure that what he is drawing on is emotionally accurate and truthful. The imaginative life is not merely remembered, rather it's *active*—the pain, the joy. It's probably the most important source.

It is indeed clear that Pennell placed text as central to the actor's preparation. Words were the avenue to his "wound." Rather than leaping to the verse and finding its meter and its stops, Pennell was more in-volved with the texture and hue of language. At this point in his life, he set himself the task of memorizing T. S. Eliot's *Four Quartets*, because he wanted to own that work, to have the poetry available at will. He savored poetic speech. It was his touchstone and his food:

> Shakespeare is astonishing in how much imagery is contained; the color of words in conjunction with one another. Each word has three meanings. It has its literal meaning—for instance, you look up the word *sea* in the dictionary and it says "large body of water," or whatever the OED definition is. Then it will have a secondary meaning, your own personal memory or an internal emotional vision of what *sea* is. For me, it's a summer's day on a place called Berry Head near Devon where I grew up, very high, with sea pinks and lichen on the rocks, the deep blue of the water with whitecaps.
>
> The third meaning is its *mantra meaning*. Here, your inner self is responding to the word and you're not relating it to a homonym. You're expressing its taste, its essence. For me, the word *sea* is an opening gate. I have no idea why.
>
> So you have to *triple* the available color you have for speaking that text. Alongside all these shadings coming to the surface, plus whatever is induced by your relationships with the other actors in rehearsal, you arrive at a point where you have too much informa-tion to process. And you have to start making decisions about this character, now, for your present performance.
>
> Eventually, one pares away the extraneous stuff collected dur-ing the rehearsal process. It will remain in that edifice that you build to support the text. It is said that there is no subtext in Shakespeare, but there has to be, because the inner life of the character is where a lot of the construction of the part sits. What people really mean is that Shakespeare leaves nothing *unsaid*: if he doesn't say it, then you're in dangerous territory if you assume that he has. There isn't subtext, as there would be in a Pinter play, where you say, "Yes. No," and there are eighty-two different emo-tions running under those two simple words.

In his essay on Shakespeare's sonnets, Auden talks about how far you can go without having to stop the thought. You have to speak the whole sonnet on a breath, but the thought process is so incredibly complex that each thought leads you to the next or deflects you to another thought or even reverses you. The old rule of thumb for verse is: go as far as you can, then regroup.

Pennell elaborated on a rich, thick, structured piece, Macbeth's soliloquy at the beginning of Act I, Scene vii:

All this is going round the houses to say that when I did *Macbeth*, in the soliloquy "If it were done when 'tis done, then 'twere well / It were done quickly," I couldn't get further than *well*. My mind kept trying to do it as it is punctuated in all editions, but I couldn't get there. In the end, my reading was "if it were done when 'tis done, then 'twere well." [Pennell put a vocalized period, a full stop, after *well*. Most editions of *Macbeth* indicate that there is no punctuation at all until "/ It were done quickly"]. So, for me, "It were done quickly" became a new development: it would be fine if it [the murder] were over when the act itself was committed, but of course, no murder ever is. This is an example of allowing oneself to speak the text as far as one can with one thought before *regrouping* that thought and letting it carry you on to the next.

There is a disparity between the speed with which you have to speak it and the speed your mind can go. The audience receives some information at a conscious level and some at a subconscious level. Their minds are catching up as well.

Pennell's love of literature and its internal shapes appears in these remarks. It is rare to see an actor who studied text with such attention to detail. This powerful literary foundation led him to explore thoroughly and to emerge with a detailed performance analysis of a piece of text in the opening scene of one of Shakespeare's comedies:

In I.ii of *Twelfth Night* [ll. 1–15], the writing is such a miracle of economy.

Viola: What country, friends, is this?
Captain: This is Illyria, lady.
Viola: And what should I do in Illyria?
My brother he is in Elysium.
Perchance he is not drown'd. What think you sailors?
Captain: It is perchance that you yourself were sav'd.
Viola: O my poor brother, and so perchance may he be!
Captain: True, madam, and to comfort you with chance,
Assure yourself, after our ship did split,
When you, and those poor number sav'd with you,
Hung on our driving boat, I saw your brother,
Most provident in peril, bind himself
(Courage and hope both teaching him the practice)
To a strong mast that liv'd upon the sea:
Where, like Arion on the dolphin's back,
I saw him hold acquaintance with the waves
So long as I could see.

That incredible image of "our ship did split"—the writing creates sound for the actor to use—listen to the I's and D's and P's. Shakespeare changed the pronouns from *our* to *you*. Is he thinking of the seamen as *we* the crew and *you* the passengers? Where *are* the passengers at this point? Who is left behind? Is Viola with the sailors? They're not coming out of the water, they're not on the beach building fires to keep warm—she and the captain and sailors have already started their movement to go get help.

Also, listen to the extraordinary way in which the dialogue flows. Notice how the word *perchance* starts and then moves through the line, traveling through the text like a ship on a journey. In the final bit, it has lost "per" and has become more strongly the random god, or fate, or *chance*.

Hear that amazing image of Sebastian being bound to a mast and compared to Arion [Orion], the poet, singer of tales, who was thrown overboard by the sailors and rescued by the dolphins. Add this to what Viola says about herself, as a twin, ending with her remark about Orsino, "For I can sing, / and speak to him in many sorts of music." Here she is comparing *herself* to Orion, talking of *her* ability to spin words into gold as early as Act I.

In the "O my poor brother" line, most editions place a comma between the phrases, making it a dead brother and a live brother, two totally opposed thoughts. Antithesis at work. She also says, "Mine own escape unfoldeth to my hope, / Whereto thy speech serves for authority / The like of him." What does this mean?

Ornate, Chinese-box language. But you realize that the openness with which she approaches everything is governed by its equal and opposite need to veil her vulnerability. With words, she goes from the utterly open to a complex verse structure which hides, which disguises, just as she is disguised. All the great emotional moments in the play occur when she has opened herself up and someone has slapped her down.

Pennell saw this kind of textual scrutiny as a voyage of discovery. He used language to accumulate information about the inner life of the character:

If you look at text closely, there is a funny pattern that runs through the so-called villains and arch-villains. Iago is a good example. As I studied that role, I kept thinking, nobody ever lies to the audience in Shakespeare. Can you think of one example? Iago may lie to other characters, but he is always truthful to the audience—either in scene or in soliloquy. Shakespeare's never dishonest, and *the text is the subtext* in that regard.

So I kept reading Iago's dialogue. When he says *three* times that Othello had an affair with Emilia, it isn't enough to say that he's using that as an excuse for his actions. Does Iago believe it, then? If so, what follows? If Iago has more than a suspicion but less than a certainty that Othello has slept with her, then I begin to understand his *under-reasons*. The text reveals the wit and the astonishing mind that character has. His mind goes like a rocket—he fascinates you.

When I saw these truthful and yet attractive things about him, that he was hurt and flawed and operating from that base, then I began to see it was not just Othello who was tragic. The more I got the audience to understand him, the more they were drawn into the play and identified with him. If they don't identify strongly, then the mainspring of the play is lost.

I found the same thing to be true with Richard III. My director Richard Bergwin made a comment about the scene with the three women (Margaret, Elizabeth, and the Duchess of York) and that incredible attack on Richard, "That bottled spider, that foul bunch-back'd toad!," and the Duchess of York talking about the pain of being pregnant with him, the horror of giving birth, and his warped childhood. At last, Richard says, "And came I not at last to comfort you?" Bergwin said, "Has it ever occurred to you that he's talking about the *crown*? That all of his achievements were an attempt to say, "For God's sake, I'll try and do *something* you approve of. I'll become king." So that line became quite pivotal for me.

Pennell instructed a group of apprentice actors, the Young Company, in Stratford. He also gave master classes and workshops in American and Canadian universities, where he taught and advised novice actors. For him, the text was absolutely the actor's to possess and use, and it was also the primary starting point:

I realized what Michael Langham meant when he talked about a good classical text being like a score. You must look at the way that it's put together and how tempo and legato and other musical ideas creep into discussions about text. I'm not talking about "singing" the text, because that's not an accepted way of performing, of course.

I'm thinking of techniques such as finding the parenthetical phrases in Shakespeare and leaving the voice up on the end of these and then letting the voice come down to close a sentence at the end of an independent clause.

In teaching text, one inevitably talks about the way one reads lines. So I always say this is the way *I* would read a line and avoid giving a student one set way of reading a line. Students really need to find their own way through to saying the dialogue.

Text relates most directly to "period styles" in acting, especially to Restoration texts and what I call "milord acting." Young actors tend to get all caught up in the red heels and foot movements and snuff boxes. Much of this can get in the way and really stultify. My advice is to *go to the script*, pull the character from the text, and *then* get into the clothes and wear them. Do not start with the flourishes—start with the text and work outwards.

Because scansion of the verse is so emphasized in actor training programs, a standard question is: Do you "meter out" the lines? Do you count out the iambic pentameter lines to discover extra beats as well as regularized beats?

It's the simplest thing in the world—daDUH daDUH daDUH daDUH daDUH. You are told that will tell you exactly where the emphasis should sit. More often, I find that the *verb* is almost always the word with the most emphasis and then the noun following hot on the heels of the *verb*. So I use meter only if I'm lost.

I find myself less wedded to metrical accuracy as I get on. It's absolutely supportive—you bounce along on top of the text almost like a trampoline. But as to getting worried if there's a foot missing—no, I don't.

Pennell researched the question of the punctuation of Shakespeare's text—specifically whether or not an actor should pay any attention to it—with meticulous interest. His conclusion was pragmatic, informed, yet demonstrated an understanding of acting as a creative art:

In the old days, I used to go through the script with Wite-Out [a liquid erasing fluid], but I don't have to do that anymore. Working in the library, I realized that there were (for any given text) from eight to fifteen versions of editors' opinions. This meant we were working from a stacked deck and often from misinformation. A comma in one version became a colon in another, or worse— even when scholars were working from the same folio or quarto edition!

The danger of *receiving* other people's punctuation is that you try and fit other people's thoughts into your noggin. Your thought process may be a word short or a half line longer, but it should be idiosyncratic to you.

Neil Freeman is a very fine scholar who has an interest in this, and he gave me a tutorial once and infuriated me so with the didactic nature of what he was saying that it sent me straight to the library.

I don't really feel you can go through life accepting all the traditional readings.

There was a moment in the epic, bustling 1994 production of *Cyrano de Bergerac* when an actor entered the stage, his back to the audience. The audience became calm, quiet, intrigued. Soon the presence of de Guiche (played by Pennell) commanded complete attention by saying nothing at all. He explains this technique:

The biggest weakness of our young actors is that they don't understand how to help the director create *focus* onstage. You can learn to *keep still* and allow focus to happen. Listen to your fellow actor intently. Help the audience focus where they should be looking or listening.

Whether one plays the play traditionally or in a more contemporary way, you come to a point where you shout and use so much muscle that you can't hear the give-and-take that sits under the text because you're too loud and have the volume at highest pitch, which obliterates all the detail you should be giving. One of the things Robin Phillips kept working on was making a statement about the *state of classical acting*. A lot of our production of *King John* was about speaking at a very naturalistic level, almost as I am now, but maintaining the same strength of thought I'm giving now. Once learned, it helps to focus an audience better because they attend to *what* you say, not *how* you are saying it.

Pennell made the point about the huge difference between personal preparation and role preparation:

When I was very young, I used to go onstage in the middle of telling a joke backstage. Now I need preparation time.

I start preparing for a role when I get up in the morning, because it takes me all day to get ready to invest the character with everything I've got. I've trained in tai chi to get myself centered and to improve my concentration. Concentration should allow you to be a hurricane onstage without destroying your calm. In Mary Renault's *Mask of Apollo*, the Greek actor sat for half an hour before the play began, staring at the mask he would wear onstage. My staring into the mirror for ten minutes before I go onstage is necessary for me.

On a larger life scale, I would say go to college first, because university will teach you to *read*. Then go train. After that, one's vocal and physical equipment can only be developed by the challenge of work with live audiences.

A healthy sense of humor and a sense of balance pervaded Pennell's accumulation of knowledge. He advocated keeping scholarly revelations in perspective:

> There is the *Variorum* edition of *Hamlet* that has a line of dialogue at the top of the page and the rest of the *entire* page is footnotes. I used to read it solemnly in my one-man show. Especially the academics would roll on the floor—without realizing they were looking at themselves in the Big Mirror (the "mirror up to nature").
>
> I got ready to open in *Hamlet* in a state of absolute terror. To take my mind off it, I decided to go back and read all the notes in the *Variorum* for the scenes that I wasn't in. I got to "Go, get . . . me a stoup of liquor"—I looked halfway down the page and I saw "Go get thee to Yaughan and fetch me a stoup of liquor (V.i.59)." Well, I'd read a historical account about this line—apparently, Yaughan was the fellow who ran the pub across the street from the stage door at the Globe theater. It was as if Shakespeare had stretched his hand across four hundred years and said, "What are you worrying about? I was writing *commercials*, for God's sake!" I had a large drink and went to bed.

I knew an actor who performed with Ben Greet's company in Stratford-upon-Avon. He went out for a drive one day and got hopelessly lost and came upon two men. The actor asked the men for directions back to Stratford, and then he asked them about their work. The thick-set hedges in England were made by cutting the hazel twigs in half on a slant-cut through the stem and then bending it and winding it in with other hazel twigs. The man said, "Yessir, that's what we do, sir, he and I work together near thirty year now. *He rough-hews them, and I shapes their ends.*" Here was a stage image [found in *Hamlet*, "There's a divinity that shapes our ends, rough-hew them how we will," V.ii.10–11] wedded directly to the earth and not available in most of the scholarly books.

The actor–director relationship changes radically from play to play. Although most people think the director simply tells the actor what to do, the process doesn't happen that way. Pennell felt that the director should induce and encourage the actor to give the best performance an actor is capable of:

There are some directors who are prepared to listen to what you have to say (as opposed to telling you what they think the script says) and to use your ideas in the production. There are others with whom you might not want to discuss the internal life of the character because they just don't work on that level or they have the play thought out in their own terms.

One thing I should like to say is that Robin Phillips has had more effect on me than any other director in my career. He's shaped my thinking more, and I think he's made me the actor I am today. I worked with him during a very important segment of my life, when I was moving out of the juveniles into the leading-man roles. He was here and available to talk to, and that was helpful to me.

Robin had that wonderful quality—as Marshall McLuhan said about computers in *The Global Village*—that they knew the an-swers but they didn't know the questions. Robin always knows the questions. He wants utterly everything you could give, wanted to talk about every detail, and would facilitate because he knows what's inside you. He waits like a rabbit with ears up, sees it, and grabs it. You get a constant feeding from him. To the other extreme of someone who says, "Go stage left or walk stage right" but who doesn't get in the way. Consequently, what comes out is absolutely unimpeded and uninterrupted. If it's right, then you're in very good shape. But you *can* be wrong.

Pennell liked another Stratford director, John Hirsch, one with a lightness of being despite years of hard living:

> I do have to mention John Hirsch because I miss him still. I did my best work with him—that sounds awful—I mean, work I was relatively satisfied with. Hirsch was all the things Robin was not. You know, you can go for either the heart or the head in a theater production, and Robin absolutely goes for the heart all the time.
>
> John came in from the world of Bruno Bettelheim, lost his family in the Holocaust, walked and sold himself throughout Europe to buy bread. When we did *Tempest*, we had the most astonishing series of images thrown at us, all kinds of craziness mixed with ideas from the classical European theater—from Bergman's *Magic Flute* to psychiatrist Vivian Rakoff from Toronto. I just loved Hirsch. He made me laugh a lot.
>
> There was humor in Robin, too—who was so knotted at the throat with Edwardian ideas and very controlled. It was extraordinary. They both came from such different places, and yet their demands were very much the same.

Although Pennell was a private man, he talked about his craft with selected friends in the theater. He felt that exploring ideas with other bright minds enhanced his thought processes and his performances:

> I worked with Maggie Smith for about four years, and she gave me a lot. If someone in the audience coughed, Maggie would automatically repeat the word that might have gotten obscured.

There was that famous statement of hers that if you didn't laugh, you'd cry. Comedy, she said, arises from the need to disguise the pain. It comes from the place that is informed by the unbearable pain of living and of relationships. It's skating along on top of the thinnest possible ice, so that at any moment it can tip into a tragic dimension, but it never does. A little like [William] Hutt going on and on [in the performance of *A Long Day's Journey*] to Mary about how she can go to any sanitarium she wants, he will pay for it, all she has to do is choose. Within *reason*. That's the brilliance of Bill's performance, apart from its reined-in quality in walking that delicate edge—that he *shares* the play so beautifully with Martha Henry.

In 1981 I bought an early edition of *Orlando* in Charing Cross Road when I was doing *Virginia* in London. An old gray envelope with a 1942 New York postmark fell out, typed on an old Underwood. It said, "Dear Miss Lust: I am writing to inform you that my husband has been unwell so he has been unable to read *Orlando* by Virginia Woolf as he is working on another project. Yours sincerely, Carlotta O'Neill." Written when O'Neill was working on the last draft of *Long Day's Journey*. This was the perfect opening-night gift for Martha Henry this season, for all my happy years of working with her.

Another actor I talk to is Brian Bedford—I feel utterly open and at peace to discuss anything at all. When Janet Wright and I were doing *King John* last year (she played Eleanor), we got into an awful lot of stuff I wouldn't normally talk to anyone about, because I trust her implicitly. She's the best kind of actress because she holds nothing back.

The other person an actor talks to a lot is the designer, who puts the finishing touches on your characterization. I discussed more what I felt about the play with Desmond Heeley than I did with Michael Langham [the director] during *Measure for Measure*. At Stratford, you are working with the very best people and the design concept is interactive and partnered.

From the center of this actor emerges very contemplative ideas about his art. Pennell thought of his profession as a personal journey as well as a historical context. As he encountered (or reencountered) a stage role, he had obviously grown and changed; consequently, his base of experience had altered. His statements reflect the ultimate byplay between his own personality and preparing to play a role:

> Yesterday, when I was driving home from the lake, I was listening to *CBC Arts Tonight* on the radio. Every time you hear a poet or a novelist, you hear about their memoirs. What are memoirs? They are autobiographical, but they are not actually autobiography. I think acting is a memoir. It's a series of reflections on your life and on what happens to you.
>
> Occasionally, I get to play the same parts again or be in plays I've already acted in. It's always amazing to me that the roles and the plays are quite, quite different from how I remembered them. People ask if it is easy to play the same role a second time, and no, it's just as hard, because the plays change, never stay still, constantly move. They're living.
>
> The fascinating thing about acting is that it's always too late. By the time you're ready to play Romeo, you're too old; by the time you're ready to play Hamlet, you're certainly too old. There is a wonderful line in Eliot's *Four Quartets*: "Trying to learn to use words, and every attempt / Is a wholly new start, and a different kind of failure / Because one has only learnt to get the better of words / For the thing one no longer has to say, or the way in which / One is no longer disposed to say it." I can think of no more accurate statement about acting than that.[4]

The following section focuses on a single role that Pennell played. In the season of 1993, he accepted the challenge of a work not performed very often, *King John*. The production became a twentieth-century benchmark for that play. Directed by Robin Phillips, it was set at the turn of the century with an Edwardian design concept using World War I uniforms and evening dress, telling a story of royal posturing over teacups and brandy snifters. Phillips used signature directing techniques, including minimalistic sets, slow-motion freeze-framed battle scenes, electronically enhanced stage whispers, and elegant period costumes—a powerful antiwar statement that made the script relevant to modern audiences by describing the fragile peace shaped by jostling power brokers.

Shakespeare's King John has usurped the throne from his elder brother, whose young son Arthur threatens the legitimacy of John's reign. Eleanor, John's mother—played by Janet Wright in the production—is his ballast and adviser. In this relationship, Pennell found a key to the development of the character:

> Robin's image was Queen Mary and an amalgamation of the tragically flawed weaknesses of the Duke of Windsor (Wallis Simpson's husband) and George VI—George with his crippling stutter and the duke with his aversion to command. Part of it was about communication—the bravery of it but the inability to do it. George went on the radio during World War II even though he hated to.
>
> I had an image from childhood. I was actually in the Mall in London, just opposite Clarence House (the Queen Mum's residence), when George VI was mourned. Groups of us, families with children, watched the procession from Buckingham Palace to Westminster Abbey. The horses came by with the gun carriage carrying this tiny little coffin.
>
> Queen Mary had been ill and was not with the cortege. As the gun carriage went up the Mall, the doors of the central balcony door opened, this figure stepped out (with the toque and egret), and, just as the coffin passed, she dropped a deep curtsy and went back in. It was one of the most moving things I've ever seen— literally the history of whatever the royal houses were. *King John* is the recognition by the mother of the powerful figure of her son. But the son *is king*.
>
> A good deal of Janet's (playing Eleanor) and my interaction was about that, a woman not wanting to give up her ability to manipulate, but at the same time she loves her son and wants him to succeed. Janet played that duality exactly right. She reminds him that the military power of England, not his questionable right to succeed to the crown, keeps him in power. "Didn't I tell

you . . . ," she says, and he says, "Leave me alone." John's subtext
is "Silence, Mother, and stop interfering!"

In the Tom Patterson Theatre, with the audience so close on
that in-the-round stage, there is a monitor constantly operating
inside my head running on free play and coming and going on
its own. I'm not conscious of it, but the camera in the monitor is
checking the audience constantly, moving, coughing, and watching their eyes.

Pennell talked about how Phillips's directing helped to find an emotional response to a delicate performance situation. Here, he is, in
essence, probing the wound. King John's mother, Eleanor, was one of
his military commanders, and in IV.ii, he learns that she has died:

> At the top of the scene, there is a long discussion with those vacil-
> lating nobles, Pembroke and Salisbury, who want young Arthur
> set free. Into the midst of this comes Hubert, whom John has just
> spoken to about the murder of Arthur. John is terribly uneasy as
> the nobles exit: "They burn in indignation. I repent. / There is no
> sure foundation set on blood, / No certain life achiev'd by others'
> death." Next, the messenger comes with Eleanor's death: "My liege,
> her ear is stopp'd with dust." Finally, he's alone. Overwhelming
> grief washes over him.
>
> We worked on this in a rehearsal hall with heavy black curtains.
> It was the first time off book, and toward the end of a long, dark,
> blustery day, Robin said, "I want everybody to leave except those
> in this scene." He pulled the curtains and turned the lights out.
> The actors remaining did just the voices, and once their part was
> spoken, they left. When we got to the Messenger's exit, I was in
> the room, except for Robin and the stage manager, entirely by
> myself in darkness. What happened is that I completely went.
> I broke down, I lost it [here, his voice trembles]. We didn't talk
> about it, but that's the way I played it from then on.
>
> Robin wanted this sense of a public obligation constantly pull-
> ing at John and never being able to expose a moment of emotion
> because you are always being watched. By myself, the grief rushed

in because it had been completely checked and reined in. There was no build. I had a long cross to a chair—all this on a short line with no beats to complete it: "My mother dead!"

Robin never allows you to think emotionally until you get to the point when you *can*. I do my best work for him, but we rarely discuss it. He simply says, "That's fine," and we go on.

Pennell talked about using one's own perspective and one's own personal materials to get inside a complicated character:

I understand all of King John's weaknesses because I have all of them myself and have probably indulged most of them. He is frail, and never for one moment do I *not* have sympathy with him. My job was to inform the audience that they must empathize. In all the histories, he is the man who is uppermost a mirror of humanity.

There's a sermon in that wonderful *Beyond the Fringe* parody, do you know that? Where he says, "Life is like a can of sardines— there's always a little bit left in the corner. Do you have a little bit in the corner of your life? I know I do in mine." It's very funny, but very true.

Pennell's narration of the death of John shows the actor using his life experience to inform characterization, a constant maxim in his approach to a role:

It's very hard for me to talk about this *because* . . . [Pennell never finished this statement.]

At the point where John says, "O cousin, thou art come to set mine eye!," I think the boat is leaving. John had been waiting for the Bastard because he's someone John genuinely loved. They knew one another pretty well. The Bastard had gone from being a cocky opportunist to one who decided to be constant.

More important, John is already starting to return to the land. All the history plays share an absolute passion for the island, a physical longing for each part of it. For example, the samphire gathering in

Lear—such a simple image but so accurate if you've eaten them—they're really rather good. There's something about little bits of stone and rock and leaf and earth that John constantly touches.

He begins with the image of fever and fire, "so hot a summer . . . my bowels crumble up." Then he sails into an extraordinary description of the northern part of England, straight up the Pennine Chain. He speaks of dying and going out into those curlew-haunted wilds with only low-down trees and that coolness and freedom and sense of height and air you get: "Let my kingdom's rivers take their course / Through my burned bosom; nor entreat the north / To make his bleak winds kiss my parched lips / And comfort me with cold. I do not ask you much: / I beg cold comfort."

That deliberate sinking back into the earth, the earth that gave form to begin with, the course of nature and the inevitable rotation of ashes to ashes and dust to dust—like Eliot in the first part of *East Coker*. John sees himself as England going back into England, the king as the outward image of the spirit of England, as King Arthur was. When the Bastard comes to "heaven he knows how we will answer him," John has abnegated all worldly interest in political power.

Such great ironies in the play: the relationship with Eleanor, the accidental death of Arthur, the back-and-forth of the byzantine territorial battles. As one gets old, one realizes that the only real humor is ironic—and irony is lost upon the young. If anything is lost on the young, irony is.

In this account of Pennell's stage death, it is tempting to wonder whether he had been forewarned of his own. At the end of 1994, he rehearsed *Sleuth* in Chicago, opened the show on December 16, and two weeks later had to discontinue performing the role. He returned to Stratford, had some medical tests, and on February 16 invited his good friend Richard Monette to his farmhouse, where he lived with his woolly dog Pook, to tell the news. Six days after, he was gone.

Tributes flowed in. His good friend Robertson Davies wrote a beautiful eulogy. Colleague Martha Henry offered insight into this eventful and productive life:

Somewhere inside him, he settled the dichotomy of what he started out as, the phenomenally gorgeous, *iridescent* leading man, who then became the elder statesman of the theater. He could have been a major international star. But he chose instead a much more private surrounding at Stratford. He believed in the idea of a theatre company. His nature pointed in that direction: He wanted to contribute to something, rather than devote all his time and energy in the race to be a star. . . . I think there was a part of Nicky that wanted to hide away from the world. He didn't go to the bars or to the pubs after rehearsals. He could have gone anywhere he chose. Well, he went where he chose. That was to Stratford.[5]

However, Pennell did not ever feel that he had gone far away:

When I was young and in drama school, I did a radio show on BBC Drama with an actress called Evelyn Russell, who had been in Sir Henry Irving's company. Irving worked in his early days with William Macready, who worked with Edmund Kean. Who worked with Sarah Siddons. Who worked with David Garrick. And Garrick had worked with an actor called Hawke, whose father had been a boy player in Shakespeare's company. So that makes me only eight generations of actor away.

Which isn't long. Is it. Really.

WILLIAM HUTT AS PROSPERO IN THE 2005 PRODUCTION OF *THE TEMPEST* AT THE STRATFORD SHAKESPEARE FESTIVAL. (PHOTO BY DAVID HOU, COURTESY OF THE STRATFORD SHAKESPEARE FESTIVAL ARCHIVES)

7

William Hutt

Our Revels Now Are Ended

William Hutt was in his lifetime the premier tragedian of Canada. He announced to me, "The secret of great acting is Truth, and once you've learned how to fake that, you've made it." A man of tremendous dignity and Wildean wit, Hutt had a career that spanned the twentieth century. He witnessed the establishment of theater as a cultural force in Canada.

At his farewell performance of Prospero in the summer of 2004 on the Stratford Festival stage, he completed his career as an icon, a mentor, and colleague of the giants—notably Tyrone Guthrie and Tanya Moiseiwitsch—in establishing that gorgeous theater. All of us stood and wept during the final curtain call. No one could finesse a line or turn the hinge of a scene like Hutt. That night and most nights he played, he was master of all. He died at the age of eighty-seven in 2007.

Hutt was best known for his roles at the Stratford Festival in Ontario. Although he'd acted all over the world, he had been an associate with the festival since its inception in 1953 and both acted and directed there. Major Shakespearean parts he played include Richard II; Titus Andronicus; Pandarus; Brutus; Feste; Jacques; Banquo; Enobarus; the Duke in *Measure for Measure;* both Ford and Falstaff in *The Merry*

Wives of Windsor; Polonius, the Ghost, and First Gravedigger in *Hamlet;* and the Fool in *King Lear.* He acted the roles of Lear and Prospero three times each. He often held court in The Church, a restaurant in the center of town of Stratford, and then sailed home in a large yellow Cadillac with his name on the license plate.

The list of his non-Shakespearean classical roles was equally impressive. He performed in numerous Molières—Argan and Tartuffe, Dorante, and the title role in *L'invalide imaginaire*—as well as Thomas More, Teazle, Volpone, Khlestakov, James Tyrone, and the Chorus Leader in *Oedipus Rex.* He literally revisioned Lady Bracknell (certainly upstaging Dame Edith Evans's portrayal in London several years earlier) in *The Importance of Being Earnest,* a singular success in his career. He created the role of the lawyer in Albee's *Tiny Alice* for its first showing on Broadway. His extensive credential has placed him in London's West End, Chichester, Australia, New York, and all over the world.

Hutt was the first winner of the Tyrone Guthrie Award for Directing (at the Stratford Festival). He was given the Governor General's Lifetime Achievement Award and was named a Companion of the Order of Canada (the Canadian equivalent of a knighthood) and of the Order of Ontario. He won the Sam Wanamaker Award in 1994. He held honorary doctorates from the Universities of Western Ontario, Ottawa, Guelph, and Toronto, as well as from Trinity College and McMaster University. His extensive career in television garnered him Genie and ACTRA awards, including the Prix Anik from the Canadian Broadcasting Company.

Although Hutt acted sporadically in high school, he was mostly enamored of the movies and would often skip school to watch glamorous stars on the silver screen. He eventually enlisted and won a Military Medal in World War II as a medic, aiding soldiers under fire during the invasion of Italy. Those duties acquainted him with death at a young age. He acknowledged those experiences as creating a well of resources from which to draw diverse characters and to develop a far-ranging emotional arsenal.

In the military, Hutt saw professional theater in London. He was attracted to the pulse of the city and mesmerized by the performances.

The gracious old theater buildings with plush seats, gilded ceilings, and chandeliers drew him into the magic of illusion.

He made a bargain with himself. He would get a degree from the University of Toronto and then give himself five years to establish an acting career. If he hadn't made it by the end of this time, he would "stop knocking his head against a wall."[1] Amazingly, by that time, he'd added nearly fifty parts to his credential. Most of his roles in college were at the Hart House Theatre in Toronto, loosely connected with the university, where artistic director Robert Gill introduced a generation of young Canadian actors to the rigors of theater work.

Hutt's most intensive training was with director Amelia Hall at the Canadian Repertory Theatre, who drew into her circle not only Hutt but William Shatner, Christopher Plummer, Donald Davis, Ted Fellows, Richard Easton, Eric House, David Gardner, and George McCowan—names that formed the early ranks of actors in regional rep in Canada.[2] Hutt learned about the constancy of the job, being in rehearsal most of the day and performing most evenings. The cast was expected to show up at rehearsal with lines learned and ready for work.

Here, the seeds of Hutt's brand of nationalism sprouted. He'd done his early work with professionals who later, as he colorfully put it, "hemorrhaged" across the border into America, a hungry giant that swallowed the blood of Canadian talent with the lure of money and fame:

> I began to sense that anybody who had any potential at all simply disappeared south of the forty-ninth parallel. The cultural history of this country would be bleak for years. . . . Along came Stratford and began to offer me roles that were challenging and interesting, coupled with the fact that I never really wanted a motion-picture career—I just really loved the stage.
>
> All those things combined in my mind to say that I wanted to stay in my country. I wanted to somehow prove that you could become part of the international scene without having to leave Canada. That made me confront all those people who constantly said that to *be* anybody in this country, you've got to leave. That makes no sense to me.[3]

Hutt contemplated the drain on the artistic pool of Canada not only as it applied to its cultural profile, but also to the national character of the place: "I remember my shock when Gretzky [the Canadian hockey player] went to Los Angeles. . . . We are very cavalier with our national treasures. . . . My God, is that what this country is all about—we develop treasures and just sell them off!"[4]

He admitted to another aggravating fact about theater, a very legitimate complaint about not documenting stage artists' work:

> Whenever a great production emerges, perfect in all its aspects in terms of casting, designing, directing—why isn't that performance routinely filmed for public consumption, as the 1975 *Importance of Being Earnest* ought to have been? Why isn't it preserved on film or television for posterity? Why can't the money be found when it is available for other popular events?

Hutt vigorously promotes "the passing on of Canadian history, reminding people constantly that we are Canadians, not Americans, not Britons, is paramount. When what we have done is unique, we often don't realize that history is being made!"[5] His was an important and persistent voice, and he was certainly correct that benchmark productions need to be recorded for posterity far more often than they are.

Regarding the business of acting, Hutt continually spoke about the play being the first guide to characterization. He believed in exploring the character within the play's circumstances: "If I do any outside research at all, it is very, very minor. I might research the period in which the director has decided to put the play—skim the history of the period. That's about all. You cannot act anything more than what is on the page."

His primary principle was that character is generated from the actor's own personality, the qualities that make the actor individual:

> You cannot divorce yourself from yourself. That is impossible. These people who say, and most of them are amateurs—"Oh, I

just felt so different—it was a totally different me." That just simply doesn't happen. It's all pie-in-the-sky imagination. What in fact happens is this—I will talk to you, I will talk to my closest friend, my minister, my butcher, the paperboy, and to each one of these I will have a slightly different attitude, but I am the same person. . . . To expand that into the field of acting, you're the same person in a different set of circumstances. So I suppose if there's any plan, it's to understand the conditions in which this character lives.

I cannot pretend that I am not Bill Hutt onstage, but so long as I wrap myself in the experience and illuminate the audience that it is a different set of circumstances, to *them* I become a different person. You cannot perform Lear, Timon of Athens, Hamlet. All you can do is *experience* those roles.[6]

Hutt had achieved that stage of mastery where he knew that the text would play itself if he was true to it. He described this act in a mystical way, claiming that it was impossible to assimilate until one has experienced it:

There's one thing first and foremost, about acting as an act of *surrender*. Most actors, in fact all actors, have very high-profile egos—basically because they don't have any ego at all. If they have spent any length of time on the stage, over a period of years they learn how to give in to the demands of the playwriting, the character, the director, and the designer. That ultimately means that your own core can dissipate, and in order to protect that, you develop a pretty high-profile ego.

Acting is a beatific surrender of one's self, not unwilling. Once that has been achieved, you can simply let the role possess you so that you are the role, the role is you. *Being the same person in a different set of circumstances* is a very superficial way of explaining what I am trying describe in a deeper, religious sense.

It is the most difficult lesson for any actor to learn, because actors feel they're giving themselves up for a period of time—

the self that they have searched so long to find from the age of twelve.

Then they recover it after the show is over. Certainly with me—I don't want to meet people very much then. Not because I don't like them, but because I just want to recoup myself.

Hutt also believed in creating a concentrated focused attention emanating from the actor, rather than using excess movement and gestures. American politician Ed Muskie once said, "I never speak unless it improves on silence." Hutt heard this remark, felt it was filled with great wisdom, and applied the words to acting. He doesn't believe in moving onstage unless it improves on stillness.[7]

You don't need much movement. In human behavior, the more emotional the moments you have in life, the stiller they are. Fear is still. Even death. You simply watch it very, very quietly. You don't roar or beat yourself against the wall. You weep quietly.

Also, I believe, amongst many things about acting, that *it's the art of being private in public.*

This singular quality is one of the hallmarks of masterful acting, often described as *acting in repose,* creating a pool of attention so highly centered in the actor that the audience is simply drawn to the character as it awaits his responses. Although the trait takes years to learn, Hutt had developed it, along with the use of the pause, to its quintessence. Hutt personifies the quality constantly, not only in characters such as Hamlet's Ghost and the Duke in *Measure for Measure* but, surprisingly enough, in his portrayal of Lady Bracknell:

I'm not just talking about pauses. . . . In early rehearsals, I pay a great deal of attention to other people—to see what they are doing. Every play—even if one is playing the leading role—is an interactory thing. You have to find out how the other characters are acting or reacting or behaving, which will automatically gauge for you what they are doing.

It is so in life.[8]

Hutt told the story of a newspaper critic who brought his young daughter to *The Importance of Being Earnest*, where Hutt's Lady Bracknell reigned. The girl remarked, "If I didn't know that was a woman, I would think it was a man." Hutt felt that was an extraordinary compliment. Later on, the father wrote and said he had only one criticism of the performance—Hutt had used his fan too much. Interestingly, Hutt never carried a fan in the production, only a handbag.

Hutt had a great deal to say about speaking the speech in Shakespeare. First of all, he did not believe in being overly attentive to the punctuation used in the playscripts:

> People do not speak in terms of commas, periods, exclamation marks, colons, semicolons. They speak in terms of thought processes.
>
> Now, what I have just stated, if I put it down on paper, would probably have a lot of commas in it somewhere, but it's all one thought. So the first thing I do in attacking any speech, including a speech of Shakespeare, is to divide it up into thoughts. What is a complete thought? A complete thought is, for example, "O, that this too, too solid flesh would melt, / Thaw, and resolve itself into a dew! / Or that the everlasting had not / Fix'd his canon 'gainst self slaughter!" (*Hamlet, Prince of Denmark*, I.ii.130–31) That line is all one thought.
>
> So, if the thought process is clear and you can speak to the end of the thought, the rhythm of the speech will simply be there. Another example, "O what a rogue and peasant slave am I! / Is it not monstrous, that this player here, / But in a fiction, a dream of passion, / Could force his soul so to his own conceit / That from her working, all his visage wann'd; / Tears in his eyes, distraction in's aspect, / A broken voice, and his whole function suiting / With forms to his conceit? And all for nothing!" (*Hamlet*, II.ii.502–4). All one thought. And whoever plays that should be able to say it all in one breath. Most actors can't. You have to be able to breathe Shakespeare like you breathe an opera. Then the rhythm will take care of itself. You don't have to beat them over the head with the iambic pentameter. *No.*

I don't pay that much attention to the beat. Maybe I have a natural sense of music. If I am on the *wrong* beat, I will know it. For instance, one would never say, "Oh, that *this* too, too solid flesh would melt. . . ." As if Hamlet is saying. "I don't care about anybody else's flesh—I just want *this* flesh to melt." Then you know you've robbed the verse—that's not what the line means. Hamlet's not thinking in comparative terms during that speech.

Also, particularly with Shakespeare's more well-known soliloquies—the best way to speak them, I have always felt, is to get into them before the audience can.

Hutt was adamant about not cutting the lines you are given (most professional companies do some cutting in the text):

You need every word that you have. *You need it.* That is a very important lesson to be learned by a lot of young actors. If there are three fies, then you need three fies, not two. Fie, fie, *fie*.

Also four *howls*—like we find in *King Lear*. Four. So many people think they don't need them because they don't know what to do with them. Instead of trying to find the reason, they *omit* words! They don't try hard enough.

One thing that Hutt was very, very precise about is finding the most important word in a speech or passage.

I pay a great deal of attention to that—I can't say it often enough because, well, it does make a difference. To a certain degree it's the same thing as emphasis. But it's not a vocal trick. It starts out with my seeking what I think is the operative word. Early on in rehearsals I will probably use that word (that I have originally chosen) and then, as perhaps my thinking gets deeper about a particular speech, I may find that the thought is better expressed by hitting another word rather than the first word I chose. There are some things that are really quite obvious, and emphasizing the right word helps the audience to realize how much cleaner and clearer the conundrum is, right from the beginning.

> An example: if you were playing Lady Macbeth and at the line, "Who would have thought the old man to have had so much blood in him," what do you think the operative word is there? What would you guess?
>
> Most actresses head for the word "blood." Some head for "so much." I have never heard anybody head for the right one. Because look at the image. He goes into the room. Where is the blood? It's all over, so in order to illuminate the horror of the image, "Who would have thought the old man to have had so much blood *in* him."

Few actors highlight this extremely pivotal technique: most lines turn on a word or phrase, and it is paramount that the performer finds a way to convey the crux of meaning to an audience.

Hutt's acting career took a leap forward when he encountered Robin Phillips. Phillips was a student at the Bristol Old Vic in 1959 and watched Hutt do one of his earliest versions of James Tyrone, though students were not allowed to mix with the professionals beyond attending the final dress rehearsals. Years after the two became acquainted, the director recounted how indelible the memory was.

When Phillips (as artistic director) arrived at Stratford, he felt it was a bit like entering a theater from the past. He'd arrived in the mid-1970s, and Shakespearean acting particularly had turned a first corner at a time when Shakespeare began to appear on film more frequently (more realistic performances were demanded by the close-up camera). There was another shift in the 1980s when a revolution in theater fare demanded still more realism in classical acting. Phillips worked with individual members of the company, suggesting alterations, opening alternatives, nudging good performances into great. He made positive and necessary changes in acting styles and brought considerable intellectual clout to the repertory. Hutt attributes his self-esteem to Phillips: "I never thought that I had a natural talent. I thought for a long time that whatever talent I had was manufactured, that I wasn't really an instinctive actor. . . . It wasn't until Robin came into the picture . . . and told me he wanted me to get back to the simplicity of my own instincts."

Hutt delivered a compliment about Phillips that many other actors echo: "I think Robin inspires freedom within the artist, which then releases discipline." Although Hutt had had a steady and substantial career up to the time Phillips arrived in 1975, he reckoned it by the years before he worked with Phillips and the years after:

> I was like a lot of actors, could have gone along and done the same old thing that I'd been doing for years. I've seen very fine actors who basically never alter their technique or their approach to a part. They never, ever change, even though the lines change.
>
> Robin came along and made me rethink all my old habits, techniques, mental and emotional processes. He wasn't implying that none of it worked. He was just saying one could find a different or a new or a more exciting way to do things.
>
> He introduced me to the *continuing future*, even though some actors say, "I don't have any future now." A lot was fulfilled. I discovered a greater depth. Things that I took away from Robin are constantly applicable to whatever part I play now: a greater flexibility of thought, a broader horizon of emotional responses, and a greater security. Confidence.
>
> They are milestones. Ultimately it means—however simplistic this may sound—the stage is my home. It's as if it were a different room in my own house.

Hutt emphasized that this does not dismiss his thirteen splendid years with Michael Langham or any of the other directors he'd worked with during his career. He had learned so much in the years before Robin came that he was quite well established in the craft of acting, certainly enough to go on performing in the way he always had. Yet Robin advised, "Don't just hold on to it because it worked in the past." And Hutt listened: "Perhaps it was a desire on my part that made me move ahead, go on to the next platform, another horizon."

Hutt worked with Phillips almost as long as he'd worked with Langham. He preferred a director who processes a great deal with the actors:

The more a director talks, if you listen carefully enough—98 percent of them just gabble, but 2 percent will drop a gem. Phillips was wonderful at talking. There, you understand, circumstances alter cases. You develop a shorthand between the actor and the director. For example, he would say to me, "Bill, that's a hairpin line." It means "take the pressure off the line." It all started from my work as Lady Bracknell fiddling with her hairpins. She was reacting to a line just spoken: "I hear her hair has turned quite gold from grief." She says, "It certainly has changed its colour. From what cause I, of course, cannot say."

Phillips meant that Hutt should say the line offhandedly, less staged, more laden with subtext than with pronouncement. "In other words, think of something else while you are saying it." It was a signal between the two artists, a metaphor for less conscious technique.

Hutt told the story of Phillips returning to monitor the 1988 *King Lear* after it opened:

He walked into my dressing room and said, "Bill, take your subconscious onstage tonight." I said, "Okay." He was telling me that my subconscious mind was more interesting than my conscious mind. My performance was becoming too self-conscious—of the effects that I was making.

Robin seems to know instinctively what the actor wants to do *almost before* he actually does it. He has a wonderful way of freeing the actor and then disciplining the speech or the gesture, allowing the actor to express what is inside, and then focusing it for him. So that the freedom does not become rampant or licensed.

The role Hutt had a great deal of experience with, next to James Tyrone in O'Neill's *Long Day's Journey*, was the ultimate paean to age, *King Lear*. Although most actors wait a lifetime to play it, Hutt began in 1962. He emphasized that one must understand the power of monarchy to understand the dynamics of Lear, that the king has absolute command over another's life or death:

The problem with the play is that very first scene. Audiences find it unbelievable. Well, I don't think there *is* a reason—Shakespeare hadn't studied Freud. He just said, "I'm going to put a king on the stage who decides to give up his kingdom on the strength of three daughters giving the best answer to 'Which one of you loves me most?'" In our analytical age, everybody says, why does this stupid old son of a bitch do *that*!

Even to contemplate the game is either the first hint of senility or of faculties disappearing. As well as a very strange mind—an unpredictable mind.

For each production of *Lear*, Hutt had to learn different thought processes, because each was directed by a different director for a different era with a unique design. His first was called the "Eskimo Lear." Hutt performed it in his early forties in 1961, with David Gardner directing:

Instead of champing and snorting horses, wind-blown heath and deer, there was barking dogs, ice, and seals. The characters wore heavy furs, hides, parkas, and mukluks. Bones, beads, and bright Inuit patterns were their special adornments. It was a chill, frost-bitten landscape at the top of the world.[9]

Scene designer Herbert Whittaker described his intentions:

We went for the cruelties and ferocities within the figures—the kind of society where life was not important. Food was torn apart with the teeth. The final Cordelia moments were on a triangular piece, and the lighting was such that you had the feeling of an ice floe. . . . At the end and when the lights dimmed, it was almost as if that thing floated off—which was an Eskimo mode of death.[10]

For a long time in rehearsal, Hutt did not emit the "howl" lines in the script (V.iii.255, "Howl, howl, howl, howl! O, you are men of stones!") until he'd gotten the part thoroughly under his belt:

He opened his massive jaws, threw back his head, and produced the type of sound that could freeze marrow. . . . The sound and pain were so bare that after he had done the long, slow, arching noises of a mighty heart bursting, everybody else onstage felt awkward—almost embarrassed to be exposed to such agony.[11]

Although this was an engrossing performance, reviews read as if the design concept engulfed the acting. Nonetheless, the production made an extensive tour of the Midwest and the eastern United States to great acclaim. Audiences were extraordinarily moved. Hutt himself felt that he was not entirely successful—in fact, to be so at his age then would have been nothing short of miraculous. King Lear is one of those roles where, once an actor is old enough to understand it, the traditional high-decibel performance is beyond his physical prowess. If an actor plays it in early middle age, he has not yet attained the life experience to understand the complete physical, mental, and spiritual transformations.

Hutt was in his sixties the second time he assayed *Lear.* The production was grand, stunningly beautiful, and filled with an emotional wallop that was almost too large for the play. Resembling a full-scale pageant or epic film, Annena Stubbs's set and costume designs soared right out of the sweep and dynamism of the art displayed just five years before at Montreal's Expo '67, clearly twentieth century but classic and powerful at once. Long cloaks of sweeping red leather swathed the principals, and soaring, cosmic headdresses of futuristic design adorned the women's heads. You saw those costumes before you tuned into the play itself, wondering at the cost and the workmanship. Director David Williams elected to use the full text of the play.

The cast, as well, reflected a pinnacle moment in Stratford's history, with some of the best and the brightest performers at the peak of their careers in the major roles. Goneril and Regan were played by veterans Pat Galloway and Carole Shelley; Kent and Gloucester by Mervyn Blake and Powys Thomas; the Fool was Edward Atienza, who seemed to mirror Lear's downward spiral into madness.

Herbert Whittaker detailed the munificence of the production, giving credit although he knew that the production choices belonged to a fading era:

> It filled us with nostalgia to recognize the old Stratford style. It has many characteristics; the dash and dispatch of exits, the unexpectedness of entrances, the crash of Louis Applebaum's off-stage music . . . the histrionic mannerisms of sudden chorus reaction, eccentric gaits, sudden changes in pitch . . . the superb properties . . . even to the Guthrie banners—all are here set in the service of the second coming of Lear.
>
> . . . Perhaps [Lear's] rages are too much for us at first, but they strengthen the line of descent the actor is following.[12]

The traditional production was enlivened by selected moments of sheer brutality, like the moment someone squished Gloucester's eyes, "vile jelly" on the floor. The acting was close to the declamatory style that younger directors would later work to humanize, perhaps a last, fitting farewell to the rhetorical mode of performance in which actors "made points" (stage business accompanied by bursts of applause). Actors were rarely still onstage and played fantastical tricks with the voice.

Hutt described it thus:

> In 1972, I believed that Lear came onstage to die. At that time, I felt the play was the longest death scene ever written. So that in terms of orchestration, it would start very high and then slowly diminish to the final death scene where there's nothing left but just him, just the bones, just the voice, just the thought.

Hutt again expressed some dissatisfaction with his work but spoke with a greater sense of fulfillment about the production of 1988. The 1967 Lear was very different:

> [It] was high fashion, high decibel level for all of us, full of rage, and all that was relative to the *space* [i.e., the monumental Festival

Theater stage]. Whereas in 1988, on the more intimate Patterson stage [which was closely surrounded by audience], the space was entirely different and dictated the nature of the production. The heath scene worked so much better, because you could be almost inaudible as you talked to *yourself.*

Thought, *focused thought,* has the energy to be *communicated* and *heard.* I know I am capable of letting the audience know what I am thinking.

Robin Phillips directed this final Lear, and that meant a different artistic sensibility at work; in Phillips's case, a modern vision and cerebral muscle were brought to bear upon the text. Hutt described the differences between the 1988 production and the prior one:

It's a different family, different lights, different sense, different director, and a different venue.

I'd said to Robin, "I want to do this Lear with your Young Company because there is such an enormous amount of talent in the group." They were all too young for the parts, but it didn't matter to me—I wanted to work with them. I also said I wanted to do Lear in a small space. I'm tired of Lears coming out and screaming at the top of their voices, even my own. By the time he gets to the end of the heath scene, "Blow winds and crack your cheeks," the only thing he can possibly do is orchestrally fade away in a very slow decrescendo.

In the middle of the production, Robin gave notes to the cast. He told Hutt:

"By the way, Bill, you're too young, you're too young, you're too young; you're too loud, you're too loud, you're too loud—do you get the point?" He was absolutely right. He told me during rehearsal, "I think Lear is more of a character part than you think he is. You are playing him too robust, too much in charge of things." Which is how I played him earlier, as a man of enormous strength and enormous command—he goes across the stage saying, "I'm going to do this and do that. Now tell me how much you love me." This later one is a total reversal.

The approach to the 1988 production was radically different from any other Lear seen at the festival or, indeed, anywhere. It was a new definition of the potency of this monarch, one who had the ultimate destiny of any given subject in his hands. Hutt pointed out that "If you've got that kind of power, you don't go around saying, 'Look, folks, I'm powerful.' Nor do you have to speak loudly nor move around a lot. The power is just *there*." In fact, this monarch was on the wane, at the twilight of an Edwardian reign, and showing some signs of touchiness and senility. The opening scene where he divided his kingdom among his daughters was reminiscent of a kind of parlor game that broke through the boredom and inertia of another royal family evening, the men in waistcoats and the women in glittering jewels on richly colored gowns, more femmes fatales than she-wolves. A Viennese waltz was playing in the background, and it stopped abruptly once Cordelia uttered her responses. The king's fury was leashed in, enormously restrained, and the holding back made him seem more dangerous.

The critical reception in one review was overwhelmingly complimentary to the newly wrought interpretation, praising its eloquent subtlety:

> The most . . . remarkable event of the Stratford Festival's opening week is William Hutt's King Lear. It is so beautiful it is almost beatific.
>
> The Young Company production has been staged . . . with delicacy and restraint. The effect on this most bombastic of tragedies is a revelation in the same league as the cleaning of the Sistine Chapel ceiling. It is suddenly possible to hear what the characters are saying; to greet them as fellow human beings; and to weep, as so much of the opening-night audience did on Saturday, when Cordelia and Lear are reconciled.[13]

Both director and leading actor were praised together, a signal that the production was founded on a solid collaboration and had artistic coherence:

> In Canada at any rate [nor, indeed, in the United States], there simply is nobody whose Shakespearean interpretations are of such consistently high quality.
>
> All this would be for naught, of course, without an actor of considerable stature [playing] Lear. And Phillips has William Hutt.[14]

Even though the vision of the play was more domestic and less filled with histrionic acting, the ultimate impact was just as devastating: "The achievement lies in Phillips' ability to scale down without diminishing and to make manageable what is by its very nature inexhaustible."[15] The production also demonstrated the journey in Hutt's modes of acting, replacing titanic rage with fitting nuance that complemented the contemporary realism that Phillips inserted into twentieth-century Shakespeare, where the smallest gesture was one of the most revealing.

Hutt was admired by audiences and valued colleagues. He had a reputation for helping young actors, dispensing careful advice, putting in a good word when a novice needed that essential role to get noticed. He was enormously coveted as an acting partner, not simply because one could claim fame by association, but because he was so rock-solid reliable and so generous onstage. Fellow actor Patricia Conolly played Viola in a production of *Twelfth Night* where Hutt played Feste:

> You never quite knew what was coming, so there was that sense of excitement and a little bit of danger because he worked so much *from* the moment. But at the same time, I felt completely safe on the stage. . . . I felt as though he owned that stage somehow. I felt I could drop my lines, fall down, and somehow he would make it all right. There was always a different twinkle in the eye, a different moment, or a subtle change in inflection. I always wished the scene would go on longer.[16]

In Canada, Hutt was a symbol of the country, looked up to as the grand old man of the theater, the elder statesman of the arts. He had a long and rich career, one that left room for both irony and self-fulfillment. He made a wonderfully insightful comment during an interview about *King Lear*:

> The rest of the play just simply illuminates the mind of this man. He's a bastard, he really is a stubborn bastard, and Robin Phillips said, "The audience must be and should be unsympathetic to you until you get to [the] 'O, reason not the need!' speech. There's an extraordinary clarity that comes through Lear at that moment when he is trying desperately to explain to his children that it isn't a question of need anymore. Not *need*. It is because I am who I am.[17]

The interviewer then continued, describing Hutt with a fabled remark: "With public age comes private wisdom."[18] The comment is eminently germane to one of the greats of North American theater and to Shakespearean acting.

MARTHA HENRY AS ISABELLA IN THE 1975 PRODUCTION OF
MEASURE FOR MEASURE AT THE STRATFORD SHAKESPEARE
FESTIVAL. (PHOTO BY ROBERT C. RAGSDALE, COURTESY OF THE
STRATFORD SHAKESPEARE FESTIVAL ARCHIVES)

8

Martha Henry

Who Will Believe Thee, Isabel?

During breakfast at Acrylic Dreams on Bay Street, my favorite B&B in Stratford, Ontario, I mentioned that I would be interviewing Martha Henry, first lady of the Canadian stage. The other residents chimed in, and a story emerged from each table. One was a narrative about the opening scene in the 1996 production of *Sweet Bird of Youth*, where Ms. Henry rose out of her lover's bed and wrapped herself in the velvet coverlet, a gesture dreamily described as "a sexual experience with a red bedspread." Eyes glazed over in memory in the room. We all knew it had been executed masterfully.

Martha Henry's performances have superlative detail and specificity, so it is easy to assume that every performance on her long and enviable credential has had that quality and exactness of preparation. She has played most of the major Shakespearean roles: Miranda, Lady Macduff, Lady Macbeth, Cressida, Luciana, Cordelia, Goneril, Joan la Pucelle, Viola, Olivia, Princess of France, Rosaline, Doll Tearsheet, Thaisa, Titania (twice), Helena (both in *A Midsummer Night's Dream* and *All's Well That Ends Well*), Desdemona, Lady Anne, Isabella, Rosalind, Beatrice, Lady Percy, Constance, Paulina, Volumnia—most of these at the renowned Stratford Festival in Canada.

She has acted in a number of Molière's plays, another specialty of the
Stratford repertory company, and in several performances of Chekov,
Miller, Tennessee Williams, and the other world-class playwrights
whose work the festival so successfully re-creates. A role that received
numerous accolades (next to the unforgettable Isabella in the 1975–76
Measure for Measure) is preserved on video, the ghostly and lumines-
cent Mary Tyrone in O'Neill's *Long Day's Journey into Night*.

Not only is Martha Henry a national treasure, she is a friend and
colleague of many of the other jewels in Stratford—including the late
William Hutt and Nicholas Pennell. She has acted and directed in the
major theaters in Canada, including the Shaw Festival, Theatre Calgary,
Citadel Theatre, Manitoba Theatre Centre, Theatre London, and Tar-
ragon Theatre. From 1988 to 1994 she was artistic director at the Grand
Theatre in London, Ontario, and she has accrued a long list of acting
performances on television and film throughout the United States
and Canada. She has collected several awards, including the Governor
General's Award for Lifetime Achievement in the Performing Arts, a
World Theater Award, three Geminis, five Genies, seven honorary
doctorates, and the Order of Ontario and Order of Canada.

Henry attributes the genesis of her interest in theater to a difficult
period in her childhood. Her mother was a musician and went off in the
evenings to play for jobs; at a certain point, Henry's parents were sepa-
rated and she was sent to live with her grandparents in Michigan:

> I had been uprooted, and nobody told me why. I had this feeling
> that there were things going on that I didn't know about because
> I was too dutiful and ineffectual to be brought into everybody
> else's secrets.
>
> My grandmother had a huge cedar chest in the dining room
> where she kept all kinds of blankets and, layered down, things
> from her life. One day, I came to two little thin books. I'd learned
> to read very early, so I pulled them out, and here was MARGARET
> in capital letters, and it alternated with CLARA—I remember
> how it looked to this day. I read through it and figured out that
> it was a conversation, people talking to each other. I also figured
> out that if I could be one of those people, I would know secrets,

because I could read the end of the book. I didn't know it was called a play.

Somehow, this was a door or a gateway. If I could find where this book operated, I could be one of the speakers. I had been to the movies, but I actually thought they were real and didn't know they were done with cameras. I now had the sense of having uncovered something huge that I could be part of. (Later on, I learned that the script belonged to my uncle, who had spent a year at Northwestern University learning about lighting design.)

When I was seven, I heard that the Brownies were putting on a play, so I joined, *not* to learn to camp and go into the woods, but because my mother had bought me a fairy costume. If there was a fairy in the play, surely they would have to cast me. I still remember the one line I had. Someone was supposed to ask me how to become a fairy. I answered, "You have to study your lessons and take examinations and get a certificate before you become a real fairy." To this day, I have trouble saying "get a certificate."

At one point I said to my grandmother, "It's just as though Mommy and Daddy were divorced." My grandmother called my mother and told her, "You have got to get up here and tell this child what is going on."[1]

This account foreshadows Henry's well-developed intuitive powers. In a later interview on CBC, she shared an insight: "I am consistently and constantly absorbing other people's anxieties and joys, and so those all *go in* somewhere, and I suppose they become another human being when I go on the stage."

Henry was born in Detroit and attended the nearby Kingswood School, Cranbrook. Later on, she auditioned for a place at Carnegie Tech University and got her BFA there. A year after, she entered National Theatre School in Canada.[2] Halfway through the three-year program, she was invited to do her first role at the Stratford Festival, Miranda in *The Tempest.* The founder of the school, Powys Thomas, told her to go with his blessing.

After being hired at the festival at a very young age, her career led to the true mentors of a lifetime. Actors like Hutt, Bruno Gerussi, and

John Colicos would kindly come up and take her by the elbow in the corridor and suggest various ways of dealing with Shakespeare: "They never sat me down and said, 'I'm going to give you a lesson on verse speaking,' but they might tip you off during coffee about pronunciation or stressing syllables, and eventually I'd figure it out."

Douglas Rain provided her with an unforgettable lesson in the textual foundations of Shakespeare. This remained the core of her acting process:

> I had the privilege of sitting with him once for about five or six hours while he talked about one of his roles. He was in the midst of rehearsals for Michael Langham's *King Lear*, and he was trying to figure out why Edgar falls for Edmund's trick with the letter. We were well into the play by this time (I was playing Cordelia) and he was very familiar with his part, so I said scarcely anything. I was fascinated, listening to how he worked out all this astonishing detail.
>
> Everything he talked about was in the text or grounded in the text. He was speaking in a kind of freewheeling way, saying things like, "Why does Edgar say this, and why does he say Poor Tom does that?" Who is Tom? I thought. He must be talking about when Edmund stops Edgar from going into the house. Douglas went back and forth over the situations of the two brothers' births to see if there was anything useful there.
>
> He never said anything like, "Maybe Edgar went to school when he was three." Never any of that. It was always about *just what was written in the text.* This kind of detective work—the ability to translate way beyond what was written—was something I'd never heard. I wish I had taken notes at the time, as he spoke. I realized that I had a way of reading the words and making *assumptions*, that if the text said one thing, then it kind of meant *another*. Even to this day, I am careful to catch myself inferring too much.
>
> Douglas did not do that. He looked at every word in every sentence for its own value, what it meant sitting alongside another word and in opposition to another word. Then he would look at a sentence where the same word had been used in juxtaposition

to a different *kind* of phrase. Why was the phraseology different in each of these cases? I realized he was making the character absolutely specific.

He took nothing for granted in his examination of the text. This way has served me ever since. I do it when I am directing as well as when I am acting. I break the text down literally word by word so I don't gloss over anything. Unless it is *written down*, I never say, "Oh, it must be daylight," or "There I am ruminating." If it is not absolutely found in the text, don't make an assumption. When you look for that specificity, it's amazing what opens up for you.

Henry found that her work process began to shift from one mode to another:

After spending those hours listening to him, I knew I had been *generalizing*. I'd read the text, and then alongside it I had my own narration that went along with my life up until then. (I was twenty-three and hadn't lived very much.) I also worked from movies that I'd seen—I'd trot them along side by side. I didn't realize that I was making up a story about the character based on outside premises. To suddenly see that the text alone would give me every ounce of information that I needed was a revelation.

Henry also realized that not all experiences in examining text are easy. Although she loved working with David William, she once spent two hours with him working on one line in *Twelfth Night*: "I am all the daughters of my father's house and all the brothers, too—and yet I know not" (II.iv.120–21):

Just that line. Not that scene, not those speeches, just that sentence. It was like repeating your own name over and over until it was a nonsense syllable. Eventually, some of the work we had done on it came back to me, but I was so rigid with fear and so confused trying to find out what he wanted that it went dead for me, and I couldn't incorporate it in any way. Oddly, you are grateful. I will never forget how important that line is. Some lines deserve a kind of impact because they are written in gold. They rise in the air.

Henry examines the iambic pentameter in the dialogue and uses that structural information to make decisions about how to say it:

> Also, when I work with the language, I meter out the lines. I've done a lot of it by now, so it comes easily. Yet there are places where I say, "Why am I having a problem with that? I'll look at it, ferret it out and bang it around, and then realize I have been mispronouncing something or putting the accent on the wrong syllable. Or the beat is not where I think it is—it's over *there* instead—and often the whole thing falls into place.
>
> But there are some things in Shakespeare where you have to take a deep breath and just go ahead and *do it*, even if you don't understand it. Inevitably, once you are in performance, it will all click. If you've done everything you can think of doing and it still isn't making any sense—well, Shakespeare wrote it, so there must be a rationale. You simply allow him to point out the solution in good time. I had a moment like that in *Othello*, which snapped into place after a month into performance!

Henry has such a theater trunk of experience with Shakespeare that a gift for his dialogue, even the sound and feel of Elizabethan language, has become part of her autonomic nervous system. Her expertise is invaluable to younger actors.

> I am often asking students in rehearsals, *"Could it mean this?"* Then I have to stop and think *why* I sense that. I found myself answering one actor with *"because Shakespeare doesn't write that way."* This fellow had decided that some phrase had started a new topic which was completely divorced from what came before. In Shakespearean dialogue, everything that is spoken comes, in some way, from what has been spoken before. Nothing is a complete change of subject—it generates *emotionally* from what has been stated previously.

For example, in a production of *Macbeth*, Vivien Leigh performed Lady Macbeth, sharing these lines from III.vi with her husband, Laurence Olivier:

Macbeth: If we should fail?
Lady Macbeth: We fail?
But screw your courage to the sticking place,
And we'll not fail.

Leigh said it as if there was a period, a full stop, following the first "fail" and *not* a question mark at the end of the sentence (which there is in most editions of *Macbeth*). That was innovative and everyone noticed it and she got great plaudits for doing it, but I think it's wrong, if anything in Shakespeare can be said to be wrong. It seems to me that inflection would push the already doubtful Macbeth over the line into anxiety. Also, she is giving a modern meaning to the word *but.* Shakespeare used that word for the most part to mean *only.* Lady Macbeth is really saying, "We? Fail? All you have to do is resolve yourself and we will not fail." She means the only thing that is keeping us from not failing is you not having any guts. This reading is much more likely.

This kind of fine tuning on a line is found in very experienced actors. It clues younger actors in to probing a line closely and making judgments about their own character context. The scrutiny of small moments in the scene guides the actor to the truth of the character's intentions.

Another mode of personal practice Henry finds helpful is doing a certain amount of preparation before each meeting with fellow actors. Her progress in rehearsal develops more quickly and more fruitfully if she arrives as prepared as possible. Her homework is done in private—she refers to herself as a nighthawk, doing the interior work after midnight, the "summoning."[3]

You do it all the time, depending on when you can and when it occurs to you. I work best in the wee hours of the morning when every else is in bed. Then, nobody's watching, the phone isn't going to ring, I feel free to let my mind go into various directions, and I don't judge.

When asked if she memorizes her lines before rehearsals begin, Henry explains:

> As I grow older, the lines tend to come in rehearsal, but in a different way than they did before. I read about actors who learn lines in rehearsal, actors who have found that if they are completely nude mentally and imaginatively, then everything happens in rehearsal. I couldn't possibly work like that. I wouldn't enjoy it.
>
> I need to have my own time with the script and with Mr. Shakespeare so that I have something to bring into myself. Once I've got something there, I can go into rehearsal and see what else is going on and try to absorb the things that are happening around me. Then I take *that*, and I go back home and I do more investigating and *then* I bring that back into rehearsal, so that it's a constant give-and-take process.

Henry is well trained in voice and technique. One mentor was Eleanor Stuart, who taught at the National Theatre School and was a great actress in her own right. Another was Edith Skinner, who influenced all voice teachers in acting training right into the late twentieth century. Both focused on using the voice to convey the text:

> Eleanor taught us, more than anything, exactly this kind of ability—to never give up on the text. She was a magnificent, extraordinary woman. She never sat down in class, even though she taught well into her seventies—because she felt that was disrespectful to the students' work. She always called the students by surname, "Miss Henry." The joke about her was when she came to be in the Stratford Company, she walked from Montreal to Stratford so as not to inconvenience the railways. We were all dazzled by her and filled with a kind of pride that we got to be in class with this astonishing woman.

At Carnegie Mellon, I also did some speech work with Edith Skinner. I learned a great deal from her about iambic pentameter.

Moreover, Henry continues to take voice classes to this day, a rare practice among experienced actors but an extremely important one:

> I've been working with a woman at the Shaw Festival this year. They have wonderful coaches in Stratford; both Janine Pearson and David Ley are very good. When I am in Montreal, I work with Louis Spritzer. He has a method of working that I feel very, well, *comfortable* is a catchy word—more *oiled by*. He is able to work with actors in a way that gives you back the warm-up. He also does body work, Reichian work; he's studied all over the world.
>
> After an hour, you know that you and he are very much in pursuit of what your voice wants to do. He releases something in you, and he comes up with a potluck of things culled from his experiences, and he gives them to you as your personalized package. I do the exercises in the morning when I get up. The first thought in my head that day is—Do I have a show? Do I have a rehearsal? Then I gear myself toward that.

The key collaboration for an actor is her relationship with the director. Henry has worked with several and has learned from each of them—about work habits, about communicating, often about the use of rehearsal time, occasionally about survival. Here, she shares some invaluable perceptions about entering the actor–director relationship:

> Each director has a different method of working. There is always a point, when I am working with a new director—and I think this happens to every actor—when you are waiting to see if this is a director you can trust. Around the end of the first week that penny drops, and you realize that either you can or you cannot. It doesn't seem to have much to do with whether or not you *like* the director—you can like them very much—but you know that you can't trust them. And that's fine. It is simply a way of knowing

what region you are in, how much of the work you are going to have to do by yourself, what kinds of questions you can ask, what you should not ask, what territories you can venture into, and those that you'd better avoid.

The ideal situation seems to be that when you get to the end of the first week—or to the end of day four or day ten, even—you surmise, "This is someone who I can put myself *into the hands of.* After that, you can go anywhere and do anything. The process isn't going to be easier, often it's more difficult with a director you know you have faith in, yet it is a process like leaping off a cliff or jumping into an ocean.

All this must sound slightly pretentious to someone who isn't in the theater. After all, you are not in an operating room—you are not skydiving. But any artist understands that there is a *psychic leaping over.* To be able to do that kind of complete transformation is a very frightening thing.

Once you've established this basic thing, and you've gone through the whole process with that director, the next time you work with him or her, you won't have to go through it all again. From day one, in fact, when you are preparing for the part, you will already have a sense of where you can go with that director. It is especially crucial that this link happens with Shakespeare. Otherwise, you can have a perfectly adequate performance, but you will never have anything *astounding.*

When John Hirsch directed, he would come and sit down with you and talk to you about very personal things in his life. You understood then, as an actor, that these were nuggets given to you to extrapolate from, to enhance your own thinking from, and to enliven your imagination.

Martha Henry's favorite director, and perhaps everyone else's in the Stratford Company during the 1970s and 1980s, was Robin Phillips. He was so exceptional as an artist and visionary that he influenced her on several levels. She worked with him in a number of productions and changed the nature and the impulse of her work forever. In 1986, Henry was his assistant director on a production of *Cymbeline*:

He was incredibly generous with me. He met with me in the prior December, even though we weren't starting rehearsals until March. He took me all through his drawings—he does detailed sketches of every scene, even moments in scenes, almost like the storyboard of a film. (Robin can design a set, make costumes, make wigs—can do anything at all connected with the theater—himself.) He was very patient, met with me many times, showed me a picture of a scene in a boat that he'd drawn that never made it into the play because the budget wasn't big enough. I always thought it was a shame to scrap that scene.

I remember another drawing from *Cymbeline* where Colm Feore, playing Iachimo, was coming through the center upstage pillars and had a yellow beach towel over his left shoulder—there was also a drawing of Colm lying facedown, on stage right, on this yellow beach towel.

It wasn't until we got onstage and were in the middle of the first technical dress rehearsal that I saw Colm walk through the pillars with the yellow beach towel over his left shoulder and then move downstage right and lie down on it. Suddenly, the sketch came back into my head, and although I'd been entirely involved in the whole process, I never *once* heard Robin say, "Now walk through those pillars, and . . ."

Henry's first experience as an actor working with Phillips was in 1976 in *Measure for Measure*, when he electrified audiences with Brian Bedford playing Angelo to Henry's novitiate Isabella. Set in Vienna at the turn of the century, it also showcased Phillips's skill with the Edwardian period:

I had not known Robin prior to this production. I remember that there was a day in which I realized that he was someone with whom you could leap quite handily—*that* area he would take care of completely.

Unlike any other director I had ever known, he never said, "Cross down here, cross up there, think about doing this, don't do that . . ." He never told you where to go, scarcely made suggestions about where to enter. However, he did come up onstage one day and talked for half an hour about his relationship with his sister. In *Measure for Measure*, the key relationship in the play is between Isabella and her brother Claudio, not her relationship with the Duke, *not* the relationship with Angelo. It's the interaction with Claudio that runs her engine.

I don't think I would have realized that without Robin. In the middle of rehearsal in an empty theater, he told me about himself and his sister. Most directors wouldn't take that long, because you have a limited amount of time. He spoke to me as long as necessary, and then he sat back down. That conversation completely altered the way I looked at the character and the part.

Phillips clearly understood the psychology of suggestion within the actor's rehearsal and character preparation:

I remember once in *Measure for Measure* Robin putting a jug of water on the desk that I was sitting at. It was the first play I'd ever done with him, but at this point in rehearsal, I knew him well enough to know that he didn't put it there idly. It was up to me to figure out why. This was in the scene between Angelo and Isabella, right after he propositions her and tells her he will not save her brother unless she sleeps with him. Indeed, at the end of the scene, I put my hands in it and bathed my face with water.

That turned out to be quite a seminal moment in the production. All from Robin's doing, but from his *not* saying to me, "At the end of this, you will . . ." He gives you a choice, gives you free will. He knows in his head exactly what the terrain is, but he allows you to *walk in it freely*. Which means the actor is constantly expanding and living and breathing. The actor is never dead. It is an amazing gift.

Henry articulates the values this inventive director offers as he guides actors through the performance process:

Robin very often does something that I've never seen another director do—which is to give you an image which is beyond the situation we're discussing. For instance, if you are talking about walking from one house to another house in a state of working something through, and the situation is that I am going to tell my husband I am pregnant, Robin would turn it into something more urgent than that, so that the message you had to give occurs in the middle of an earthquake or a huge avalanche.

He is constantly encouraging your body or your mind to enlarge its *thinking*—not its behavior. He is very specific about human behavior; he never asks for something that is in any sense declamatory—quite the contrary. He is looking for something which will *ground* the actor in the true moment. He wants the imagination and the thinking in the mind to be bigger, because the mind of Shakespeare is bigger. Bigger than we are used to.

What Robin achieved was to keep the actor alive beyond the rehearsal state. Later on in the run, things constantly came back to you that you hadn't been able to use initially. They were lodged somewhere in the back of your brain. In September or October, when you had come to what you thought were the limits of the scene, something else would kick in which opened a whole new door for that experience or that character or that relationship or that moment onstage.

However, there are occasional trade-offs in working with virtuosos:

Robin is a master at personal psychology. He can be very hard. Nonetheless, once you've worked with him, all other directors seem slightly dull in comparison. He rehearses in a unique way, one that means *you are creating all the time*. I have no other phrase for it. You are allowing or making things happen all during the work session—something is always going on. It is an exciting rehearsal process.

As with many great artists, Phillips did keep his actors guessing at times. Henry related this incident from a rehearsal with actor-director

Brian Bedford, with whom she shared a close friendship and a wry sense of humor:

> I always felt, working with Brian Bedford, as though I was being put into his pocket, an experience I really adored. I don't know if I can describe working with him in any other way. After our first time working together on *Measure for Measure*, we had this odd experience when we did *Richard III* together the following year.
>
> We were doing the scene over the coffin with Richard and Lady Anne. As I said, Robin does not block things in the traditional way. He doesn't say move there, do this, none of that. We had tried the scene many different ways, and we felt quite free to go anywhere we wished, because we knew that was Robin's way. We did that for several rehearsals, and one day, suddenly, Robin became extremely angry and he said, "Why aren't you doing the blocking?" Brian was never rattled by Robin and said, "Blocking?" Robin said, "Yes, the blocking." Brian responded, "I don't remember that we ever *set* blocking." Robin said, "It is written down in the book."
>
> Well, of course, stage managers write down everything we do! Robin must have seen something in a prior rehearsal that he liked, and he assumed we would know what that was. To him, we had changed what we'd done and the scene wasn't being revealed as well. Robin called a coffee break, and I said to Brian, "Had we ever set blocking?" Brian shook his head.
>
> That was another lesson in working for Robin. What it does is snap a place inside of you so that you never again feel as relaxed. I've thought later that was probably what he wanted. Perhaps I was feeling as if I could do absolutely anything. I was not exercising that outside ear and eye that says, "Now pay attention and *understand* when something is right or is most creative for this scene at this moment."
>
> You can't also be just pudding and do anything that you damned well please onstage. That doesn't work any better than rigidity.

Henry has roles that are her favorites. She offers a caveat—sometimes the one you enjoy rehearsing the most is not the one the audience enjoys most, so the varnish is taken off the experience. At other times, an actor's greatest triumphs are the ones that are well received.

> Playing Isabel was one of my absolute favorites. Of course, I was working for the first time with Robin, and it opened up a whole new world of playing. Performing Mary Tyrone in *Long Day's Journey into Night* was a perfect experience, because things meshed so well in rehearsal. The ensemble—William Hutt, Peter Donaldson, and Tom McCamus—sensed that we were present at an unusual and invigorating event. When you feel that you are doing better work than you have any right to deserve, things come together magically.
>
> I loved playing Desdemona because I imagined I understood her so well. However, my Othello was not English-speaking and was struggling to make the lines meaningful in a language other than his own, so the atmosphere and ambience were not conducive. I was performing the role at a time when my mother had a stroke. I was on my back and being strangled by Othello when I saw someone come across backstage to speak to the stage manager. I knew immediately it was a message for me.
>
> I found my first Volumnia extremely hard. I found Constance very hard. But the balance was not exactly right in either situation. Once Robin Phillips entered the Stratford scene, our world changed—our view of acting changed. The full experience—working with actors you know and trust, having a visionary director, good writing. That is what creates the ideal situation.

One benefit of having a track record with an established company is learning how to use its performance spaces and finding what works within them. The Stratford Festival Theatre stage, designed by Tanya Moiseivitch and Tyrone Guthrie, was famous for its sightlines.

> When I was hired to be involved in my first season as an actor, Peter Donat took me from the reception [area] . . . to the empty theater. He said just sit in here and look at that stage and watch for a few minutes. Peter had worked there for a number of years

by then. I did that, and I began to see the stage breathe. . . . At
that point, it was still the original thrust stage . . . [it] had a life
to it that pulsated. While I indeed have a sometimes overactive
imagination, it wasn't that. It was the amalgamation of everything
in the theater coupled with the fact that the stage knew I was
sitting there and knew I was watching it. What it was saying to
me was: "If you come to me straight, I will support you. If you
cheat while you are on me, I will throw you right off." And I saw
that happen again and again in the years that I worked there.
The people that were able to address the stage cleanly, the stage
supported and helped. And the people who tried to get the best
of the stage just got tossed away.[4]

The Festival Theatre was altered, just before the millennium, and
actors and directors discovered they had to learn all over again how
to manipulate the performance space, to adjust technique to the con-
verted area:

Somehow the balance of the house with the stage has changed.
It all worked on paper, and when I first heard about the plans, I
thought, "Good for you!" The decision had been taken deliberately
to make the house smaller, which was quite daring in a day and
age when everyone wants to make more money and to sell more
seats. However, something had happened to the mystery of that
stage—it is still quite wonderful, yet different from what it used
to be. It's more stolid, a bit less nimble, a bit less wieldy, more
set in its ways, a little more earnest and forefront and not quite
so playful as it used to be. It's as if it has six legs where it used to
have eight.

On the older stage, I remember sitting there—you could get a
seat for two dollars! I wanted so much to see Siobhan McKenna,
but I saw mostly the back of her head. Now sightlines have gotten
much better. Yet the actors are discovering that the staging has
been affected slightly—the diagonals are no longer exactly what
they used to be [actors moving diagonally across the stage floor],

although a few very good directors have figured out how to use the diagonals and can make the entrances and exits work.

You can still use the stage, but it's as if the formula has been altered and the effects are not the same. As if the stage is now grown up and mature, whereas before it was mischievous and youthful. The circles still work well—look at how they enhanced *Hello Dolly!*

Nevertheless, change is good for actors, very good.

Henry remarks on the shifting face of theater from the time she began acting up to the present. She has encountered this art form from the angle of actor, administrator, and director. Naturally, different customs and mores have evolved:

Acting styles have changed, so this is a difficult topic to tackle. Over the decades, we have tried to become more naturalistic onstage. That gave rise to a whole movement, the "Stanislavsky method," which was a reaction to the declamatory fashion of speaking Shakespeare. When I was young, I had actors and directors saying to me, "Oh, no, you need to stand with your upstage foot slightly ahead of your downstage foot."

Now that is laughable, but there was a time when learning conventional stage technique was de rigueur. You mastered certain ways of moving and being onstage. I am still saying to actors, "No, just turn the easy way." It continues to be difficult for some experienced actors on a proscenium stage to turn their backs to an audience. They have been trained to do it the hard way.

On the other hand, we interviewed dozens of young actors at the Grand Theatre who might have been innately gifted but were essentially untrained. They were trying to behave onstage as if they were in your living room, because that was what they saw on TV. They lacked the ability to communicate or to explore a character, without any diction or voice training that would work on a stage. That can become a soggy, uninteresting lump sitting in the middle of the room. To be an actor that goes beyond television work takes as much skill as a ballet dancer. Yet you can still get a lot of jobs that don't require it—that's the ridiculous aspect.

The sublime aspect is that there is presumably a Laurette Taylor or Kate Reid or Susan Wright or another great artist out there who can make you believe that they've dropped something on the floor that never has fallen before and then burst into tears, and it persuades you that this is the first time it ever happened.

I remember in England many years ago when I first saw Peggy Ashcroft onstage, I was floored at how modern she was. I had expected something much more old-fashioned and stately and grand.

To the great pleasure of acting students in training, Henry has been invited for teaching stints at both the National Theatre School and at her alma mater, Carnegie Mellon University. She is now the director of the Birmingham Conservatory at the Stratford Festival:

I am a good person to be with in a rehearsal hall, especially for a young actor who is just starting out. I can see the traps before they can, because I've been there, I've done every stupid thing in the book. Somehow I struggled my way through it, by the grace of God. There are certain things I can nip in the bud before they become large problems.

I adore young actors, feel very nurturing toward them. I try to create an atmosphere in which they can do their best work.

Her combined talent of being an actor and having directed has given her valuable perceptions to share with students: "When I direct, I think acting is easier; when I act, I think it's directing. Neither is easier, but I do find one feeds the other." Directing has taught her to be less difficult as an actor, now that she knows how vulnerable a director can feel: "I give a lot more leeway now. I'm sorry it took me so long."[5]

As a director, Henry is very open to production concepts that create a unique and nontraditional time period as well as a design vision for Shakespeare's plays:

What does Shakespeare care? He's not insisting that everyone do it the same way. [The plays] withstand all kinds of stretching and annotating and setting in strange periods. Sometimes [the concept] illuminates and sometimes it makes it fuzzy, but I don't think it matters.[6]

Henry is a role model for theater artists. She is refreshingly outspoken and even edgy and political, as the whole Canadian Stratford tradition appears to be. She is also committed, experienced, articulate, and an important voice in world theater:

Well, it's certainly my vocation, there's no question about that. It's my profession, it's my job. It's also my sorrow, my anguish, my source of humor. You get a very strong sense of family in the theaters I've worked in.

You work extremely closely with a number of people that you get to know very well. You work with other actors and directors over and over again, and you expose yourself to them in ways you don't even do with people you have relationships with!

So you perceive colleagues in a very particular way. You understand people's courage and people's frights, and that's a very delicate thing to hold. It carries a lot of responsibility with it, so you protect it.

The theater has a great tradition of sheltering its own, because you realize how difficult it is to be an artist in any event. You are exposing a part of yourself. You are creating something to put up there in front of people so that they will have a communicative experience.

One that we hope might even change them significantly.

TONY CHURCH AS FALSTAFF IN THE 1984 SHAKESPEARE
SANTA CRUZ PRODUCTION OF *KING HENRY IV, PART ONE*.
(PHOTO BY SHMUEL THALER)

Tony Church

Mend Your Speech a Little

Tony Church's career was decidedly trans-Atlantic. British-born, he was part of the Royal Shakespeare Company in the early 1960s (through 1987) under Peter Hall's artistic directorship, and he was one of those exceptional character actors whose work was essential to the consummate Shakespeare production. In England he performed in a wide range of roles, including Henry IV, Polonius (twice), Falstaff, Sir Toby Belch, both Ulysses and Pandarus, Friar Laurence, John of Gaunt, Cymbeline, and the title role in *King Lear*, a part that he played several times. Over the years, he recorded major roles in over twenty-six of the Shakespeare plays for the Argo recording company. He worked in repertory in England, on the BBC "Shakespeare Plays" series, and at the Royal National Theatre. During the 1980s, he was director of drama at the Guildhall School of Music and Drama in London and served on the Arts Council of Great Britain. He died in the spring of 2008. There is a memoir in progress titled *A Stage for a Kingdom*.

Church was one of the founding directors of ACTER (now Actors of the London Stage), the group of Shakespearean actors who toured college campuses in the United States. He spent the latter part of his career there, most notably as education director at the National Theatre

Conservatory and associate artist with the Denver Center Theater Company, and he also performed across the United States in regional theater and Shakespeare festivals.

Since Church grew into the profession in England during his teens, he spent valuable time among the trendsetters when the Royal Shakespeare Company was making huge transformational shifts in acting and production, beginning with Peter Hall's directorate in 1958. He was then in the cadre of English actors who mediated many of those ideas into American classical theater. His great talent was communicating, with elegant clarity, both the origins and the vibrancy of this historical shift.

Teaching and acting are professions that often interblend, complementing each other with facility. Actors who have taught are greatly articulate about the profession. For Church, these dual vocations were prophesied early on:

> When I was in the army, I met up with a schoolmaster in Singapore who had directed me as both Polonius and Faulconbridge. He said to me, "You're going to be an actor and a teacher. I have no idea which you will do first, but once you've done one, you will do the other."
>
> He was right. I was an actor for donkey's years, and then in the middle 1970s, I found myself teaching in colleges in America. Before that, I ran the Guildhall School in London and then eventually came to Denver. I'd never taught before and never thought of doing it.[1]

Although his career as an actor provided him many opportunities, Church mentored aspiring and high-achieving Shakespeare actors, including actor Simon Russell Beale as well as Paul Whitworth, who was the artistic director at Shakespeare Santa Cruz for several years.

Church's idol and role model was Ralph Richardson, one of the best known of the classical actors working on the English stage during the middle decades of the twentieth century. Richardson had an extensive film career, playing Buckingham in Olivier's 1955 production of *Richard*

III in addition to being a regular at the Old Vic. The young Church rarely missed a performance:

> I'd seen Richardson's Cyrano and his Falstaff, the greatest things
> I've ever seen onstage. I also saw his John of Gaunt in *Richard II*
> and Bluntschli in *Arms and the Man*. I can hear him saying [in
> a high, thin tenor voice, Church imitated him exactly], "When I
> was about thy years, Hal, I was not an eagle's talon in the waist;
> I could have crept into any alderman's thumb-ring: A plague of
> sighing and grief! it blows a man up like a bladder" (*1 Henry IV*,
> II.iv.330–31). I'd seen all his movies during the war, and he was a
> great, great film actor.
>
> We all had three great gods: Olivier, Gielgud, and Ralph Rich-
> ardson. I saw Gielgud's 1944 *Hamlet*, which Dadie Rylands di-
> rected, and I also saw *The Duchess of Malfi*. But Richardson was
> my exemplar.[2]

Church's early years were crammed with performance experiences. He was obviously histrionically inclined, and his English masters at school recognized his talents and pointed him toward acting:

> I read aloud, recited poetry, I played Grumpy in a *Snow White
> and Rose Red*, a production done by the local YMCA when I was
> seven in 1937. I loved reading stories and poetry aloud. I read to
> the cleaning woman but never to my parents (I was too embar-
> rassed). I read Kipling to people when I was eight or nine. I liked
> doing characters. I started acting when I was in a private boys'
> boarding school at age nine or ten.
>
> My first Shakespeare role was Lorenzo in the last act of *The
> Merchant of Venice*. Lorenzo in 1941, a one-hour version of *Mac-
> beth* in 1942, a ninety-minute version of *1 Henry IV*, *2 Henry IV*,
> and *Henry V* (doing Falstaff), and so on it went! When I went to
> "big school" (called "public school" in England), then I did Faul-
> conbridge in *King John*, Polonius in *Hamlet*, Petruchio in *Shrew*,
> Falstaff again, and Othello. I also directed and starred in an Edgar

Wallace thriller when I was fifteen. I was always acting my socks off, but my passion was invariably Shakespeare.

After returning from the National Service, Church enrolled at Cambridge, where he studied for degrees in English and history and got his MA. Performance was so popular that a great many societies got formed because each was limited to doing one production per term:

> At Cambridge, I did a lot of Shakespeare but also other parts like Creon in *Antigone* and Vanya in *Uncle Vanya*. I did twenty-six plays in three years! Ian McKellen did twenty-eight. Trevor Nunn directed a huge number, as well. I used to do my academic work at night and frequently rehearsed during the day.

One Cambridge club was noteworthy, the Marlowe Society. To perform in that group, one had to be asked. Young actors were honored with an invitation, and they knew they would be working with one of the foremost professors of Shakespeare in terms of actually coaching actors about speaking the verse, a man named George (Dadie) Rylands. So Church's academic career connected him with a mentor who influenced the careers of celebrated classical actors and directors, shaping the direction of Shakespearean production throughout the twentieth century. Rylands was, most importantly, the student artists' networking link to the professional stage in England:

> Dadie was a huge influence and had tremendous connections in the theater. He was close friends with both John Gielgud and Peggy Ashcroft. He knew Noël Coward, he gave a party one day at lunch and the Oliviers came. He was our liaison to the world of great stars, our power in the land. When I went to his ninetieth birthday party in the Swan Theatre in 1992 [in Stratford-upon-Avon], Gielgud performed several of his favorite speeches onstage in honor of Dadie.

Rylands not only mentored and taught, but he also performed. Peter Hall said about him, "To be honest, heroic actor he was not—but he was very good at playing nutters." Hall added, "He was a setter of standards, and someone who made us all appreciate the beat and structure of verse."[3] Rylands fostered an entire generation of young theater hopefuls—Hall, Trevor Nunn, John Barton—who later created outstanding seasons at the Royal Shakespeare Company and the Royal National Theater. His great contribution was to focus young actors' attention on analyzing the Shakespearean line. He was especially attentive to what Church called *rhythm*, which encompassed a variety of verse functions:

> Rylands had a way of talking that was highly pitched and often in a monotone. But the spring of the rhythm in the line when he spoke was unbelievably interesting.
>
> He could also hear the length of vowels in lines, long vowels as well as short vowels. I remember doing that great, long speech of Richard of Gloucester in *3 Henry VI*, parts of which were knit together by Olivier for the opening speech of *Richard III* on film. In the end of the speech he says, "Can I do this and cannot get a crown?" The way I worked with Rylands made me see that I could say: "CAN / AYE / DOO / THIS / (four single accented monosyllables, you see) andcannotgetacrown?" I would never have seen those possibilities before—the value of long versus short syllables.
>
> Rylands also attended to rhythm within a scene. John Barton was directing a production of *Julius Caesar*, and Rylands came in and worked with the cast. All the conspirators were standing there, washing their hands in the blood of Caesar, when someone says here comes a man of Antony's. There we were, a load of murderers, and Brutus said, "Soft! Who comes here" (III.i.121), and we all jumped.
>
> That appearance of Antony's servant was a traumatic moment. Rylands said, "Listen to the number of times the servant says the word 'Antony' in that speech, right down to 'So says my master Antony' (III.i.122–36). The words are like bells of doom. What are we going to do with this man Antony, the conspirators are thinking, and then Antony appears. He takes the hand of each of

them, slowly going all around the conspirators' circle. He's putting his mark on each one of them. Those names will not be forgotten. Then Antony says, "Gentlemen all" (III.ii.190).

These were the kinds of clues Rylands revealed to actors in his close textual readings—words repeated and finding out what that meant, stage directions contained within the actual dialogue, and so on.

Rylands talked about *timing*, never about music. He talked about images, also, but more about rhythm and timing. All of us who came through the Marlowe Society were very marked by that attention to rhythm.

We paid attention to whether or not a speech had an extra beat in it—we all did that sort of poetic analysis. I didn't know about feminine endings, but I understood the extraordinary rhythmic construction that was playing syncopation over the basic iambic pentameter.

Cicely Berry talks about it in her book *The Actor and His Text*. Everybody writes about it now, but in those days we were the first people who were beginning to discover these things. We had text classes with John Barton regularly each week at the Royal Shakespeare Company, where we worked with him during the 1960s and 1970s—discussing the importance of and how to use alliteration, assonance, all those literary devices.

Church emphasized the importance of this one basic tenet highlighted by Rylands and assimilated by his various pupils:

The rhythm is there, it doesn't matter what your interpretation is; if you don't attend to the rhythm of it, the whole thing falls apart. Especially in comedy—rhythm is everything. The audience is led from one point to another via rhythm. It is much more than iambic pentameter—it is the counterpoint in rhythms. *Love's Labour's Lost* will not work unless those couplets ring against one another. There is a joy and a delight in it that is like children's sound games and songs.

In the clickety-clickety-click of the lovers' scene in *A Midsummer Night's Dream*, if you get out of sync with the rhythm by one scintilla, the comedy will not work. You cannot make a move nor do any business except at the end of the line. If it's a couplet, you've got to wait until the end of it, then do the business. If you do it in the middle of the couplet, you've completely wrecked it. This is the thing Rylands emphasized. Whenever I direct, I am adamant about it.

But the most important thing was how those changes of rhythm are character indications. The greatest play for understanding this is *Julius Caesar*. Look at the actual rhythmic construction of the speeches of Antony and Brutus:

> *Antony*: Friends, Romans, countrymen, lend me your ears!
> I come to bury Caesar, not to praise him.
> The evil that men do lives after them,
> The good is oft interred with their bones;
> So let it be with Caesar. The noble Brutus
> Hath told you Caesar was ambitious:
> If it were so, it was a grievous fault,
> And grievously hath Caesar answered it.
> Here, under leave of Brutus and the rest
> (For Brutus is an honorable man,
> So are they all, all honorable men),
> Come I to speak in Caesar's funeral.
> (III.ii.73–84)

> *Brutus*: Romans, countrymen, and lovers, hear me for my cause, and be silent, that you may hear. Believe me for mine honor, and have respect to mine honor, that you may believe. Censure me in your wisdom, and awake your senses, that you may the better judge. If there be any in this assembly, any dear friend of Caesar's, to him I say, that Brutus' love to Caesar was no less than his. If then that friend demand why Brutus rose against Caesar, this is my answer: Not that I lov'd Caesar less, but that I lov'd Rome more. (III.ii.13–20)

You will find two *totally different human beings* being indicated by the way the verse is written. Once you start to comprehend these things, you look for them all the time.

Rylands emphasized finding the appropriate punctuation as the actor learned what the lines meant. Church seconded him in this and underscored it with his own students:

> Rylands was very keen about punctuation, which he modeled on George Bernard Shaw. I remember we were doing *Pygmalion*, and the man who was playing the character of Doolittle was giving a very good Cockney performance. Rylands said, "No, no no, no, no. Remember that you are preaching sermons. Look at the speech again, Peter—one count for a comma, two for a semicolon, three for a full stop. That's what Shaw said. Never fails." And the actor went back, strictly adhered to the punctuation, and doubled the amount of laughs he got.
>
> I make my students do speeches from *The Art of the American Folk Preacher*, written in the 1940s—southern Baptist ministers' speeches. They all claim to be inspired, but the speeches are all tightly scripted and controlled. It lets the students know that they have rhetoric in their own tradition.

Church had very decided views about punctuation and went far beyond what Rylands promoted, since the argument about punctuating Shakespeare rages on and probably always will:

> When I was directing *As You Like It*, my Rosalind said to me, "I've gone back to the folio," since she wanted to see the actual punctuation there. "'Come every day to my cote and woo me, [comma]' is what all the paperbacks said, but in the folio it is 'Come to my cote: [colon] and woo me.'"
>
> She was looking for all the aids she could find in speaking the text, and she did this by examining a number of different editions of the play. That change from one punctuation mark to another opened up many more possibilities for the actor acting Rosalind.

Neil Freeman, who specializes in Shakespearean punctuation, would say, of course it is all there. The use of the colon as a *breathing punctuation* is now being taught by a lot of people. I discovered when I was doing *Twelfth Night* in Cambridge in 1954 that the punctuation in the folio for Malvolio is entirely actor's punctuation. It is not academic punctuation or reading punctuation—it is definitely *actor's pointing*. Time and time again when the sense would be a comma, there is a full colon in the folio.

We've always said that nobody knows what the actual punctuation was in Shakespeare—but the one thing it *isn't* is an editor's punctuation. Most academic editors, who have entered the picture long after Shakespeare wrote, have added mostly literary punctuation, and the punctuation in the folio is entirely *theatrical*. The purpose of the punctuation in almost all of the modern editions has been for readers to read the plays, *not* to act them. The folio is not intended to be *read*. It's a *play script*.

I believe that if Shakespeare punctuated the scripts at all, he was much more likely to punctuate them for actors than readers.

There isn't any indication that he cared a tuppenny about being published.

Clearly, Church believed that in Shakespeare, every method of character analysis begins with the language in the texts.

Students should be given a great deal of information and guidance and especially encouraged to find things on their own. As an historian, I want them to read as much background as possible. The words the characters say are what we have to follow as an actor.

There is nothing on the page but who is speaking and who is listening—and note that both the speaker and the listener are equally important, because there are very sparse stage directions in Shakespeare, and no descriptions of the listeners. So you must discover what the relationship is between each character; how the speaker affects the listener. There are long speeches, of course, but these, too, must be considered as dialogue. There are no Pinter pauses or Beckett silences—if they are there in Shakespeare, they are indicated by broken lines—half lines or parts of lines without the full five iambs.

One of the things I teach, and I also do for myself, is the idea of finding in any given line the *seed* of the next line. I teach my students to play it one line at a time, a thought at a time. They are not to move on to the next thought until they have found the reason for it in the current thought—the one they are actually on. If they don't find it there, something that leads to the next thought, then don't go on to it. Does the reason come from something else that is going on onstage? Or someone else's reaction or lack of reaction? *What* is it that causes the next line to happen?

Church also exhorted his students to imagine and comprehend images. These must be looked at in terms of how they operate and resonate within each character's way of speaking. He warned students that they not only have to be Marc Antony or Casca, they have to be Shakespeare:

You see Shakespeare's mind doing these little jumps, making bridges, linking one idea to another, not going in a straight path. It's quite clear if you examine a line, looking for the odd thing in it, looking for what gives you the spring to the next line. You have to say to yourself: If I were writing this, why would I write it like that? You have to think in terms of writing the play. You have to get back into what happened in Shakespeare's mind as you go from one thought to the next.

The other way to do it is artificially to stop yourself whenever you come to a junction and say, Which way is the track now moving? If you go back and find out how a thing is written, you find out how it is thought, and then you have a staircase, a scaffolding. You learn to track on the playwright's mind and find out how thoughts build on each other.

For example, look at how the first part of the Prologue in *King Henry V* is structured in a pattern of "rising" images (I.i.1):

Chorus. O for a Muse of fire, that would *ascend*
The brightest heaven of invention,

A kingdom for a stage, princes to act
And monarchs to behold the *swelling* scene!
Then should the warlike Harry, like himself,
Assume the port of Mars; and at his heels,
Leash'd in like hounds, should famine, sword and fire
Crouch for employment. But pardon, gentles all,
The flat, *unraised* spirits that have dared
On this unworthy *scaffold* to bring forth
So great an object: can this cockpit hold
The vasty fields of France? Or may we cram
Within this wooden O the very casques
That did affright the air at Agincourt?
Suppose within the girdle of these walls
Are now two confined mighty monarchies
Whose *high*, *upreared* and abutting fronts
The perilous narrow ocean parts asunder:

You have a muse, one which ascends, fire going up, burning upwards. You have this amazing staircase going up to this fantastic "heaven of invention." Instead of simply saying, "I want to invent," Shakespeare gives you this other ascendancy of phrases, and you climb the staircase. These are not necessarily obvious thoughts. Each one of these little nicks takes you up and up, and you've got to get inside that engine of creation (the mind of the playwright who made this verse) and re-create it yourself.

If you work out the nuts and bolts, your performance is always fresh. You have to drive the thing eventually so you have to find out what drives *it*, how many pieces of coal give it that particular speed.

I believe that if you follow these notions, that's fifty percent of your character analysis. These are links of understanding, parts of the process of what makes the language, the words, come to life.

Now there are thousands of other things you need to do to put all this information into the blood bank. Eventually, it's all about choice. One word is not another word, so you have to make choices about that. You have to justify what you are saying. If you do enough of that work, you will discover a lot about the character. You don't invent character out of the air and stick it on. You take Antony's character from *what Antony says*. That dialogue will tell you something pretty bloody specific.

Church was not a great believer in the theories of Stanislavsky. He felt that this approach had some strong points but that its original essence had been greatly compromised:

> I'm not saying you cannot do a lot of wonderful things with the kind of psychological preparation Stanislavsky discusses.
>
> The world was in the grip of a huge interest in Freudian psychology at the time when Stanislavsky's theories were being transferred to the United States, so it's not surprising that the Stanislavskian technique of "emotional memory," recalling a traumatic event from your past and using that memory to call up a corresponding emotion, is mixed up with Freudian psychiatry.
>
> This method worked wonderfully for film acting, but stage acting is shared with a live audience. In film you only have to share with the camera. These two kinds of acting are two *drastically* different projections of the actor's energy.

Church categorized certain Stanislavskian tenets as inapplicable for Shakespearean acting:

> The journey of discovery that every Shakespearean character makes is actually discernible in the text—you don't have to look behind or underneath it. It is a great mistake to begin playing the subtext *that Shakespeare actually intends for the audience.* You should play what's written; you always have to play the intention if you can find out what it is.
>
> For example, if you are playing Leontes—Tim Pigott-Smith was right when he played Leontes in *The Winter's Tale* in 1988 at the National Theatre—the intention is to make everybody *understand* that he has discovered his wife is unfaithful. It's absolutely

necessary for everyone to see that Leontes is, *in his own mind*, totally right, perfectly sane, making an absolutely logical judgement, a well-thought-out proper thing for a king to do.

When the audience listens, they think, this man is going round the twist. The "saner" he gets, the more complicated the language gets, the more detailed and precise it gets. It sounds like a brilliant psychological case study of jealousy. But the actor does *not* play "I am in the grip of sexual jealousy"—because that's a generalization.

In that scene with Paulina where he is calling her all those names, he is very funny at her expense—he calls her "Dame Partlet," and so he plays these jibes at the lords, who are aghast. Yet from the point of view of Leontes, everyone around him is stupid, fake, barmy, doesn't get the picture. He even laughs at them and says they are ridiculous. When Tim played it that way, with total clarity, it was one of the most alarming characters I've ever been onstage with, a serious madman. It comes from playing exactly what is said with no *commenting on* the role.

A rehearsal period, for Tony Church, had very definite means and ends. Having done a good deal of directing, he knew what he wanted to achieve each day and how to manage the cast toward those ends:

Two things should happen in rehearsals: one thing is *discovery*, and the other is *practice*, and you need quite a bit of both. The French call rehearsal *répétition*. The opera people call the man who plays the harpsichord in rehearsal the *répétiteur*. I tell my students that they have to be prepared each time to offer new things in rehearsal. They also have to remember what they did during the preceding rehearsals. Although every rehearsal should be fresh, each should build on what you have "discovered" before. That doesn't mean the actor "locks it in"—but she/he doesn't throw away good discoveries, either.

Remember that performance is an entirely different entity. Performance expands on the groundwork you've already set in rehearsal, especially if the rehearsals are productive.

Church emphasized that acting is also about reacting, a product of good listening onstage:

> The actor who listens onstage is going to be twenty times better than any other. I can remember Christopher Plummer coming to Stratford-on-Avon to play Richard III in 1961. The most remarkable thing about him was that man standing with his head slightly to one side, listening all the while. For opportunities. The great improviser. His eyes would be following you, the ears would be listening, this enormous attention riveted, nothing was too small for him to notice, he could make capital out of a whisker. It was a marvelous thing to watch Richard being played as a *listener*.
>
> Of course, all this is learnt and perfected in rehearsal, where a director can watch you and let you know what is working and what is not.

Rehearsal should not lock the actors into set patterns of movement and vocal intonation. Rather, it aids in solidifying character and also sets a direction for each scene to move toward, in order to keep that focus clear throughout the run of the play:

> The point is that if the rehearsal has been done well, with all the intentions and objectives made clear, the actors can then move about quite a bit within the actual performance. The ways of achieving those objectives, the stress or importance of one word or one line rather than another, can vary considerably, but the intention of the character never varies.
>
> I had three scenes as Flavius with Paul Scofield's Timon in *Timon of Athens* in 1965. He never played these remotely the same, but within consecutive performances they were absolutely within the context of the situation. I don't remember his ever repeating the same inflection in his lines from one night to the next. He never knew exactly what he was going to *do*, but he was always in character and always right with the text.
>
> Actors have told me that it was extraordinary to have been in *Dance of Death* with Olivier when he was ill. The producer

reduced his number of performances as much as possible, so Olivier would come in once every ten days and give one or two performances. He never re-rehearsed, ever. He sometimes used different blocking and came in from different doors from what had been rehearsed. Every night was like a first night, but he was always in character and always in the situation.

In my opinion, some of these were the greatest performances of his entire career.

Since Church was a very strong character actor, he had also played old men in his youth. He knew well how to physicalize a character, how to find bodily qualities that were appropriate for that persona, and how to actualize those onstage:

If I find out the real inner rhythm or inner springs of the way the character talks, then I know how they move. Peter Brook had an exercise that he used in the opening rehearsals where he had the actor walk across the stage the way he ordinarily walked. That walk was peculiar to that person just as a character had its own basic inner rhythm. If an actor finds a character's rhythm (and each actor's rhythm will be different from another's), then he will find out how the character moves—what kind of feet he's got, how he gestures, the speed of his reaction to things.

For example, in *Julius Caesar*, Cassius thought quickly and moved like a ferret; Brutus was more deliberate and liked to work things out in linear cogitation. Antony improvised. Casca put everyone down—he made everyone wait for what he was going to say, he stood there clenched as he waited, all the muscles tight. That affected the way he moved. So, each of these character traits should be matched in the way they think and the way they move onstage.

When I was playing Peter Quince in *A Midsummer Night's Dream*, I realized that he always wanted to impose his authority. He was always asking questions of people and then judging: "You can play no part but Pyramus" (I.i.85). When I know a character's verbal rhythms, then I know his physical rhythms. That rule applies to characters outside of Shakespeare, as well.

Church explained that wearing a costume piece could also help an actor with finding the correct movement for a character:

> One of my students was playing the banished Duke in *As You Like It*. Although he was wearing skins and leggings, he wore his coat like Noël Coward, across his shoulder, making him look wonderfully aristocratic. The Duke was the sort of man who could make the meanest garment look as if it were made by a Savile Row tailor, because he had a natural *style*.
>
> Then, when he became the aristocrat talking about enjoying the birds and the babbling brook while he was in exile—"Is not this life more sweet than painted pomp"—it gave the line its full value and also let the actor experience it. That forest rhythm was far different from what was going on in the court.

A more personal example was Church's appearance as Falstaff in a modern dress production at Shakespeare Santa Cruz. He made the transition from Elizabethan England to contemporary America with ease and panache:

> Falstaff turned out to be an aging biker. I wore a disreputable pair of old army boots, a huge Guatemalan vest, and a vast pair of jeans. . . . Over the top, I wore a biker's jacket decorated with medals from random campaigns, and I had a terrible old hat stuffed with all sorts of badges. Instead of Falstaff's beloved sack, a villainous ancient brew of terribly alcoholic sherry, I carried underneath my arms packs of beer which I'd drink straight from the can and pass round till my store was depleted. The gang of thieves and ruffians in Mistress Quickly's dosshouse was a wonderful collection of riotous ne'er-do-wells from the back end of nowhere in contemporary America. . . . Paul Whitworth as Prince Hal came on dressed remarkably like Boy George, riding a small motorcycle. . . . The audience sat in a grassy slope . . . and when it came to the battles, we had shootouts in the trees around them.
>
> At the end . . . I joined in the victory parade as [the actors] turned to leave the stage . . . [I] withdrew a huge Churchillian cigar

which I stuck in my mouth and lit, making the victory V sign to the audience before swaggering off.[4]

Church directed many productions, a number for professional actors and many for students. He also worked with some of the finest directors in England and America. On the basis of all this experience, he articulated valuable ideas about the director's responsibilities to the actor:

> I dislike a director talking the thing to death—I like one who believes primarily in doing. When an actor says to him, "What I think I'd like to do . . . ," his answer should be, "Show me." Let the actor do it. Try it out. Talking can dehumanize and even mystify an idea.
>
> As an actor, you have to be a magician. You have to be in a position to receive messages: from your psyche, from the smells in the rehearsal room, from somebody's costume, from touching their hair, from something the director says. The actor should be alive to these influences.
>
> The director's primary job in any production is to be the audience. The director shouldn't say what he liked or didn't like; he should say what he *noticed*, what he *did see*, what he *did hear*. The director has an agenda, of course, and is after getting some results, but should not direct by *giving results*. The director should direct by sending the actors off on a journey and then responding to that.

Church talked about an ideal experience with a young director he worked with in the 1970s at the Royal Shakespeare Company. Buzz Goodbody offered an imaginative work process and strong support since he was playing *King Lear* at a very young age:

> She was, politically, an extreme left-winger and focused on the underbelly of prosperous Elizabethan society, at the outcasts and the indigent. When Lear strips off his royal trappings, becomes a wandering beggar and encounters Poor Tom, he becomes aware

of the underside of a world he's ruled for perhaps fifty or sixty years. There's nothing to suggest that he or anybody else in the play has ever thought of those people before. Lear becomes the voice and conscience of Shakespeare in a world in which beggars are whipped from tithing to tithing and treated as criminals. The needy of Elizabethan society were pariahs. This was Buzz's interest in the play.

This *Lear* was a stripped-down, nihilistic version performed in the Royal Shakespeare Company's black-box theater called The Other Place. The cast was reduced to just nine people, with only Lear's part remaining mostly complete:

> Buzz was the first director to work with me through improvisation . . . She told me to lie down while she sat by my head and talked me into a dream state where first of all the Earl of Kent, my second in command, saved me from being killed in battle. Next, the Earl of Gloucester, my chief minister, got me out of an appalling political fix. I went on to dream about the mothers of my three daughters. I'm certain the girls each had different mothers who all died in childbirth. It all came to me during those dream sessions with Buzz. . . . There were a number of extraordinary moments in that production.[5]

One of the most delightful things about Tony Church was his love of talking about the theater. He remembered, in vivid detail, story after story about famous colleagues. He came from that important generation of the four "greats": Gielgud, Richardson, Ashcroft, and Olivier. He performed onstage with them and learned from them as an actor in training, so he felt responsible for transferring the value and content of their gifts to younger actors and directors.

He passed the torch from the period of the earlier style of rhetorical acting of the early twentieth century to the more contemporary and more realistic style of acting Shakespeare of the twenty-first century, taking the best of both and adding these qualities to his teaching repertory, always weighing what worked best, always giving forward the most useful pieces to the next generation.

Church was vitally important as one of the great remembrancers of stage personalities and stage practice. An hour spent with him was always rich with history and discovery and laughter.

GEOFFREY HUTCHINGS AS BOTTOM THE WEAVER IN THE 1981
A MIDSUMMER NIGHT'S DREAM AT THE ROYAL SHAKESPEARE
COMPANY. (PHOTO FROM THE JOE COCKS STUDIO COLLECTION ©
SHAKESPEARE BIRTHPLACE TRUST)

Geoffrey Hutchings
I Met a Fool i' the Forest

When I was a young scholar, I spent one magical summer studying at the Shakespeare Institute in Stratford-upon-Avon with the crusty Kenneth Muir, the genial Dr. Fox, and the ruddy-cheeked Russell Jackson. I was in heaven in my heather purple Scottish crewneck on a crisp June morning, running to the post office prior to class. I realized suddenly that standing in line in front of me was Geoff Hutchings, the man who played the clowns at the Royal Shakespeare Company for fifteen of its most important years. In the midst of all that heavy theatrical history flowing through my mind, I swayed with the weight of tradition and eyed him closely. Years later, when I interviewed Hutchings, he had only one response to this schoolgirl story: "Was I behaving myself?" I rather doubt Hutchings ever behaves himself, and those of us who love to laugh are the richer for it. Nonetheless, remembering that day planted in my mind the idea of having a Shakespearean clown in this collection.[1]

As you read reviews about Hutchings's work, you sense that after his first clown performance was over, future successes were simply taken for granted. He is witty, sly, and he sees life as an opportunity for mischief. A raconteur of the first order, he regales listeners with tales of himself and his friends feigning loud snores when Royal Shakespeare Company (RSC) director Trevor Nunn gave notes to the assembled company.

Hutchings places his roots squarely in Dorchester, Dorset, in the West Country of England. His grandfather was a member of the Hardy Players. The Hardy novels were adapted into scripts performed by an amateur company that held forth at the Corn Exchange in Dorchester, which is exactly where Hutchings first performed, in a school play. It was originally built for the buying and selling of grain, is referenced in Hardy's *The Mayor of Casterbridge*, and eventually became a venue for local amateur theatricals, light operatic groups, and other visiting professional companies. Hutchings's grandfather performed to Thomas Hardy, Siegfried Sassoon, and T. E. Lawrence. Inscribed over the door is a motto from Defoe: "A man might as well spend his time . . . in Dorchester . . . as in any other town in England." The troupe was welcomed into London in *The Daily Sketch* with this notice on February 22, 1924:

> Whenever The Hardy Players pay one of their flying visits to town they remind us that Hardy not only rediscovered Wessex but made the Dorset Society in London a living thing. Their entertainments bring a breath of country air and are not dramatic performances in any conventional sense. Dorset men and women went to St. George's Hall yesterday as to a family gathering, and it was a joy merely to mingle with them for an hour.

These early beginnings uncover a family thread throughout Hutchings's life that began in a rural setting and was then deftly woven into his performances of the rustic clowns in Shakespeare.

Small-town England had a wondrous variety about it, replete with country characters and local movers and shakers. School offered many performance opportunities, and Hutchings was involved in plays directed by the history master David MacOwan (coincidentally the brother of the head of LAMDA, the London Academy of Music and Dramatic Art). The whole community attended these.

Later, Hutchings entered the University of Birmingham as a "musclehead" because that school had the only degree course in physical education in the country. He got interested in the university theater group and met John Russell Brown, scholar and author of several books about Shakespeare, including the iconoclastic *Free Shakespeare*. One of the early proponents of teaching Shakespeare through performance, Brown showed Hutchings what he wanted onstage by demonstrating. Naturally, Hutchings was very good at physicality—well trained and very expressive—and he could translate his professor's directions: "I credit him with being responsible for my becoming an actor, and he credits me with his becoming a director—but I keep quiet about that part." At university, Hutchings began his track record of working with Terry Hands on *Everyman*, an association that continued through his later RSC roles as Hands made his mark as a director there.

After performing in a dozen undergraduate productions, Hutchings went to France to study at the University of Montpelier (combining French and physical education) and attempted to start a drama group. Alas, the bureaucracy interfered, and the dean of the arts faculty decreed that he could not do any plays with religious, political, or sexual content. Saying to himself, "Then what is *left*?," Hutchings returned to England and to the Royal Academy of Dramatic Art (RADA).

In those days, it was still possible to find the odd student who was using RADA as a kind of finishing school where you could get training in voice, elocution, and even posture. However, the actual curriculum was more practically oriented toward theater performance and was taught by eminent teachers who were to be influential in Hutchings's later career. There were classes in voice (Clifford Turner), speech (Barry Smith), technique (Robin Ray and Peter Barkworth), Shakespeare (Nellie Carter), and Laban (Yat Malmgren), all influential names in actor training in England, and also a variety of offerings in fencing, makeup, stage management, and mime. Plays there were directed by well-known theater practitioners, including the principal, John Fernald.

At RADA, Hutchings was in a production of Kafka's *The Castle*, which drew glowing reviews from Kenneth Tynan and got noticed by David Storey, providing his first professional job, cast as D. H. Lawrence in a film. He was cast in repertory at Nottingham, Colchester, and Bournemouth (working with Frank Dunlop, John Neville, and Richard Eyre). Hutchings tells a story about performing in Richard Rodgers's *No Strings*, where the great man came in and conducted the group in a rehearsal of the songs, which he insisted on directing to a very strict rhythm. The composer concluded the session by saying, "Thank you very much," and, as he left, "And God help you all." The show did not get good reviews.

Then there was a call from artistic director Peter Hall at the RSC to play John of Lancaster in the newly devised *The Wars of the Roses*. However, Hutchings could not be released from the show he was in, so it wasn't until four years later that he joined the RSC, in 1968, when the company was illuminated with a galaxy of directorial talent in Terry Hands, Trevor Nunn, John Barton, and Peter Brook.

The atmosphere at the RSC at this time was heady and provocative, creating hallmark productions and well-trained actors:

> In the late 1960s and early 1970s when I was there, there was a top level of actors who played the protagonists. Some had worked their way up through the company, and others had come in at a higher level and maintained that. People like Ian Richardson, Alan Howard, Janet Suzman, and Richard Pasco were invited to play certain parts and occasionally stayed on for more seasons. Then there was a middle band of heavyweight character actors who supported the leads, and finally there were the bit players— understudies, walk-ons, spear carriers, who had been taught by the middle band of experienced actors.
>
> Terry Hands said that for every five parts offered, there would be four that you were perfectly cast for and that you would do well in and were, in effect, for the company. Then there would be a fifth part for you, which stretched you by taking you into more challenging territory.

Hutchings's "middle band" roles included not only character/clown roles such as Autolycus, Bottom the Weaver, Feste, Launce, Lavatch, Fluellen, Dromio of Syracuse, and both Doctor Caius and Peter Simple (*Merry Wives*), but also Bosola in *Duchess of Malfi*, Black Will in *Arden of Faversham*, and the Dauphin in *Henry V*.

Hutchings notes that one of the huge advantages of being in the company was the superlative level of continuing education available:

Buzz Goodbody, the most gifted up-and-comer, was an assistant director taking the understudy rehearsals.[2] One season we were all doing yoga and movement classes with John Broome, who had worked at RADA for some years and eventually was hired away by the Stratford Festival in Canada. John Barton would do sonnet classes which focused on text. Cic Berry, by now the best known of the voice coaches, was giving classes. Apart from being prepared for specific skills required by the plays, you had to learn to fight in the battles and engage in combat. Because of these kinds of instruction, I grew as an actor through the company. These were the fringe benefits that came my way and gave me vital training in my craft.

One positive aspect was that you became part of an extended family of coworkers. I had done a script for TheatreGoRound in Aldeburgh in Norfolk with Ian Richardson and Richard Pasco, and we drove through the night so I could be married the next day—in Stratford in front of Shakespeare's tomb! There was a huge party in the manor house in which we were staying. A chamber group from the company played, there was jazz in the barn—the trees and the grounds were lit by the RSC electricians. When my mother died, the company gave me two trees to plant in our garden in memory of her.

We even played football and cricket matches against the local stars. The social side of it was very good because we were stationed up there in the Stratford company for most of the year.

In addition, we did plenty of work with the touring troupe TheatreGoRound, which traveled to smaller venues in the region. Larger "main-house" productions played across England as well as toured abroad: Japan, Australia, France, Germany, Belgium, Holland, and New York. There were many delights and compensations in being an RSC company member.

In one particular season, Hutchings played Bottom, Feste, Lavatch, Launce, and the Clown in *Titus Andronicus*, an assignment that probably would not have been achieved by a single actor, even in Shakespeare's time. There is a general belief that Shakespeare's fools and clowns got adapted to the personality and skills of whichever actor was the reigning comedian in Shakespeare's company when the play was being written. The detailed history of these engaging performers is more complicated than that, as all three occasional company "members"—Tarleton, Kemp, and Armin—were sometimes very much within the company and sometimes traveling or otherwise engaged. Most clowns depended on local gigs in a variety of public arenas as much as on being cast in a stage role, and they all arranged freelance endeavors whether or not they were cast in a play sponsored by a particular company.

Although he did not have a favorite role, Hutchings has a theory about the roles he played:

> I'd like to think that I brought to the clowns and fools that I played a sense of being brought up in a rural setting. Certainly Lavatch (*All's Well That Ends Well*) was a rustic. There is the implication that he was not so much a clown as a fool, that is, he was actually *hired* and *retained* there to make merry, because the countess says, "My Lord that's gone made himself such sport out of him; / By his authority he remains here." According to clown tradition (Enid Welsford's book *The Fool* is the bible on this subject), there are only five "professional" jesters in Shakespeare: Lear's Fool (which I've never played), Feste, Touchstone, Yorick (in Hamlet, whom everyone forgets about), and Lavatch. Feste has been around a bit and is not an urban character, necessarily. This was a challenging role, because I had to learn to play the lute, the ocarina, and accompany myself as I sang—all in six weeks' time!
>
> Launce can be played either as a country bumpkin or as more urbane and witty. Those comic characters Launce and Speed in *Comedy of Errors* are a lesson in pure comedic script writing, complete with timing and pauses. They are the template for a double act in stand-up and music-hall comedy. That speech about taking the dog to Madame Julia is pure pathos and bathos.

Regarding the way he forms his Shakespearean clowns, Hutchings made this comment:

It was from [these] dense and complicated text[s] that I had to glean something of the character that I was eventually to portray. The work of an actor on a text is like that of a detective. You have to look for clues to the character's behavior in what he says, to a certain extent in what others say about him, in what he does and in the way that others react to him. You then have to interpret those clues and bits of information and create in your own mind an "identi-kit" picture, which is then processed through your senses. Using your own experience, talent, and ability, you arrive at a comprehensible and recognizable human being as near as possible to the dramatist's original intention.[3]

Clearly, one of Hutchings's triumphs was Bottom the Weaver in a 1981 production set at the turn of the century. Although the play is set in Athens, Hutchings expands on the core of Bottom's character:

Bottom is truly a member of the working class in Shakespeare's England. There is a sense about all of the Mechanicals in *A Midsummer Night's Dream* being the kind of fellows John Shakespeare presided over in Stratford City Council meetings, tradesmen just as he was a glover and maker of leather goods. And like himself, the men were community-minded but not above using influence to settle disputes. Loyal to the monarch, of course, provided he or she did not get sticky about what religion one was in sympathy with. They were largely men of simple needs and desires, eager to show their skill as performers and to represent the city as members of their own guild, as well as being up and coming citizens in the social structure. They did not think of themselves as country bumpkins but as folk who have a duty to represent their town in a positive and (if possible) sophisticated manner.

True to the materials that all artists create from—what they know and what they have experienced—Hutchings explained:

My approach to a character is to place Bottom *vocally* somewhere. Give him a regional location in England, usually. I toyed with making Bottom rural West Country, which are my own roots and which I have done with other characters. But then I thought, no, he's a weaver. He deals with cloth. So where was the cloth trade, manufacturing and making wool fabric, in Victorian times? Remember that the production was to be set around 1900. That would have been in the north, in Lancastershire—although I pitched him more Yorkshire than Lancastershire because he did not have to be urban. He could be rural and in an area connected with sheep farming. So that helped me locate him, in terms of accent and gestures.

It is traditional in English productions to begin with an accent for a comic character, usually something from the countryside or somewhere considered less sophisticated, and then to provide costume clues to support that choice:

In performance, you have to justify your own ends and come up with the character's actual motivations. If you are playing a character with a large ego, you have to remember that he doesn't see himself that way. Furthermore, you have to enjoy playing this weird and charismatic character in Shakespeare. Bottom's primary need is to "get it right." He wants to make sure that his friends are going to do the best possible production of *Pyramus and Thisbe* that can be achieved. So what he says is *not* actually egotistical, not actually self-promoting, but said in the interests of creating the best achievable production for the entire group's reputation.

Then, you see, he thinks to himself: If I am the best person to play this part, then it stands to reason that I am the best actor *in Athens*! The play must be as perfect as it possibly can be *throughout*, so it is my job to shore up the weaker people within our rehearsals. Bottom does this for the good of the company. He does not do it to put himself forward. This is not to say he doesn't enjoy acting and showing off, but rather that he has slightly purer motivations for performing.

This handle on the character also fits in with that North Country attitude of speaking your mind and not being upset if you hurt someone else's feelings, because you are actually informing them *for their own good.* So you are, in reality, doing them a favor. In most of my roles, I try to find somebody in my past that I knew to base the character on. So Bottom was an amalgam of people I knew from the North Country.

Since the production was set around the turn of the century, the tradesmen (the Mechanicals) were dressed in suits. For Bottom's transformation, when the ass's head appears, we had a sort of woolly rubbery thing that completely covered my head, and we tried to put a snarly mouth on it.

We did not dwell overly on the phallic side of Bottom and Titania's mating, although there are productions where that sexual angle comes through very strongly. I frankly think that was the least of our problems, given the Victorian setting of this production. We chose to suggest that the romance was humorous rather than salacious.

Hutchings found a special challenge in one speech:

The soliloquy I found most difficult and don't think I ever cracked was the "Bottom's Dream" speech, the core of which are these lines: "I have had a most rare vision. I have had a dream, past the wit of man to say what dream it was: man is but an ass, if he go about to expound this dream. Methought I was—there is not man can tell what. Methought I was—and methought I had. . . . But man is but a patched fool, if he will offer what methought I had. The eye of man hath not heard, the ear of man hath not seen, man's hand is not able to taste, his tongue to conceive, nor his heart to report, what my dream was."

In a way, the meaning is endemic to the speech itself, and maybe that is what Shakespeare intended—that Bottom doesn't *want* to remember. So he's not even sure it *was* a dream and is still wavering about whether or not he wishes it were. The syntax is fractured in such a way that his mind is almost pushing that memory *back* rather than bringing it forward and analyzing it. At this point, he's just surfacing from that foggy analysis of what did and what didn't happen as he returns to reality.

Perhaps I was picking up on the speech without realizing just that: I was having problems because I was working so hard on conveying my complete understanding of the speech when it was *about* something I didn't really want to deal with.

There were clear indications that the actors were spurred by their own capability for comic invention in the production. At one point, bowler hats thrown by Puck went sailing out over the audience's heads and then snapped back onto the stage, accompanied by a slide-whistle sound. Comedic ideas were borrowed from London music hall comedy at the turn of the century. Also, there was a running gag of nobody being able to remember Snug's name, culminating in "Let . . . um . . . Him that plays the Lion . . ."

Hutchings added, "We all knew each other really well, so the rehearsals also were laced with much off-text mirth, very obvious behind the scenes, hopefully less so in performance." Each of the gentlemen had a very specific comic talent, and they would brainstorm and pool creative ideas. He added, "If you remember, this production used bunraku-like puppets for fairies. It wasn't easy talking to a puppet with a voice coming from behind a mask, let alone making comedy out of that."

Hutchings's experiences reveal a great deal about the inner workings of the leading Shakespeare company during the pinnacle of their successes in the twentieth century. Times have changed over the latter half of that century, and he witnessed those shifts and periods of growth, both internal and structural within the theater business. For one thing, directors at the RSC during the 1960s through the 1980s had the power to cancel a show if it was not meeting a certain standard, and the actors in residence at that time witnessed this upon occasion. The directing corps would meet and decide when a production was not up to snuff. Explanations would be made, but a substandard show simply did not continue in the repertory.

Verse speaking, of course, changed radically over the middle of the twentieth century. When Hutchings was at RADA (ca. 1961–63), there was the famous "stage voice" that everyone had been taught to create, because it worked to eliminate any cultural stigma of social class. However, with actors like Tom Courtenay and Albert Finney preceding Hutchings's tenure, it was becoming acceptable to hear regional accents onstage from characters that were not playing comic characters or house servants. Prior to the advent of more realistic and grittier "kitchen-sink" drama, as it was called, "actors had to study these accents as they were set down in phonetic spelling in G. B. Shaw's dramas, and these were never very good models." Hutchings, however, had heard them on the street and had a keen ear for reproducing accents.

So, from the new cultural freedom to use accents for major characters that were *not* comic came more freedom within the physical context and also more variety in the subject matter of the plays.

> Also at RADA, the voice coach dealt with voice production and breathing. We used to lie on the floor, and Clifford Turner would say, "Put your hand over your *epigastrium*." Most of us had no idea what that *was*, let alone where it was located.
>
> Barry Smith dealt more with pronunciation and vocal dexterity, learning the riddles and tongue twisters and how to say them very quickly and accurately. He did everything *on the breath*, which created a kind of refined voice. So, we all had thorough training in voice technique, which works in any performance situation once you've got it down.

Later on, Hutchings was introduced to the National Youth Theater and played several roles there. The director was Michael Croft, who was most insistent about the correct speaking of Shakespearean verse:

> He was similar to Peter Hall and Cic Berry. They trained us initially in the right way of verse speaking, using breathing from the diaphragm and "rib reserve," a technique for supporting the

sound on a cushion of air retained in the expanded ribs, rather like the mechanics of the bagpipes. Then breathing became second nature, automatically and anatomically correct. According to Peter Hall and Cic Berry, it should become so natural that you don't think about a weak line ending or a caesura. Only in that way can you embrace the rigidity of the form and the flexibility of it, as well as the naturalness of it. If you can accomplish all that, people will understand it. Even if they don't understand the words, they will understand the meaning of the sentence.

I don't mark the end of a verse line with a slight pause, because that will accentuate it. I've always found that if you have a problem with a piece of verse and you are not quite sure *where* to stress the right word to achieve the right meaning, if you use the pentameter as a guide to which words you need to stress, more often than not, the sense of the sentence comes out. Most of the Shakespeare stages had awfully good acoustics, so audiences would hear your emphasis. Start with the sense of the line, is my opinion.

The clown language is mostly not metered and does not jump back and forth between verse and prose except when you have songs, like Feste does, or Lear's Fool's rhyming couplets, which are more like folk sayings or riddles or rhymes that came from old songs.

The thing about verse speaking is that if it's not done well, you notice it. Cic Berry used to work more on the verse than the prose, but most of the clowns and the fools speak in prose.

Production values have also changed in the second half of the twentieth century. Design concepts could overwhelm a production where every detail was graphic and lots of money was spent on costume and props, making every dress or uniform "authentic." Nowadays, scene design can be more indicative, can suggest an epoch but not lock the production into a specific time period. Ideas about makeup have changed along with that. Hutchings had once played Shylock complete with a rubber nose, a custom that went back as far as the seventeenth century. Today that would be frowned upon as racist and antique.

Furthermore, there was a shift regarding character portrayal and character interaction within the plays:

> The psychology of the plays was very elementary in the early days when I was acting, if it existed at all. Stereotypes were accepted, and standard ways of playing a part got passed down through other actors. It was a matter of learning your part and not bumping into the scenery—coming in on cue, always louder and faster.
>
> Today, with updated ideas found in contemporary scholarship—especially people's more general awareness of social, family, and cultural structures—there are modern relevancies which can be punctuated within the plays. They can be explored and exposed in a way no one bothered to do before.

Interestingly enough, historian Samuel Crowl talks about what he observed watching rehearsals led by director Ron Daniels, who was working at the RSC at that time and directed Hutchings as Bottom in that 1981 *Midsummer Night's Dream*:

> The other central precepts of Daniels's approach . . . were: be natural, be specific, keep your energy level up, concentrate on telling the rich humanity of your character's story, capture the natural rhythm of Shakespeare's line by being vocally alert to the second and fifth beats, provide a little caesura before central verbs to make them race, and don't stress pronouns.[4]

One sees in Hutchings's earlier career with the company the seeds of such a detailed doctrine, certainly having some of its history actualized in both Cic Berry's books and John Barton's fastidious text analysis and dramaturgy. Hutchings's tour of duty at the Royal Shakespeare Company is a snapshot of some of the most exciting and formative years of that group, with enterprising and innovative personalities defining its mission and direction.

Since leaving the company in 1985, Hutchings was cast as Nym in Kenneth Branagh's 1989 film of *Henry V* and also played Bardolph in a BBC-TV production of *Henry IV, Parts 1 and 2.* He has performed regularly in productions at the National Theatre and in London's West End, most recently in *Endgame* and *Cabaret,* winning the coveted Clarence Derwent Award. He has made more than fifty appearances on film and television.

Notes

Chapter 1: Kevin Kline

1. Joe Klein, "The Pirate King of Broadway," *New York*, January 19, 1981: 27.
2. R. Wetzsteon, "Kevin Can Wait," *New York*, May 10, 1993: 40.
3. "Rousing the Troops," *New York Times*, July 6, 1984: C3, l.
4. Wetzsteon, 41.
5. Kevin Kline, personal interview, June 7, 1990. This discussion happened just as the run of the 1990 *Hamlet* was concluding in New York.
6. Rob Edelstein, "High Approval Rating," *Total TV*, June 11–17, 1993: 10.
7. Howard Kissel, "'Much Ado' About Kline," [New York] *Daily News*, July 10, 1988: 5.
8. Most of the personal remarks for this chapter were taken from an interview of Kevin Kline in New York City on December 14, 1995. Unless otherwise indicated, his commentary comes from that interview.
9. Kevin Kline, personal interview, June 7, 1990.
10. John Lahr, "The Great Guskin, *The New Yorker*, March 20, 1995: 46.
11. Lahr, 46.
12. Kline had performed it in 1983 at the Newman Theater in New York. In 1990 he directed it at the Anspacher Theater (New York Shakespeare Festival) and then adapted it for PBS, codirecting

with Kirk Browning. For a thorough documentation of the PBS *Hamlet*, see my two articles "Kevin Kline's American Hamlet: Stage to Screen," *Shakespeare on Film Newsletter*, 15.2 (April 1991): 12-13; and "At Last, an American Hamlet for Television," in the special issue on "Shakespeare on Film," *Literature and Film Quarterly* 20.4 (1992): 301-7. For a close analysis of how Kline performed the soliloquies, see his chapter in my book *Modern Hamlets and Their Soliloquies* (Iowa City: University of Iowa Press, 1992; expanded ed., 2002).

13. On July 26, 2007, I interviewed Kevin Kline in New York about his performances of Falstaff in the 2004 production of *Henry IV* and of Lear in *King Lear* in 2007. All remarks on these two characters, which are dealt with in full further on in this chapter, are from that interview.

14. Kevin Kline, personal interview, June 7, 1990.

15. Kevin Kline, personal interview, June 7, 1990.

16. Matthews was the dramaturge on this production and also played a role.

Chapter 2: Kenneth Branagh

1. I interviewed Kenneth Branagh in London in July 2005. Unless otherwise indicated, his remarks are from that interview.

2. His Royal Highness Charles, Prince of Wales, eventually became a patron of the Renaissance Theatre Company.

Chapter 3: Derek Jacobi

1. Pam Clarke and Yvonne Parkin, "Beauty, Royalty, and Genius," *Stage Struck* (Newcastle upon Tyne: Penguin Press, 1990), 26.

2. "The Diffident King Finds Refuge from Unscripted Reality," *Sunday Times* [London] December 4, 1988: C1.

3. As described by actor Julian Glover, who played Claudius on tour with the Prospect Theatre production. Julian Glover, personal interview, November 7, 1985.

4. "Breaking the Jacobi Code," *Guardian* [London], November 10, 1986: A18.

5. Clarke and Parkin, 20.

6. Ian Woodward, "You Can't Judge Jacobi by Appearances," *Good Housekeeping*, April 1977: 49.

7. I interviewed Derek Jacobi for this book at the Theatre Royal, Newcastle-on-Tyne, on June 23, 1994. Unless otherwise indicated, his remarks are from this interview.

8. Sheridan Morley, "Derek Jacobi—Going Through Hoops," [Sunday] *Times Magazine*, May 28, 1977: 9.

9. Morley, 9.

10. Clarke and Parkin, 4.

11. See the discussion of the stage and television role in my book *Modern Hamlets and Their Soliloquies* (Iowa City: University of Iowa Press, 1992; expanded ed. 2003). Jacobi also gave a peerless performance of *Richard II* for the BBC series.

12. J. C. Trewin, "To Be the Best Hamlet," Saturday magazine, *Birmingham Post*, June 10, 1977: 6.

13. Clyde Vinson, "Clyde Vinson Talks to Derek Jacobi," *Text and Performance Quarterly* 9.1 (January 1989): 72. Reprinted by permission from the copyright holder, the National Communication Association via Taylor & Francis, Ltd.: www.tandf.co.uk/journals.

14. Roger Lewis, *Stage People* (London: Weidenfeld and Nicholson, 1989): 22.

15. Lewis, 236.

16. Lewis, 236.

17. Lewis, 22.

18. Lewis, 226.

19. I interviewed Jacobi for my book *Modern Hamlets and Their Soliloquies* in London on July 5, 1988, and certain referenced remarks are taken from that interview.

20. *Derek Jacobi at the National Press Club*, video recording of question-and-answer session in Washington, D.C., on April 29, 1997, broadcast on the Bravo channel.
21. James Rampton, "Old Habits Die Hard," *The Independent* [London], August 16, 1996: 24.
22. Derek Jacobi, personal interview, July 5, 1988.
23. Derek Jacobi, personal interview, July 5, 1988.
24. Derek Jacobi, personal interview, July 5, 1988.
25. Derek Jacobi, personal interview, July 5, 1988.
26. John F. Andrews, interviewer, "Derek Jacobi on Shakespearean Acting," *Shakespeare Quarterly* 36.2 (1985): 134-40. Quotations are from pp. 137, 138, and 140. Copyright Folger Shakespeare Library. Reprinted with the permission of the Johns Hopkins University Press.
27. Andrews, 138.
28. Andrews, 140.
29. Andrews, 140.
30. Andrews, 140.
31. Vinson, 79.
32. Woodward, 51.
33. *Derek Jacobi at the National Press Club*.
34. Derek Jacobi, personal interview, July 5, 1988.
35. Hugh Hebert, "Late Starter Ahead by a Nose," *Guardian* [London], July 22, 1983: 9.
36. Hebert, 9.
37. Quoted in Morley, 9.
38. "Breaking the Jacobi Code," A18.
39. Rampton, 24.
40. Hebert, 9.
41. Derek Jacobi, personal interview, July 5, 1988.
42. Vinson, 68.
43. "Breaking the Jacobi Code," 18.
44. Clarke and Parkin, 12.
45. Derek Jacobi, personal interview, July 5, 1988.
46. *Derek Jacobi at the National Press Club*.
47. Vinson, 76.

Chapter 4: Stacy Keach

1. I interviewed Stacy Keach on February 12, 2007, in Los Angeles. Unless otherwise indicated, his comments are from this interview.

2. Jackson R. Bryer and Richard A. Davison, eds., *The Actor's Art: Conversations with Contemporary American Stage Performers* (New Brunswick, N.J.: Rutgers University Press, 2001), 160.

3. Chris Jones, "Extreme 'Lear,'" *Chicago Tribune* review online, September 21, 2006.

4. Charles Isherwood, "Shakespeare in 2 Houses, Bloody and Plain," *New York Times* review online, October 18, 2006.

5. Tom Creamer, interviewer, "Growing Madness: An Interview with Stacy Keach," *Onstage*, Goodman Theatre subscriber publication, September–December 2006: 9.

6. Tom Williams at www.theatreinchicago.com/review, filed December 19, 2006.

Chapter 5: Zoe Caldwell

1. Zoe Caldwell was interviewed in New York City on July 26, 1995. Unless otherwise indicated, her remarks are from that interview.

2. L. S. Keast, "Zoe Caldwell: A Great Taste for Life," *After Dark* (July 1970): 16.

3. An art form in which the performer interpreted music via rhythmical, improvised bodily movement, in the style of Isadora Duncan.

4. Jackson R. Bryer and Richard A. Davison, eds., *The Actor's Art: Conversations with Contemporary American Stage Performers* (New Brunswick, N.J.: Rutgers University Press, 2001), 3.

5. Zoe Caldwell, follow-up telephone interview, August 16, 1995.

6. Paul D. Zimmerman, "Zoe in her Prime," *Newsweek*, February 5, 1968: 81.

7. Walter Kerr, review of *Cleopatra*, *New York Times*, September 17, 1967: II:l:l. Caldwell was reviewed so well for this role that she

named her subsequent memoirs after it: *I Will Be Cleopatra: An Actress's Journey*, by Zoe Caldwell (New York: W. W. Norton, 2001).

8. Ronald Bryden, review of *Cleopatra*, *London Observer*, September 13, 1970: 28.

9. Keast, 42.

10. Zoe Caldwell, follow-up telephone interview, August 16, 1995.

11. Jan Breslauer, "When Two Legends Meet," *Los Angeles Times*, June 11, 1995, *Calendar* magazine: 86.

12. Zoe Caldwell, *I Will Be Cleopatra*, 166.

13. Zimmerman, 81.

14. Leonard Foglia quoted in Paula Span, "Zoe Caldwell: A Class by Herself," *The Washington Post*, September 10, 1995: G1.

Chapter 6: Nicholas Pennell

1. Donal O'Conner, "Something About Theatre 'Absolutely Incomparable' Says Nicholas Pennell," *The [Stratford Festival] Beacon Herald*, 1994 season: F68.

2. Pennell was interviewed on two occasions during August 1994 in Stratford, Ontario, Canada. Unless otherwise noted, his comments are from that interview. For greater detail about Pennell's working career as a classical actor, see the biography *Nicholas Pennell: Risking Enchantment*, by Mary Z. Maher, published in 2005 through PublishAmerica.

3. Pennell and Richard Monette played the role of Hamlet in tandem. For more information on this interesting juxtaposition, see chapter 7, "The Play's the Thing," in Pennell's biography *Nicholas Pennell: Risking Enchantment*.

4. These words are excerpted from Section V of "East Coker" in *Four Quartets*, copyright 1940 by T. S. Eliot and renewed 1968 by Esme Valerie Eliot, reprinted by permission of Houghton Mifflin Harcourt Publishing Company, p. 16.

5. Quoted in Lawrence Devine, "Pennell in His Time Played Many Parts," *Detroit Free Press*, Sunday ed., March 12, 1995: 5G.

Chapter 7: William Hutt

1. William Hutt was interviewed in Stratford, Ontario, on August 12 and 17, 1995. Unless otherwise indicated, his remarks are from that interview.
2. Keith Garebian, *William Hutt: A Theatre Portrait* (Oakville, Ont.: Mosaic, 1988), 81.
3. William Hutt, interview on video by Pat Quigley, "William Hutt: Portrait of an Actor," *Behind the Scenes*, Rogers Cable, August 10, 1992, Stratford Festival Archives copy. These quotations reprinted courtesy of the William Hutt estate.
4. William Hutt, video interview with Pat Quigley.
5. William Hutt, video interview with Pat Quigley.
6. Garebian, 269.
7. William Hutt, video interview with Pat Quigley.
8. Garebian, 269.
9. Garebian, 151.
10. Quoted in Garebian, 152.
11. Garebian, 153.
12. Herbert Whittaker, "An Imposing, Old Style King Lear," *Toronto Globe and Mail*, June 8, 1972: A5.
13. Ray Conlogue, "A Remarkable King Lear," *Globe and Mail* [Stratford], June 6, 1988: A24.
14. Robert Crew, "Hutt's Lear Magnificent," *Toronto Star*, June 6, 1988: C4.
15. Robert Reid, "A Tragic Masterpiece," *Kitchener-Waterloo Record*, June 6, 1988: 16.
16. Garebian, 294.
17. Keith Garebian, *Masks and Faces* (Oakville, Ont.: Mosaic, 1994), 11.
18. Garebian, *Masks and Faces*, 12.

Chapter 8: Martha Henry

1. Martha Henry was interviewed in July 2005 in Stratford, Ontario, Canada. Unless otherwise indicated, her comments are from this interview.
2. Henry eventually took Canadian citizenship.
3. Christopher Rawson, "Leading Lady," *Pittsburgh Post-Gazette*, October 1, 2003: E1.
4. Interview, *The Forest City News*, August 10-016, 1964: 8.
5. Rawson, E1.
6. Peter Birnie, "Cue Martha the Magnificent," *The Vancouver Sun*, January 2, 2002: 9.

Chapter 9: Tony Church

1. Tony Church was interviewed in London on December 12, 1994. Unless otherwise indicated, his remarks are from that interview.
2. Church speaks about Gielgud's 1944 *Hamlet* and Ashcroft's 1945 *Duchess of Malfi*, both hallmark performances.
3. John Goodwin, *Peter Hall's Diaries* (Cambridge: Harper & Row, 1983), 395.
4. From Tony Church's personal papers.
5. From Tony Church's personal papers, with the permission of Mary Gladstone. Alas, Ms. Goodbody committed suicide at age twenty-eight, just as her *Hamlet* with Ben Kingsley took stage in 1975. On the strength of her work in this *Lear*, she was awarded an artistic directorship, making her the first and only woman director in the company at that time.

Chapter 10: Geoffrey Hutchings

1. Geoffrey Hutchings was interviewed in London on June 23, 2004. Unless otherwise indicated, his remarks are from that discussion.

2. Goodbody's suicide in 1975 is still considered one of the tragic moments in RSC history. She was the first aspirant woman director with the company during its modern renaissance.

3. Hutchings is quoted from his chapter titled "Lavatch in *All's Well that Ends Well*," Philip Brockbank, ed., *Players of Shakespeare* (Cambridge: Cambridge University Press, 1987), 80.

4. Samuel Crowl, *Shakespeare Observed: Studies in Performance on Stage and Screen* (Athens: Ohio University Press, 1993), 74.

Grateful acknowledgment is made to the following for permission to reprint previously published material:

Taylor and Francis, Ltd.: Excerpts from "Clyde Vinson Talks to Derek Jacobi," *Text and Performance Quarterly* 9:1, © 1989 by the National Communication Association. Reprinted by permission of Taylor and Francis, Ltd.

The Johns Hopkins University: Excerpts from John F. Andrews, "Derek Jacobi on Shakespearean Acting," pp. 137, 138, 140, *Shakespeare Quarterly* 36:2 (1985), 134-40. © Folger Shakespeare Library. Reprinted by permission of the Johns Hopkins University Press.

Houghton Mifflin Harcourt Publishing Company: Excerpt from "East Coker" in *Four Quartets*, © 1940 by T. S. Eliot and renewed 1968 by Esme Valerie Eliot, reprinted by permission of Houghton Mifflin Harcourt Publishing Company.

Faber and Faber, Ltd. / © The Estate of T. S. Eliot: Excerpts from "East Coker" in *Four Quartets*, © 1940, reprinted by permission of Faber and Faber, Ltd. / © The Estate of T. S. Eliot.

Additional thanks are offered to those who granted permission for use of materials but who are not named individually in the acknowledgments or in the notes. While every reasonable effort has been made to contact copyright holders and secure permission for all materials reproduced in this work, we offer apologies for any instances in which this was not possible and for any inadvertent omissions.